D0296381

Capital, the State, and Late Industrialization

Social Change in Global Perspective

Mark Selden, *Series Editor*

Exploring the relationship between social change and social structures, this series considers the theory, praxis, promise, and pitfalls of movements in global and comparative perspective. The historical and contemporary social movements considered here challenge patterns of hierarchy and inequality of race, gender, nationality, ethnicity, class, and culture. The series will emphasize textbooks and broadly interpretive synthetic works.

The Transformation of Communist Systems: Economic Reform Since the 1950s, BERNARD CHAVANCE

The Challenge of Local Feminisms: Women's Movements in Global Perspective, edited by AMRITA BASU, with the assistance of C. ELIZABETH MCGRORY

Power Restructuring in China and Russia, MARK LUPHER

Capital, the State, and Late Industrialization: Comparative Perspectives on the Pacific Rim, edited by JOHN BORREGO, ALEJANDRO ALVAREZ BEJAR, and JOMO K. S.

FORTHCOMING

African Women: A Modern History, CATHERINE COQUERY-VIDROVITCH

Japanese Labor and Labor Movements, KUMAZAWA MAKOTO

Human Families, STEVAN HARRELL

Capital, the State, and Late Industrialization

Comparative Perspectives on the Pacific Rim

EDITED BY

John Borrego,
Alejandro Alvarez Bejar,
and Jomo K. S.

WestviewPress
A Division of HarperCollins*Publishers*

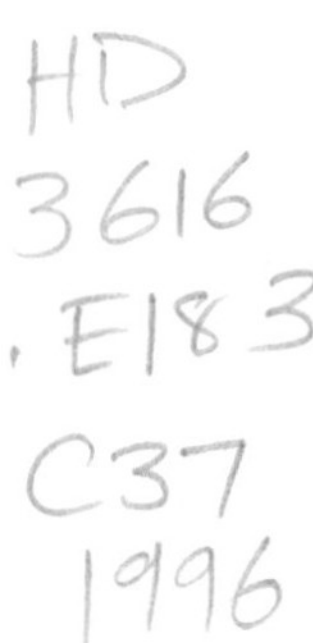

Social Change in Global Perspective

Published in 1996 in the United States of America by Westview Press, Inc., 5500 Central Avenue, Boulder, Colorado 80301-2877, and in the United Kingdom by Westview Press, 12 Hid's Copse Road, Cumnor Hill, Oxford OX2 9JJ

Library of Congress Cataloging-in-Publication Data
Capital, the state, and late industrialization : comparative perspectives on the Pacific Rim / edited by John Borrego, Alejandro Alvarez Bejar, and Jomo K. S.
p. cm. — (Social Change in Global Perspective)
Includes bibliographical references and index.
ISBN 0-8133-2961-2 (Hard)
1. Industrial policy—East Asia. 2. East Asia—Commercial policy. 3. Capitalism—East Asia. 4. Industrial policy—Latin America. 5. Latin America—Commercial policy. 6. Capitalism—Latin America. I. Borrego, John. II. Alvarez, Alejandro (Alvarez Bejar) III. Jomo K. S. (Jomo Kwame Sundaram) IV. Series.
HD3616.E183C37 1996
338.95—dc20 96-11299
CIP

The paper used in this publication meets the requirements of the American National Standard for Permanence of Paper for Printed Library Materials Z39.48-1984.

10 9 8 7 6 5 4 3 2 1

We dedicate this book to the memory of our good friend Antonio Gutiérrez Pérez whose enthusiasm for investigating the global significance of the Pacific Rim we share. Antonio died unexpectedly on February 27, 1994, in Mexico City at a time when he had reached both full maturity and creativity in his work. We're sure he would have been pleased with the publication of this book.

Dedicamos este libro a la memoria de nuestro querido amigo Antonio Gutiérrez Pérez, con quien compartimos su entusiasmo por investigar el significado mundial de la Cuenca del Pacífico. Fue sorprendido por la muerte el 27 de febrero de 1994 en la ciudad de México, cuando estaba en una etapa de gran madurez y creatividad. Estamos seguros de que hubiera disfrutado con la publicación de este libro.

Contents

Acknowledgments

This volume was born out of an initiative of John Borrego and Alejandro Alvarez to meet with and engage likeminded students of development and industrialization in East Asia. After several aborted attempts, a meeting was convened at the Institute of Advanced Studies, University of Malaya, Kuala Lumpur by Jomo K. S. Over three days, a dozen Mexican researchers met with East Asian counterparts, addressing a range of issues of common interest.

In preparing this volume, however, we have made two important changes. First, we have excluded many interesting papers prepared on very specific developmental problems in Mexico and Malaysia, partly because many were only written in the Spanish language. Second, we have invited and included several chapters related to the main theme of this volume, namely, capital, the state, and late industrialization in East Asia in comparative perspective.

In other words, while the seeds of this volume were sown at the June 1992 conference, it has taken on a life of its own, changing its identity, expelling and drawing in, not unlike the process of capital accumulation itself, with its attendant inequities.

After this brief background to the volume, it remains therefore to thank all those who have made it possible: the University of California (UC) system, the Universidad Autónoma de México (UNAM), the University of Malaya, the conference participants, especially the contributors, our families, our assistants, Cheryl Van De Veer and Zoe Sodja at the Word Processing Center at UCSC, Barbara Crum, Carter Wilson, Mark Selden, series editor, and Susan McEachern, the senior editor at Westview, who have been critical for the preparation of this volume. To all of them, abrazos.

John Borrego
Alejandro Alvarez Bejar
Jomo K. S.

1

Introduction

John Borrego, Alejandro Alvarez Bejar, and Jomo K. S.

Major changes have occurred in the international political economy since the end of the 1980s; the collapse of the former Soviet Union, the break-up of Eastern Europe, the creation of the Asia Pacific Economic Cooperation (APEC) Forum, the formal integration of the European Community (EC), the signing of the North American Free Trade Agreement (NAFTA), the conclusion of the Uruguay Round of the General Agreement on Tariffs and Trade (GATT), and the establishment of the World Trade Organization (WTO). These events will have far reaching consequences and they will continue to impact the global economy and politics for some time to come. Each event signals a fundamental transformation in the political, military and economic environment that has been in place since the end of World War Two (WWII).

Although these and other recent developments seem to be unsurpassed in their importance for world affairs, other less visible, but no less profound developments have been occurring in the Pacific Rim, many of which are rooted in the 1960s. It was at this time that the Japanese economy began exhibiting its early vibrancy and dynamism. By the mid-1970s, despite the OPEC crisis, the Japanese economy had not only taken off, but it was later joined by the growing industrial competence of economies such as Taiwan, South Korea, and Singapore. In 1985, the major industrializing countries, including Japan, had signed the Plaza agreement, resulting in a substantial appreciation of the yen, which set off a massive outflow of Japanese foreign investment into the region, further accelerating economic growth in East Asia. By the late 1980s, rapid economic growth in East Asia had extended to the Association of South East Asian Nations (ASEAN)—led by Malaysia and Thailand—and into the Peoples' Republic of China and Vietnam, involving a new regional division of labor. By 1995, assumptions of Japan's industrial strength and technological prowess were commonplace.

The role of investments in fueling the recent industrialization of East Asia (including South East Asia) is self-evident at one level. Yet, the debate on the major factors contributing to East Asian industrialization continues unabated. As might be expected, there is much at stake in this debate. The debate is essentially ideological in nature and largely centers on the role and contribution of state intervention to late industrialization.

Free Market?

On one side, one finds the economic liberals, the *laissez faire* free marketeers who insist that East Asia's spectacular economic growth and industrial transformation in recent decades have been primarily due to free market forces at work. While not denying state intervention in the provision of public goods (especially infrastructure and education), as suggested by neoclassical welfare economic theory, they generally claim that the Northeast Asian economic miracle has been despite, rather than because of other kinds of state intervention, especially government identification and promotion of selected strategic industries. They also claim that the Northeast Asian success has been largely due to the nation's ability to extricate themselves from distortionary import substitution to allegedly non-distortionary export orientation in their industrialization strategies. Furthermore, they generally ignore the significance of national (public and private) ownership of many of the manufacturing firms concerned.

There has been an important and interesting variation of this argument best articulated by Bhagwati, which Wade (1990) has described as the simulated market thesis. It concedes that at least the South Korean state has been distortionary, but argues that the distortionary effects of import substitution have been adequately negated by the same government's export promotion and subsidization efforts. Needless to say, this is a most peculiar argument, which Edwards (1993) has compared to suggesting that a person must be comfortable on balance if one leg is immersed in ice cold water while the other is put into hot boiling water.

Developmentalist States?

There has been a growing literature since the mid-1980s which has responded to the growing neoclassical and other economic literature on state failure by emphasizing instances of "state success" as well as market failure. Drawing primarily from Gerschenkeron's economic history and the Northeast Asian experiences, but also those of Singapore (e.g., Rodan, 1989) and even Hong Kong (e.g., see Castells, Goh and Kwok, 1990), they have emphasized the critical role of "developmentalist states" in achieving late industrialization. The polemical nature of some of this literature is best captured by Alice Amsden's (1989) rejection of the World Bank neoclassical economic formula prescription of "getting prices right" by advocating "getting prices wrong," when she actually means "getting prices wrong correctly," in the sense of rejecting comparative static determinations of comparative advantage in favor of a more dynamic understanding of comparative advantage as historically created, rather than as immutably given.

Hence, the debate has sometimes deteriorated into claims and counterclaims about the efficacy or failure of either the state or the market depending on one's ideological and political position. In September 1993, the World Bank published *The East Asian Miracle: Economic Growth and Public Policy*, a study apparently commissioned at the insistence of the Japanese government, probably after years of frustration with the neoclassical economic orthodoxy and free market conservatism which has long dominated the Bank. Though it is still unclear whether the publication is indicative of a more deep-rooted shift in Bank thinking, as some would like to believe, the book was nonetheless important for explicitly acknowledging and incorporating many of the arguments made by proponents of the developmental state thesis, thus legitimizing a position previously considered beyond the pale of economic orthodoxy. Nevertheless, most critics of neoclassical economic and Bank orthodoxy would argue that the publication did not go far enough, as it sought to reconcile the developmental statist position with much of free market orthodoxy.

Region?

Although there has been considerable unevenness in growth and industrialization in the East Asian region, the fact of rapid and sustained growth in much of the region is not without significance and begs explanation. Although the chapters in this volume do not address this question directly, many assume or point to significant economies of location, i.e., being in the right place (region) at the right time. There is, of course, an important pan-East Asian dimension to much of the economic growth and the relations involved, not surprisingly coinciding with Japan's wartime "Greater East Asian Co-Prosperity Sphere" (Friedman and Lebard, 1991: 27-34).

It is not coincidental that Japan's economic and diplomatic activities have been most intense in the Asia-Pacific region. Perhaps sensing this, the U.S. administration took over the Japanese-Australian proposal to set up the Asia Pacific Economic Cooperation (APEC) Forum in the late 1980s. This has managed to keep Japan in check, thus effectively subverting the Malaysian Prime Minister's efforts to set up an East Asian Economic Grouping (EAEG) and then, after initial rebuffs, an East Asian Economic Caucus (EAEC) within the APEC framework. Thus far, the U.S. has succeeded in reasserting hegemony in the post-Cold War world as well as the emerging regional blocs in East Asia. After committing APEC to regional economic liberalization in Jakarta in November 1994, the U.S. secured a similar commitment from all (North, Central and South) American governments (except Cuba, which was not invited). Thus, while the U.S. still dominates both regional blocs directly, it has also deterred regional collective action in East Asia as a possible countervailing force within APEC. Some APEC proponents privately argue that the U.S. can thus be deployed against either Japanese or Chinese hegemony in East Asia, but this view assumes the U.S. role to be essentially benign, disinterested and even altruistic, which it certainly is not.

This region is sometimes referred to as a "yen bloc," but this image may actually obscure much of what is actually taking place. For one thing, most international economic transactions in the region—including many of those involving Japanese companies and non-Japanese parties—continue to be denominated in U.S. dollars, with little likelihood or even inclination by any party for substitution with the yen. However, in so far as much of the finance in the region—both private corporate and government—is Japanese in origin, one might refer to a Japanese economic bloc in a different (i.e., non-monetary) sense. Yet, Japanese hegemony in the region is more akin to the status of Germany in the European Union, rather than the United States in North America, not least because of the countervailing influence of China and the constitutional constraints on the "normal" development of Japanese political, especially military strength.

Ethnic Networks?

At a sub-regional level, the economies of location, but also culture, must surely figure in the southern pan-Chinese zone, i.e., involving Hong Kong and Taiwan besides Guangdong and Fujian in China's South. Again, while the chapters in this volume do not directly address the question of trans-border Chinese economic networks, these are implied, if not assumed. This hints at a possible distinctive characteristic of much of contemporary Chinese capitalism. There undoubtedly still are statist rentiers—the infamous "bureaucrat capitalists" in the Maoist lexicon—and the recent spectacular performance of township and village enterprises in China, often run by state or former government officials, reminds us that the formal "public sector" is hardly dead. However, there is also considerable evidence that much capital accumulation by Chinese is proceeding regardless of or even despite, rather than because of state intervention. While the Communist Party of China on the mainland, the statist Guomindang on Taiwan and the *laissez fairish* British colonial state in Hong Kong are all encouraging capitalist accumulation, most observers would be hesitant to portray these states as mere capitalist instruments. Of course, it was precisely this "relative autonomy"—from the interests of the capitalist class as a whole, or even its dominant elements—which has been crucial in both Japan and South Korea in ensuring rapid accumulation and late industrialization in the image of the state. But, it also appears that the three states on Chinese territory have been far less corporatist than their Northeast Asian counterparts.

In Southeast Asia, the situation is more varied. It seems that "Chinese" capital is more ascendant in Thailand, even though ethnic Chinese only command a demographic majority in Singapore, where the state's strategy for growth and industrialization seems to have privileged foreign, especially technologically dynamic capital. Yet, Chinese capital accumulation is proceeding rapidly in the rest of the region, despite the apparently hostile Muslim Malay-dominated states of Indonesia, Malaysia and Brunei. While there are Chinese who have bought themselves political influence and lucrative business or rentier opportunities in these states (the Indonesian "chukongs" or the Malaysian "(Ali) Babas"), it seems fair to say that the vast majority resent, evade and bypass the state, and have consequently developed a distinctive "Overseas or Southeast Asian Chinese" business idiom heavily reliant on informal credit and contracts based on personal trust and kinship, real as well as contrived (*Forbes*, 18 July, 1994: 138-182).

Yet, despite the important differences in context among, say, China, Taiwan, Hong Kong, Singapore and possibly Thailand on the one hand, and Muslim Malay Southeast Asia on the other, the relations between capital and the state in both situations are nevertheless quite different from those in the Northeast Asian economies of Japan and South Korea, especially in terms of the absence of strong corporatist arrangements. And especially where the state is less sympathetic, or even hostile, this idiom may well take on the characteristics of insurgent or guerrilla capitalism based on institutions rooted in culture and community sanction, rather than systems of law and regulation enforced by the state.

Comparative Advantage

The rejection of development economics as well as economic rationales for developmentalist state intervention is largely based on liberal economic arguments, especially neoclassical international trade theory. The rationale for economic liberalization, including the doctrine of "free trade," is theoretically based on fairly simple reasoning. In contrast with Adam Smith's theory, based on the absolute advantage a country can obtain from the production of certain goods, David Ricardo's theory maintains that relative or comparative advantage guides countries toward specialization. Ricardo's theory was further developed in the twentieth century, influenced by neoclassical economic thinking (Heckscher, Ohlin, Samuelson), that emphasized not only "natural" comparative advantages, but also comparative cost as the determinant of international trade and geographical specialization.

Certain unrealistic assumptions were made in developing the theory. First, that although there exists free mobility of factors of production within national economies, the same does not exist among countries. Second, that all countries benefit from the free trade of goods and services. Third, that both perfect competition and constant returns to scale of production exist, the only exception being the possibility that increasing returns may be an independent cause of specialization and trade.

Recent developments in international trade theory further call into question the validity of comparative advantage after consideration of endogenous technological change and economies of scale as independent influences on trade development and specialization, thus also challenging the idea that "free trade" is always better than government intervention.

There are four important tendencies within the international economy involving the evolution of comparative advantage and recent global changes which must be considered in analyzing Latin America. First, the growth of world trade has outpaced production itself. This restructuring has been made possible by the fragmentation of production processes and the greater use of increasingly sophisticated transportation and communication technologies. Second, this strong tendency toward a globalization of production processes has radically transformed world markets, differentiating consumers with greater precision. Corporations have gone from the notion of "economies of scale" to that of "economies of scope," which involves achieving greater production volumes based on increasing the variety of products offered. Third, contradicting these two tendencies has been the tendency toward the formation of great regional trade blocs in which intra-firm trade plays a major role. Consequently, the main actors are adopting strategic specialization criteria to confront three simultaneous processes: at the sectoral level, because of drastic changes in product, scope and national hierarchies; at the geographical level, because of the appearance of a new world economic map; and finally, at the global level, because of the velocity of changes in information technology and the development of mutual interdependence. Fourth, falling tariffs, rising non-tariff barriers, new free trade areas and the development of powerful protectionist legislative instruments in the developed world has propitiated a profound reordering of North-South economic relations, marginalizing Africa, Latin America, Eastern Europe and the rest of Asia (except East Asia) from the growth of international trade.

Competitiveness?

It is well known that there is a tremendous ongoing competitive struggle for economic hegemony among Germany, Japan and the United States (Thurow, 1992). Internationally, they are the principal exporters of manufactured goods. But if we expand this list to thirty, we find seven "developing countries," five in Asia (Taiwan, Hong Kong, Korea, Singapore and China), and two in Latin America (Mexico and Brazil), some due primarily to transnational corporations relocating investment and production sites oriented to the world market (Kreye, et al., 1987; Dicken, 1992).

Taking this into account, and looking at the future of competitive struggles, it is clear that the notion of comparative advantage is a relative one, i.e., it defines the competitiveness of one economic player in relation to another, be it a corporation or a nation. But today, the notion of competitiveness takes both the economic behavior and the economic capacity of a country or a corporation into consideration. In addition, there are both dynamic comparative advantages and static ones, with the former due to technical progress in productive processes. Wage differences are also very important, but usually considered as mainly affecting static comparative advantage because there is always some rigidity due to workers' basic survival needs.

There are, then, many very different indicators of dynamic comparative advantage and competitiveness, such as the degree of production specialization (according to resource endowments, product price and quality), and the productivity of corporations and countries. Fernando Fajnzylber (1989: 20) and others linked to the Economic Commission for Latin America (ECLA) have interpreted the idea of competitiveness as the capacity to successfully participate in the international market, with a parallel growth in the population's standard of living. The indicators of competitiveness therefore include the capacity to participate in the international market, defined in terms of the technological density of production, or the number of manufactured exports in relation to total exports, the rate of penetration of imports, etc. Analysis based on all these indicators can give us a more contemporary and meaningful notion of comparative advantage.

Pacific Rim Comparisons

Now, we consider the factors determining comparative advantage in Latin America and East Asia. In the 1970s, there were no major differences between the growth rates of Latin America and East Asia (including Southeast Asia). In the 1980s, however, growth in East Asia as a region was more than five per cent above that of Latin America, which averaged "zero growth" in that decade. Per capita incomes, which were around $1000 for both regions in the 1970s, widened between the two regions in the 1980s, the East Asian countries had an average per capita income of about $4,000, while Latin America averaged only $2,600. Furthermore, though the rate of inflation in Latin America was higher than that of East Asia in the 1970s, this took a dramatic turn in the 1980s. In East Asia, the inflation rate was only single digit, while the average reached 100 percent in Latin America.

The external debt problem has undoubtedly been a key factor in reducing the growth rate in Latin America. In East Asia, there were also coun-

TABLE 1.1. Latin America and Asia: Total Foreign Debt, 1980-92 (US$m.)

Country	Total debt in 1992	GNP percentage		Percentages of goods and services exported		Debt service total as % of goods & services exported		Interest payments as % of goods & services exported	
		1980	1992[c]	1980	1992[d]	1980	1992	1980	1992
Mexico	113378	30.3	34.1	259.2	235.6	49.5	44.4	27.4	16.4
Brazil	121110	31.2	31.2	304.8	293.8	63.1	63.1	33.8	9.2
Argentina	67569	48.4	30.3	242.4	449.8	37.3	34.4	20.8	11.7
Peru	20293	51.0	92.7	207.7	440.6	46.5	23.0	19.9	10.7
Colombia	17204	20.9	36.9	117.1	166.4	16.0	26.4	11.6	12.3
Venezuela	37193	42.1	61.1	131.9	214.8	27.2	19.5	13.8	12.5
Chile	19360	45.2	48.9	192.5	148.3	43.1	20.9	19.0	10.4
Korea	42999	48.7	45.8	130.6	14.2	19.7	7.4	12.7	3.0
Hong Kong	N.A.	N.A.	N.A.	N.A.	N.A.	N.A.	N.A.	N.A.	N.A.
Thailand	39424	25.9	35.2	96.3	90.5	18.7	14.1	9.4	6.4
Malaysia	19837	28.0	35.2	44.6	41.5	6.3	6.6	4.0	2.4
Singapore	N.A.	N.A.	N.A.	N.A.	N.A.	N.A.	N.A.	N.A.	N.A.
China	69321	1.5	12.8	22.1	76.8	4.3	10.3	1.5	4.2
Taiwan	400[b]	9.4[a]	0.2[b]	18.5[a]	0.5[b]	4.9[a]	0.1/2	N.A.	N.A.

N.A.- not available.
[a]Data for 1984.
[b]Data for 1993.
[c]Net present value of total external debt as % of GNP.
[d]Net present value of total external debt as % of exports.
Source: World Bank, *World Development Report 1991; Taiwan Statistical Data Book,* Council for Economic Planning and Development, 1994.

tries that had significant external debt, but the relative magnitudes were not as large as in Latin America, where debt servicing amounted, in some cases, to more than half the value of all exports. The ratios of debt servicing and interest payments to exports were much less in East Asia, as shown in Table 1.1. While high debt levels in East Asia were accompanied by important productive investments, in Latin America the combination of international debt contraction and high budget deficits led to an expansion of internal debt. This, on the one hand, worsened the budget deficit and, on the other hand, deflected investments toward speculative ends.

The general tendency for employment in both regions was upwards, with similar relative levels. In Latin America, Brazil, Chile and Colombia experienced the highest growth, while in East Asia, Thailand and Korea had the highest increases. However, in Latin America, there was an increase of employment in services, and a drop in the occupational ladder from higher to lower productivity levels in both industrial and service sectors. In East Asia, the increase of employment essentially involved industrial occupations, though there were also significant increases in the services sector.

TABLE 1.2. Latin America and East Asia: Income and Productivity per Employee, 1980-91

Country	Growth rate[a]	Income per employee index (1980=100)			Total income as value added percentage			Gross production per employee (1980=100)		
	1980–91	1989	1990	1991	1989	1990	1991	1989	1990	1991
Mexico	–3.0	72	75	79	19	20	21	132	139	144
Brazil	–2.4	93	81	80	20	23	23	97	95	97
Argentina	–1.3	76	82	N.A.	16	20	N.A.	88	113	N.A.
Peru[a]	–3.0	86	95	N.A.	N.A.	N.A.	N.A.	N.A.	N.A.	N.A.
Colombia	1.2	117	116	110	15	15	14	158	168	161
Venezuela	–5.3	63	58	61	21	16	21	103	121	118
Chile	–1.0	102	105	106	15	17	17	N.A.	N.A.	N.A.
Korea	7.9	191	209	225	31	28	27	193	231	245
Hong Kong	4.9	150	153	152	55	55	55	N.A.	N.A.	N.A.
Thailand	6.5	171	173	N.A.	28	28	N.A.	107	110	N.A.
Malaysia	2.4	128	129	135	26	27	27	N.A.	N.A.	N.A.
Singapore	5.0	165	175	185	30	32	33	129	135	135
China	N.A.	N.A.	N.A.	N.A.	N.A.	N.A.	N.A.	N.A.	N.A.	N.A.

No data on Taiwan is available.

N.A.- Not available.

[a]For Peru, growth rate is from 1980-88; income per employee index corresponds to 1986, 1987, and 1988.

Source: World Bank, *World Development Report 1994.*

Table 1.2 compares income and employee productivity levels during 1980-91, when the income growth rate in Latin America either remained stagnant (as in the cases of Venezuela, Argentina and Brazil), or negative (as in the cases of Mexico, Peru and Chile), while East Asia generally grew quite rapidly. Comparison of production per employee is generally difficult, with data for Asia generally considered quite controversial. Latin American data shows significant improvements in Venezuela and Colombia, while production per employee remained stagnant in other countries, particularly in Mexico, Brazil, Argentina and Peru. Comparison of the labor contribution to total value added is also difficult. Although the percentage of value added by workers was maintained in some cases, there were falls in the gross level of production in all cases.

Table 1.3 shows value added in manufacturing during 1970-91. The highest increase in value added occurred in South Korea and Singapore, with over 100 per cent increases in both countries. Hong Kong and Taiwan followed with over 50 per cent. In Latin America, growth in manufacturing value-added was much more modest, with the highest increase in value added occurring in Brazil, followed by Mexico, Colombia and Venezuela with similar rates, and Peru and Chile at the end.

TABLE 1.3. Value Added in Manufacturing Industry (US $m.)

Country	1970	1991	Average growth rate 1970–91
Mexico	8449	63784	29.8
Brazil	10429	90062	34.7
Argentina	5750	46266	32.0
Peru	1430	6101[a]	18.1
Colombia	1487	8393	21.1
Venezuela	2140	8232	12.9
Chile	2092	N.A.	N.A.
Korea	1880	77821	183.6
Hong Kong	1013	12159	49.5
Thailand	1130	27779	107.2
Malaysia	500	N.A.	N.A.
Singapore	379	11701	135.8
China	N.A.	N.A.	—
Taiwan	N.A.	N.A.	—

N.A.-not available.
[a]Data for Peru for 1988.
Source: World Bank, *World Development Report, 1994.*

As Table 1.4 shows, if we leave out the formerly centrally planned economies such as China and Vietnam, manufacturing labor was generally cheaper in Latin America than in East Asia by 1990 whereas the reverse had been true in 1981. Wages rose in Latin America in the 1970s before suffering from the adjustments in the early and mid-1980s. In Latin America, Colombia and Brazil had the largest relative rise during the 1980s. Peru and Chile also had upward tendencies, though much smaller than Mexico's. In East Asia, there was a spectacular rise of wages in South Korea, Hong Kong and Singapore, with South Korea and Thailand beginning at very low levels at the beginning of the 1980s. In the East Asian countries, wage increases were more than compensated for by increases in productivity (as measured by value-added in Table 1.3) and, reputedly, quality as well, which have enabled the region to become dominant in areas like consumer electronics, electrical appliances, textiles, electrical and non-electrical machinery and, arguably, even the automotive industry.

The newly industrialized economies (NIEs) in East Asia (South Korea, Hong Kong, Taiwan and Singapore) are the first developing countries to have "really closed the gap" with the developed economies. For the original East Asian NIEs, the lack of natural resources as well as privileged relations with Japan and the United States facilitated their industrial tran-

TABLE 1.4. Latin America and East Asia: Real Wages in the Manufacturing Industry, 1981-90

	Monthly real wages in each country's currency			Average real wage growth rate	Real wage rate in 1990 compared	Wages in US dollars[a]		
Country	1981	1987	1990	1981–90[b]	to 1981	1981	1987	1990
Mexico	9366.4	5300.3	5000.2	–5.2	–46.6	489.3	177.9	267.7
Brazil	30.3	30.1	28.5[c]	–.6	–5.8	373.3	273.7	290.7
Peru	3430.0	35.0	1557.5[d]	–6.8	–54.6	147.5	122.5	175.0
Chile	12303.3	18772.7	20555.4	7.5	67.1	377.6	296.2	428.3
Korea	144881.6	220010.7	321764.7	13.6	122.1	258.7	399.6	834.7
Hong Kong	1145.0	1780.0	1977.5[d]	8.1	72.7	230.0	385.0	502.5
Thailand	1328.0	N.A.	2145.2	6.8	61.5	69.0	N.A.	132.2
Singapore	N.A.	665.0	793.5	6.4	19.3	N.A.	366.2	546.8

[a]To obtain the U.S. currency numbers, we used the nominal wages data divided between each year's average type of exchange ("rf" statistical series from the IMF).

[b]The growth rates correspond to available information.

[c]Data for 1988.

[d]Data for 1989.

Sources: ILO, *Labor Statistics Yearbook, 1991*. IMF, *International Financial Statistics, 1990*.

sition from import substitution to export-oriented industrialization. They were "graduated" from the General System of Preferences (GSP) in the late 1980s. Meanwhile, Malaysia and Thailand seem to be becoming part of a second generation or tier of NIEs.

Ironically, the apparent advantage of Latin America's abundant natural resources and U.S. domination may have restrained such industrial progress. In the cases of more or less successful transitions to export-oriented manufacturing (Mexico and Brazil), the new accumulation model still poses many development problems, involving a hyper-inflationary environment, with very low wage and productivity levels, and high social costs. In addition, the transition mainly involves a smaller group of companies linked to transnational corporations; most companies operating at the national level have been unable to compete successfully in the new increasingly liberalized international economy.

East Asian Lessons?

At the most stereotypical level, the conventional image is of a tremendous economic dynamism among the East Asian countries, which have capitalist economies and have generally had authoritarian governments. Their rapid economic growth and industrialization are, in turn, viewed as presenting an increasing commercial challenge to North America, Europe and Oceania, which can take cold comfort from the economic and political demise of their erstwhile communist rivals.

Can Latin America draw some lessons from East Asia, particularly the first generation NIEs? To do so, we must go beyond the "stereotype" of East Asia to understand the nuances and even contradictions in the region. The chapters in this volume indicate important qualifications to the conventional image of East Asia. Very significant variations exist, and these differences themselves tell us something about recipes for national progress in the contemporary world economy. The glow of aggregate regional statistics hides considerable unevenness which must be taken into account as well.

The economies differ significantly in terms of the timing and the nature of their transitions from import substitution to export-oriented industrialization. East Asian state success in encouraging and rewarding growth in the export capacity of import-substituting industries has attracted a great deal of attention to the *dirigiste,* but also developmentalist role of the South Korean, Taiwanese and Singaporean states. Consequently, the manufacturing sectors seem to differ in terms of degree of national ownership and control, labor intensity, technological sophistication, and domestic value-added content. Long-term success seems to depend crucially upon an ability for continuous economic upgrading and transformation.

However, development strategies have also varied greatly, especially in the case of Hong Kong and, arguably, the second generation NIEs, where the developmentalist role of the state appears to be less significant. Differences also extend into substantial variations in economic performance. Despite their general authoritarianism, the political differences among East Asian regimes are quite substantial in such important areas as the role of bureaucracies, the efficiency of "developmentalist states" and regime responsiveness to popular pressures.

Given this more nuanced view of East Asia, what lessons can be drawn? East Asian success reflects a combination of flexibility, foresight and fortuna. These economies cannot be conceptualized in terms of any single theoretical paradigm or development strategy. The modernization approach touts *laissez-faire* capitalism and cultural change; in contrast, although markets have played a key role in East Asian dynamism, the state and, perhaps, culture are also essential elements in this development pattern. The East Asian economies have explicitly and vigorously sought incorporation in the global economy, though some states have also tried to control foreign capital.

Mistaken government initiatives and outright failures throughout the region, private entrepreneurial successes, and blatant corruption suggest the need to do more than bring the state back in (Evans, Rueschemeyer, and Skocpol, 1985). Instead, in different ways East Asian states have unbundled and selectively recombined the injunctions of apparently opposed approaches, by combining private capital and market processes with state planning and other forms of intervention in shaping and pursuing national development projects. Many of the recent economic accomplishments of the East Asian capitalist economies are rooted in their pragmatic, effective and successful combination of the state and market coordination of public and private sectors. They have both encouraged private enterpreneurship and insisted on governmental economic tutelage.

This pragmatic flexibility or eclecticism seems to be the hallmark of East Asian success. A reluctance to be boxed in by any given orthodoxy and an openness to the "received wisdom" presented by competing paradigms offer important insights into the policy capacities of these nations. Another central feature of East Asian development has been the ability to find new niches of comparative advantage in the global economy, which is rapidly evolving. Such economic flexibility, of course, operates within the framework of domestic politics and international linkages. Beyond the national level, intense economic interactions are creating new and highly successful "natural economic territories" which cut across traditional political boundaries, suggesting a new type of "international flexibility." This implies that East Asian governments have exercised foresight in promoting (or at least not retarding) economic flexibility and adaptability.

Finally, fortune has affected East Asian economies in the sense that many have evidently benefited from factors over which they have had little or no control. The ability to benefit from the international system is also relevant for evaluating current alternatives for structuring the world economy, in particular the choice between maintaining and advancing an open trading system and moving toward regional trading blocs in East Asia, North America, and Europe. Flexibility, foresight and fortune therefore seem to interact (Clark and Chan, 1992: 203-212).

Latin American Emulation?

Latin American and East Asian NIEs are now among the most industrialized nations in the developing world, but have followed different paths of industrialization. Latin American regimes were generally so involved with the import-substituting manufacturing interests that they were unable to push them to develop export capacity. Instead, such interests often remained content with continuing accumulation within the realm of the "protected" national economies or moving their often ill-gotten gains abroad for security, thus exacerbating capital flight and the debt crises.

In addition, industrial growth in the two regions has had some disparate economic and social consequences. During the 1980s, Latin American nations found it difficult to maintain their previous levels of economic expansion as they confronted staggering external debts, high rates of inflation, shortages of investment capital, and growing social and economic marginalization of large segments of their populations. In the social realm as well, the East Asian countries have performed significantly better than their Latin American counterparts in terms of standard indicators of development such as GNP per capita, income distribution, literacy, health and education.

Latin America lost at least a decade with the debt crisis while the East Asian NIEs raced ahead to consolidate their gains as the rest of the region joined the surge, especially after the *endaka* or yen appreciation from 1985. With the grinding burden of $400 billion of debt spread out on easier terms, Latin American countries still need billions in investments from home and abroad to rebuild their economies at a time when they are in stiff competition for investments with countries ranging from Eastern Europe to East Asia. To compete, Latin America—led by Chile, Mexico and Argentina—is quickly remaking itself into a magnet for foreign—including repatriated capital—investment. In short, since the late 1980s, Latin American governments have been adopting liberal development strategies by privatizing, crushing inflation, slashing tariffs, opening doors to foreign investment, and signing free-trade pacts with neighbors and with the U.S. For many, the ultimate goal is a vast, unified market, probably mediated by the U.S. (*Business Week*, 15 June 1992: 51-52).

Most research in the past decade comparing the performance of the East Asian and Latin American economies attributes the superior economic performance of the East Asian over the Latin American NIEs to the different economic policies in the two regions (Ranis, 1985; Ranis and Orrock, 1985; Sachs, 1985; Evans, 1987; Gereffi and Wyman, 1987; Lin, 1988; Harberger, 1988; Fishlow; 1989, Whitehead, 1989; Gereffi and Wyman, 1990; Haggard, 1991). Specifically, these writers argue that East Asian NIEs have adopted "outward-oriented" export oriented policies while Latin American countries have been wedded to "inward-oriented" import substituting industrialization, and that the East Asian NIEs have been characterized by market-oriented policies whereas those of Latin America have involved substantial "distortions" as a result of extensive state intervention in economic activity. The consensus is that Latin America should follow the example of the East Asian NIEs by liberating their economies and reducing the role of the state.

There are two problems with this view. First, it attributes the success of East Asian NIEs almost entirely to good policies and the market, and not at all to favorable circumstances and a good start (Little, 1981: 25). The second is the failure to provide an adequate explanation of why policies have differed between the two regions (Jenkins, 1991b: 198).

The argument that East Asian NIEs' success required "getting the prices right" and a minimal role for the state has been widely challenged, particularly for Singapore, South Korea and Taiwan (Amsden, 1985; Harris, 1987; Pack and Westphal, 1986; White, 1988). The only area in which the free market ideology appears to prevail in practice is in the labor market, which could be a reflection of an authoritarian industrialization strategy—"bloody Taylorism"—in which the influence of trade unions is minimized.

Nor is it the case that the East Asian NIEs (except for Hong Kong and Singapore) have adopted general free trade. The contrast between export-oriented industrialization (EOI) and import substituting industrialization (ISI) is an oversimplified dichotomy. South Korea and Taiwan both experienced periods of ISI before launching their successful export drives (Gereffi and Wyman, 1987). Moreover these countries both promoted exports and provided considerable protection to producers for the domestic market (Wade, 1988; Luedde-Neurath, 1988; Gereffi and Wyman, 1990). Fajnzylber (1981) also suggests that when policies toward direct foreign investment are considered, it is South Korea and Taiwan which appear "inward oriented" in comparison with Latin America.

There is strong empirical support for the view that state intervention has in fact been substantial in the East Asian NIEs, and that this has played a crucial role in their successful industrialization. In addition, Jenkins (1991b) argues that the better performance in East Asia is not simply due to differences in trade orientation or the degree of state intervention, but rather to the effectiveness of the intervention. This effectiveness, he argues, is rooted in the relative autonomy of the state and the structuring of the state apparatus in the two regions, e.g., the historically determined class structure and the international context, which led to much greater state autonomy in East Asia than in Latin America. Consequently, the state in East Asia played a major role in directing investment into productive activities with a view to long-term development which contributed to rapid industrial growth in East Asia. Conversely, truncated development in Latin America resulted from less effective state intervention.

Jenkins (1991b) notes that effective national industrial policies in East Asia are characterized by four key features which contrast sharply to the situation in Latin America: flexibility, selectivity, coherence and an emphasis on promotion rather than regulation.

1. *Flexibility.* Flexibility is expressed in the willingness and ability of East Asian NIEs to change policies when they are not producing the desired results. Latin American industrialization, on the other hand, is full of examples of government policies continuing to support industries despite substantial foreign exchange costs and inefficiency (Villarreal, 1990; Aspe, 1993).
2. *Selectivity.* East Asian countries have operated policies that have been highly selective, favoring particular industries and even particular firms at different times (Wade, 1988: 53; Ludde-Neurath, 1986). These highly selective and protectionist policies of East Asia have been contrasted to the indiscriminate protection given to consumer goods in Latin America (Anglade and Fortin, 1987: 219; Wade, 1989).
3. *Coherence.* There is a high degree of coherence and agreement on the economic goals, and policies have been coordinated to achieve those ends in the East Asian NIEs. In Latin America, on the other

hand, policies are often inconsistent and contradictory (Macomber, 1987: 478; Villarreal, 1990).

4. *Promotion.* The policies in the East Asian NIEs have been directed towards the promotion rather than the regulation of private enterprises. One aspect of this is the reluctance of governments in East Asia to bail out firms that get into difficulties. This stands in sharp contrast to the Latin American situation where states often rescue firms from bankruptcy in order to maintain employment (Balassa, et al., 1986; Lustig, 1992). In Latin America, controls prevent behavior which is regarded by government as undesirable ("market repressing"), rather than promoting what is desirable ("market sustaining") as in the case of East Asia.

Jenkins argues that the question is not how to explain policy differences, but rather how to account for *different economic policies* in the two regions. In short, he asserts that effective state intervention to bring about economic transformation requires that the state: (1) be able to both formulate and implement coherent economic strategies; (2) have a degree of autonomy from the dominant class or class fractions, enabling the state to pursue goals that do not reflect the interests of these groups and may even go against their short term interests; (3) undertake an internal restructuring of the state apparatus so that an efficient and cohesive bureaucratic machinery along with effective policy instruments give the state the capacity to implement economic strategy.

In sum, the key to superior industrial performance in the East Asian NIEs is the ability of the state to direct the accumulation process as required at specific points in time. This, in turn, requires the existence of a developmentalist state with a high degree of autonomy from both the dominant and subordinate classes. To begin with, a high percentage of East Asian and Latin American exports in the 1980s went to the U.S., which has declined economically relative to Germany, Japan and the East Asian NIEs. While Latin America and Canada contributed 43.4 percent of total U.S. imports in 1967 (with 17.5 percent from Latin America), by 1988, the percentage had fallen to 30.6 percent (with 11.5 percent from Latin America, i.e., six percentage points less). In 1967, the U.S. received 21.5 percent of its total imports from East Asia including Japan, with 9.9 percent from other countries of East Asia. By 1988, 42.1 percent of U.S. imports were from that region: the four NIEs had raised their share to 15.5 percent while Japan raised its share to 20.3 percent and the percentage from the ASEAN four (minus Singapore and Brunei) fell a little to 6.9 percent. Interestingly, 30 percent of Taiwan's trade surplus with the U.S. and 40 percent of Japan's were accounted for by exports from these countries to the U.S. made by subsidiaries of U.S. corporations (see Wilkinson, 1991: 72).

The claim that East Asian growth has been completely due to the adoption of a model based on free market forces is widespread, but inaccurate. South Korea, Taiwan and Singapore present examples of strong government intervention in industrial policy, involving real exchange rates, clear policy objectives and precise incentives, as well as other government influences on the scope and pace of industrial development (see Naya, 1987).

Latin America, on the other hand, must overcome simplistic and dogmatic prejudices regarding the character and extent of government intervention. In some cases, state intervention became so extensive that it became very costly and even counter-productive in terms of industrial policy. Yet, limited government intervention has also left great holes, e.g., in terms of public infrastructure relating to education, health care, communications, transportation, etc. (For more on this theme, see the work of Urrutia, 1987.)

The structure of world trade has also changed, with the decreasing importance of food products, agricultural raw materials, minerals and metals, while fuels are returning to their historical level of importance, and there is a clear rise in the importance of manufactures. The deterioration of Latin America as a producer, as well as an importer of export manufactures, is notable. Latin America is still primarily an exporter of primary products. Latin America's specialization is based on agriculture, energy products, textiles as well as iron and steel (where it has some comparative advantage). However, Latin America shows a comparative weakness in mechanics, auto production, electrical products and electronics, in short, in production areas requiring more advanced technological applications.

Therefore, we can say that Latin America's weakness is two-fold. On the one hand, there is an obvious lag in activities where the technological factor is critical, while on the other hand, it has an export structure dominated by primary products, at a time when primary products are losing importance in international trade and, even worse, when prices of primary products have become increasingly subject to speculation in the developed countries (see Kuchiki, 1987). This is in stark contrast with East Asian NIEs, which are increasingly driven by technological innovation as opposed to cheap labor.

Book Outline

This book probably represents the first ever volume seeking to compare recent Latin American and East Asian experiences primarily by authors from the two regions coming together to explore some dimensions of their respective development experiences. Considered together, the chapters in this volume provide new "takes" on the relevant debates in several different ways. Comparison between East Asia and Latin America is explicitly important to the chapters by Alarcon, Gutiérrez, and Lippit, while it is more implicit in other chapters. The papers in the first part of the volume review various regional trends, including Japanese investments and firm strategies, financial liberalization, technology issues as well as income distribution trends.

Since the late 1980s, Latin Americanists Maria Patricia Fernandez-Kelly 1983, Peter Evans 1987, Gary Gereffi [1987, 1989a, 1989b, 1990], Fernando Fajnzylber [1981, 1989, 1990], Alejandro Alvarez and John Borrego 1990, Rhys Jenkins 1991, and Legorreta 1991 seeking to understand the apparent regression of "their" continent compared to their counterparts on the other side of the Pacific Ocean, have led the way in comparing East Asia and Latin America, although less well known initiatives in Japan and South Korea deserve mention (e.g., see Kim 1987; Fukuchi and Kagami 1990; Kagami 1995). This volume supplements this literature by extending the comparison to China (Lippit) and Southeast Asia (see the chapters by Alarcon and Gutiérrez in this volume).

The crucial role of the financial sector in late industrialization is still poorly recognized. Antonio Gutiérrez's "Financial integration and deregulation in Latin American and East Asian countries" argues that the 1980s was a decade of profound changes in the world's productive, commercial and financial activities. Recent years have witnessed redefinition of financial notions of time and space—the significance of distance has been practically eliminated and borders have been virtually erased. Among the most important changes have been deregulation of national economies, regionalization of markets and globalization of competition. Gutiérrez argues that the internationalization of production and finance and the concomitant development of a network of global interdependence requires us to redefine the role of states, the impact and limits of national economic policies and the significance of borders. He foresees the global economy, regional blocs and national sovereignties becoming the key constituent elements in the coming years. The strength and proliferation of regional agreements, compared to the weakness and problems of multilateral agreements and forums, express the real difficulties involved in trying to harmonize these divergent tendencies. It is within this new context that most developing countries have been redefining their national development strategies and forms of insertion in the international economy. Gutiérrez further argues that within this new global framework—from the global reach of megabanks to certain niches for banks specializing in special functions and operations—the differences among institutions will be more determined by the growth strategies they follow than by government regulation.

Gutiérrez then compares the processes of financial integration and deregulation in Latin America and East Asia, specifically in Mexico, South Korea and Taiwan, within this new global financial structure. He argues that the forms assumed with each country's financial sector liberalization will determine the course and the characteristics of its role within the financial globalization process. One remote possibility is that they will become truly open financial systems, yet capable of articulating national development. Another option is that they could become systems integrated with and subordinated to hegemonic centers. He argues that what is at stake in this process, even more than financial liberalization or the freeing of capital flows, is control over monetary circuits, and with that, a country's financial stability and its potential for exercising economic sovereignty.

Anuwar Ali's chapter, "Globalization and technology acquisition by the developing countries of East Asia," argues that economic globalization has led to greater economic integration and changing investment flows among countries of the Asia-Pacific region. He posits that changing investment flows will negatively impact on the industrialization process and the technology acquisition capabilities of developing countries in the region. He then outlines the major policy areas which must be emphasized by developing countries of the Asia-Pacific region if they are to become technologically competent in an ever changing global economic scenario: first, the state must take a leadership role in enhancing technological change; second, this must be complemented by "extensive and visible" mechanisms to increase public sector and private industrial collaboration; third, the state must support technological innovation through creation of demand, subsidies to firms, regulation, technical and scientific infrastructure plus support for small and medium-scale manufacturing firms; and fourth, it should help develop a banking system well adapted to the needs of innovative industries.

Anuwar concludes that the most important role of the state will be to establish an environment that stimulates firms and specialized technological agents such as engineering firms and intermediate goods suppliers to engage in ongoing technological development efforts and to enhance technological capabilities. The state should also intervene directly to induce choices of techniques that are socially most appropriate, to foster imports of technology on the best possible terms, and to stimulate the development of specialized technological agents. In short, he argues that only the state can ensure that a developing country wishing to industrialize will benefit from the correct mix of incentives, price signals, infrastructure, human resource development, and institutional framework for science and technology.

Radical critics of economic liberalization often presume that its consequences will be inequitable. Diana Alarcón's "Trade liberalization and income distribution in the East Asian economies" argues that the impact of trade liberalization on the distribution of income depends largely on the structural linkages of exporting sectors to the rest of the economy, and on institutional factors, including the structure of ownership of the means of production and the role of government in promoting human resource development. She, however, sees no unique or a priori relationship between trade liberalization and income distribution. Whether trade liberalization has an equalizing or disequalizing impact on income distribution depends on how it is refracted through the institutional framework of the economy.

Six East Asian countries (Indonesia, South Korea, Taiwan, Philippines, Thailand and Malaysia) are used to illustrate her discussion of the likely effects of trade liberalization on development in Mexico, which has recently adopted similar policies. She concludes that countries can reduce protectionist trade distortions that adversely effect economic efficiency while achieving a more egalitarian pattern of income distribution. Trade liberalization is compatible with greater equality when it is accompanied by policies oriented to promoting human resource development, thus raising the incomes of broad sectors of the working population.

Alarcon offers three important lessons from her analysis: first, exporting sectors have the greatest effects on the development of an economy when comprehensive policies of trade liberalization are adopted; second, trade liberalization is more likely to have an equalizing impact on the distribution of income when productive assets in agriculture and industry are more equally distributed; and third, contrary to some of the most publicized misconceptions about the experience of East Asia, the relatively egalitarian effects of trade liberalization have partly been due to active government intervention. She concludes that significant complementaries can be developed between economic efficiency and equity in the process of trade liberalization. Hence, dismantling a system of protectionism that breeds inefficiency can be achieved with equity, but there must be political will to ensure such an outcome.

The second part of the volume considers the role of developmentalist states in relation to nationalist economic projects, particularly late industrialization. The idea of national—as opposed to international—economic integration in Korea, industrial policy in South Korea and Taiwan, the possibilities for East Asian NIE emulation, and the crucial role of state intervention and rents in both import substituting and export-oriented industrialization are considered in turn. Lippit's comparison of the different distributional outcomes of marketization in China and Mexico supports Alarcon's observations about the East Asian-Latin American contrast, while Guyton's survey of technology transfer due to Japanese manufacturing investments in Malaysia elaborate on Tateishi's regional observations.

In sub-regional or spatial terms, many of the contributions move the discussion South from Northeast to Southeast Asia, especially to the ASEAN (Association of South East Asian Nations) economies, and to southern China, including Hong Kong. Together, they add much nuance to and even contradict the popular, but simplistic view of the East Asian economies as being in some kind of "flying geese" formation, with Japan in the lead, Taiwan and South Korea just behind, and the other economies in the region following behind and gaining from capital and technological flows down the line, i.e., a new version of "trickle down" (Ozawa 1993). Although the boom in Southeast Asia and southern China since the late 1980s has been fueled by investments from Japan and the East Asian NIEs, especially since the appreciation of the yen and the other NIE currencies after the second Plaza Hotel agreement in September 1985, foreign investment has certainly not been entirely benevolent. In pursuit of profit, jobs have been created and incomes have been raised, but not without resorting to the *mailed fist* of the state—rather than the *invisible hand* of the market—to keep labor and other recalcitrant communities obstructing further accumulation (e.g., forest communities), among others, in check (Deyo 1989).

Kim Dae Hwan's chapter, "The idea of national economic integration: the experience of South Korean development" argues that economic integration at the national level is required before international economic integration. Kim argues that most underdeveloped countries have tried to pursue national economic integration since independence from colonial rule, while the international economic system encourages international integration instead. Notwithstanding its export orientation, South Korea has also had a strong nationalist heritage. Kim argues that South Korea's economic success has to be understood in this context, even though its national integration has been accompanied by export-oriented industrialization.

In general, however, efforts towards national economic integration have been neglected because of the belief that development requires international integration. Kim criticizes this belief and instead proposes national economic integration, arguing its significance for development in underdeveloped countries. He admits that economic nationalism in South Korea was not well organized and did not emphasize distributional equality. Thus, despite relative equality at the outset, South Korea has been experiencing deepening inequality, and intensifying social conflicts, which in turn threaten national development. He argues that structural integration can only be secured when distributional equality is combined with close interconnectedness among economic sectors. Kim concludes that national economic integration continues to be an important condition for national development.

Michael H. H. Hsiao's chapter on "Agricultural reform in Taiwan and South Korea" analyzes the specific circumstances in the two countries which facilitated the land reforms of the early 1950s but also saw the emergence of subsequent policies to squeeze agriculture. He highlights the "counter-revolutionary" imperative for reform in the face of rural support for the communist enemy, the "non-indigenous" nature of the American Military Government in South Korea and the Guomindang regime in Taiwan, the weakness of landed interests after decades of Japanese colonialism as well as civil war and their inability to block reform, and the relatively painless and attractive option of land sales for the landed interests willing to transform the nature of their economic assets for industrial capital accumulation. He also considers the agriculture squeezing strategies introduced after the land reforms, noting that the net gains were enough to ensure continued rural support for the regimes despite urban-industrial capital accumulation at the farmers' expense.

In his chapter, "Industrial policy in South Korea and Taiwan," Tan Kock Wah looks critically at the neoclassical economic paradigm and seeks to incorporate the findings of another growing stream of literature which emphasizes the directive role of the state in East Asia. Tan argues that the prescription of economic liberalization to realize comparative advantage is a static proposition more concerned with the present situation than with future change. It does not give enough weight to the possibility of dynamic gains from short-term distortions, and the possibility of creating comparative advantage through rapid structural change for countries desiring long-term development. He points out that the "capital debate" which questioned the very foundation of neoclassical economics also undermined the internal logic of the Heckscher-Ohlin-Samuelson theory, identified earlier as the linchpin of the neoclassical approach to international trade theory. For if factor abundance cannot be defined independently of factor prices, a crucial building block of the theory, it is put into serious question. The neo-Ricardian critique has also shown that comparative advantage does not arise naturally, but is determined by differences in technology, consumer preferences and determinants of wages and profits, i.e., it can be deliberately created by economic policy.

Tan shows how industrial policy in East Asia has been concerned with creating dynamic comparative advantage, as opposed to the static neoclassical notion of comparative advantage, in which natural or factor endowment differences are reflected in the global division of labor. He shows why industrial targeting became an important tool for East Asian economies. The government "picks winners," identifying and promoting certain industries and technologies that they anticipated would be important for the competitiveness and well-being of the economy in the future. The positive or explicit industrial policy characterizing the East Asian NIEs has involved the infusion of coordinated goal-oriented strategic thinking into economic policy to leverage up the productivity and competitiveness of the whole economy through particular key industries. Tan argues that the cases of successful industrial policy in Taiwan and South Korea show that the state in developing countries can indeed play a positive and crucial role in late industrialization. He concludes that the missing element in the less impressive performances of other Third World countries is a "strong state committed to development with considerable autonomy in public policy formation."

Victor Lippit's chapter, "China and Mexico: Comparable Development Strategies, Disparate Results," outlines how both countries have undertaken similar reform programs in response to the serious economic and social problems associated with previous development strategies, even though China claims a "socialist" development strategy and Mexico is clearly pursuing a "capitalist" one. Both are seeking to reduce the scope of government intervention in economic activities, to enhance the role of market forces and the private sector, and to move away from earlier policies of limited participation in the capitalist world economy by sharply increasing the role of international trade and investment. The similarity of their development strategies is clear (e.g., both have linked their economies with the capitalist world economy and benefited from the upsurge in international trade and investment): both are seeking ways to reform inherited industrial structures while retaining a role for the state in planning or industrial policy, but also promoting the role of market forces in allocation decisions.

Yet, despite some similarities, there are major differences between the two countries. Lippit argues that in China the benefits of reform have largely accrued to the working classes—peasants as well as industrial workers. Although there is indeed a group of capitalist "nouveaux riches" benefiting from the reforms, a substantial share of the gains go to the mass of population. In Mexico, by contrast, capitalists have been the primary beneficiaries during the early stages of reform. In fact, the unequal distribution of income and wealth at the start of the reform period has intensified, while many workers have been dismissed because of restructuring. Lippit thus argues that the class impact of the reforms in the two countries have been strikingly different. He shows how the inherited collective and egalitarian institutions in China have, until recently, created the conditions for mass gains from economic reform. In Mexico, by contrast, the inegalitarian statist capitalist social formation that was the object of reform ensured that its primary beneficiaries would not be the producing classes, but the capitalist elite. He concludes that while ordinary people have been the major beneficiaries of the reform program in China, the reform program was built on the backs of such people in Mexico. Lippit argues that even though China has been able to maintain high rates of real growth, the government has been unable to restrain inflation. This has initiated an intensification of social problems such as crime, corruption and the exploitation of labor which are calling into question the very character of the transformation China is experiencing. In the case of Mexico, a new financial crisis emerged despite the approval of the North American Free Trade Agreement (NAFTA), and once again, the burden of the crisis fell disproportionately on the poor.

Thus, with Latin America very much in mind, both Alarcon and Lippit acknowledge and highlight the relatively equitable outcomes of economic liberalization both in some East Asian economies and until recently in China. But they are also careful to emphasize the preconditions (e.g., land reform) and the very nature of the liberalizations (e.g., privileging human resources) which have ensured such outcomes. However, Lippit suggests that the development trajectory that China is now following is more likely to lead to the emergence of welfare state capitalism than the officially endorsed market socialism.

Moving beyond the Bhagwati "simulated market" argument mentioned earlier, Rajah Rasiah takes on the myth that import substitution policies are distortionary while policies promoting export-oriented industrialization are not. Reviewing the Malaysian experience, he documents how the state intervened first to promote import-substituting industrialization from the late 1950s, and then to encourage export-oriented industrialization from the late 1960s. He acknowledges that the nature of the interventions and the distortionary rents generated have necessarily been different, but his main point is to emphasize that the latter is far from being undistortionary, as suggested by most of the neoclassical economic literature. He also does not agree with the common characterization of the Malaysian Government's heavy industrialization efforts from the early 1980s as a second round of import substitution because the new heavy industries have not been strategically linked with the rest of the economy, especially the rest of the manufacturing sector, and hence do not have the potential of significantly advancing Malaysia's industrialization efforts.

In her chapter reviewing technology transfer by Japanese consumer electronics manufacturing firms operating in Malaysia, Lynne Guyton carefully analyzes firm interests, *keiretsu* organizational structures, production strategies, management practices, the attitudes of Japanese as well as Malaysian managers, and the adequacy of government technology policies. Drawing from her survey results, she doubts that Malaysian technological capacity will be significantly enhanced on the basis of existing technology transfer policies, considering the attitudes of Japanese firms and managers towards technology transfer and the nature of Malaysian technological capacities, including the quality of human resources. She concludes by making various recommendations to various parties involved to enhance and facilitate technology transfer, especially by Japanese manufacturing firms in Malaysia.

Besides the usual focus on regions and states, the last two chapters in this volume by writers from Hong Kong provide insights of local-level, often trans-border developments in what is arguably the fastest growing region in the world in the early 1990s. Both chapters highlight the dynamism of capital in this rather peculiar historical and geographical conjuncture, especially when the fetters imposed by states are lifted.

Thomas Chan's "The Southern Chinese Quadrangle: Fujian, Guangdong, Hong Kong and Taiwan" shows the integration of "South China"—consisting of the four "local" economies of Fujian, Guangdong, Hong Kong and Taiwan—as a transnational economic region since China adopted economic liberalization and open door policies in the 1980s. Chan argues that Taiwan, a latecomer investor on the China scene, has begun relocating many of its export-oriented labor-intensive industries in Southeast Asia and China, mainly in Fujian and Guangdong. In contrast, Hong Kong has almost completed its industrial relocation into South China and has concentrated on the development of service industries in Hong Kong and even in Guangdong.

Chan links the structural transformation of Hong Kong's economy with the economic development and export expansion of Guangdong in the second half of the 1980s. He shows how Hong Kong's economy has been transformed from an industrial economy into one increasingly dominated by the fast growing service sector rooted in China business since the 1980s. The greater opening up of China has strengthened Hong Kong as the main link between China and the outside world, further integrating Hong Kong into the emerging regional division of labor. Finally, Chan suggests that the combination of export-oriented labor intensive industries with the emerging secondary import-substituting industries in Guangdong could create a dynamic regional economy that would in turn force a further restructuring of the economies of Hong Kong and Taiwan.

In their chapter, "Merchants, small employers and the non- interventionist state: Hong Kong as a case of unorganized late industrialization," Tai-Lok Lui and Stephen W. K. Chiu focus on the process shaping industrial development in the British colony. They show how industries in Hong Kong have been restructuring in response to changes in their competitive advantages in the changing global and regional environment. There have been two key changes. First, what were once the competitive edges of Hong Kong firms, particularly low labor costs and attractive terms for foreign investments, were rapidly eroded in the 1980s. Second, with changes in their comparative advantages, NIEs such as Hong Kong have had to restructure their industries. Hence, conditions and policies conducive to rapid growth and development in an earlier phase of industrialization are no longer sufficient for overcoming the new problems.

Lui and Chiu find that after the exodus by manufacturers to offshore assembly in China (especially to the Shenzen Special Economic Zone and other areas of Guangdong Province) in the 1980s the manufacturing activities remaining in Hong Kong continue to be labor-intensive and have not significantly "moved up" to more technologically sophisticated products. Clearly, the China factor and the abundant supplies of cheap labor and land in China's Pearl River delta make the continuation of labor intensive production viable without reshaping production strategies. Yet, the Hong Kong manufacturing sector has still been able to attain reasonable growth. This enigma of Hong Kong's industrialization is explained by the continued flexible importation of labor and the firms' abilities to serve the growing and rapidly changing requirements of flexible specialization. They argue that local manufacturers have almost been left on their own to cope with problems arising from increasing protection abroad, rising local production costs and changes in global capitalism, suggesting that Hong Kong is a case of unorganized late industrialization. They argue that, notwithstanding the massive spending on housing, medical care, education and social welfare by the colonial government supporting industrial development, the Hong Kong government falls far short of being a capitalist developmentalist state.

The overall picture emerging from this volume then is complex and nuanced. It calls for greater, more multidimensional and hence, more subtle understanding of the myriad relations and processes involved in late industrialization. It requires abandoning many of the simple and convenient dogmas on which so much analysis has been built. And it also reminds us of the difficulties of emulation, especially in a fast changing world economy in which transnational capital has been increasingly able to set the rules of the game.

At the present time, the only way to make generalizations from the varied situations and experiences in the diverse East Asian region would be to ignore the important political, geographic, cultural and other specificities of the moment. The ability to distinguish the particular from the general and the generalizable is another important quality possessed by the authors of this volume. Their analyses prove quite different from the often ambitious and sometimes pretentious claims at theorization, generalization or policy formula making.

References

Agalde, C., and C. Fortin. "Accumulation, Adjustment and the Autonomy of the State in Latin America." In *The State and Capital Accumulation in Latin America*, edited by C. Agalde and C. Fortin, Vol. 2. London: Macmillan. 1990: 211-332.

Alvarez, A., and J. Borrego. *La inserción de México en la Cuenca Del Pacífico.* Mexico D.F.: Facultad De Economia, Universidad Nacional Autonoma de Mexico. 1990.

Appelbaum, R., and J. Henderson. *States and Development in the Asian Pacific Rim.* Newbury Park: Sage Publications. 1992.

Amsden, Alice. "The State and Taiwan's Economic Development." In *Bringing the State Back In,* edited by Peter Evans, Dietrich Rueschemeyer & Theda Skocpol. Cambridge: Cambridge University Press. 1985: 78-106.

____. *Asia's Next Giant: South Korea and Late Industrialization.* New York: Oxford University Press. 1989.

Aspe Armella, P. *El camino Mexicano de la transformation economica.* Mexico, D.F.: Fondo De Cultura Economica. 1993.

Base, Chelem, and Gerard Lafay. "Commerce international, la fin des avantages acquis." In *Economie Prospective Internationale.* Paris: Centre d'Etudes Prospectives et d'Informations Internationales. 1989.

Bellassa, B., G. Bueno, P. Kuczynski, and M. Simonsen. *Toward Renewed Economic Growth in Latin America.* Washington, DC: Institute of International Economics. 1986.

Bello, W., and S. Rosenfeld. *Dragons in Distress: Asia's Miracle Economies in Crisis.* San Francisco: Food First. 1990.

Bird, Graham, and Ann Helwege (eds). *Latin America's Economic Future.* New York: Academic Press. 1994.

Business Week. "Asia Wealth." November 29, 1993: 20-37.

Castells, M., L. Goh, and R. Y-W. Kwok. *The Shek Kip Mei Syndrome: Economic Development and Public Housing in Hong Kong and Singapore*. London: Pion. 1990.

Chomsky, N. *Deterring Democracy*. New York: Hill and Wang. 1992.

Clark, C., and S. Chan, eds. *The Evolving Pacific Basin in the Global Political Economy: Domestic & International Linkages*. Boulder: Lynne Rienner. 1992.

Deyo, Frederick. *Beneath The Miracle: Labor Subordination in the New Asian Industrialization*. Berkeley: University of California Press. 1989.

Dicken, Peter. *Global Shift*. London: Harper & Row. 1992.

ECLA. "Panorama Social de America Latina." *Notas sobre la Economia y el Desarrollo* No. 517-518. November 1991: 2-3.

Edwards, Chris. "State Intervention and Industrialisation in South Korea: Lessons for Malaysia." In *Industrialising Malaysia: Policy, Performance, Prospects,* edited by Jomo K. S. London: Routledge. 1993.

Evans, Peter. "Class, State, and Dependence in East Asia: Latin Americanists." In *The Political Economy of the New Asian Industrialism,* edited by F. Deyo. Ithaca: Cornell University Press. 1987.

Evans, Peter, Dietrich Rueschemeyer, and Theda Skocpol, eds. *Bringing the State Back In*. Cambridge: Cambridge University Press. 1985.

Fajnzylber, Fernando. "Some Reflections on South-east Asian Export Industrialization." *CEPAL Review*. December 1981: 11-132.

____. "Sobre la impostergable reestructuracion industrial de America Latina." Santiago, Chile: ECLA. Mimeo. 1989.

____. *Unavoidable Industrial Restructuring in Latin America*. Durham, NC: Duke University Press. 1990.

Fernandez-Kelley, Maria Patricia. *Una Comparacíon del Paralelismo entre Las Zonas de Procesamiento de Exportacíon de Asia y de La Frontera México-Norteamericana*. Tijuana: Centro de Estudios Fronterizos del Norte de Mexico. 1983.

Fishlow, A. "Latin American Failure Against the Backdrop of Asian Success." *The Annals of the American Academy of Political and Social Science* 505. Sept 1989: 117-28.

Forbes. "Overseas China: The Giant Economy That Knows No Borders." July 18, 1994: 138-182.

Friedman, G., and Meredeth Lebard. *The Coming War with Japan*. New York: St. Martin's Press. 1991.

Fukuchi, Takao, and Mitsuhiro Kagami. *Perspectives on the Pacific Basin Economy: A Comparison of Asia and Latin America*. Tokyo: Institute of Developing Economies. 1989.

Gereffi, Gary. "Development Strategies and Global Factory: Latin America and East Asia." *The Annals of the American Academy of Political and Social Science* No. 505. 1989a.

____. "Industrial Restructuring and National Development Strategies: A Comparison of Taiwan, South Korea, Brazil; and Mexico." In *Taiwan: A Newly Industrialized State*, edited by H. Hsiao, W. Chen, and H. Chan. Taipei: National Taiwan University. 1989b.

Gereffi, G., and D. Wyman. *Manufacturing Miracles: Paths of Industrialization in Latin America and East Asia*. Princeton, NJ: Princeton University Press. 1990.

____. "Determinants of Development Strategies in Latin America and East Asia." *Pacific Focus* 1, No. 2. 1987.

Gerschenkron, A. *Economic Backwardness in Historical Perspective.* Cambridge: Harvard University Press. 1962.

Gomez, Alain. "The Case Against Free Trade." *Fortune* 4. May 1992: 32.

Haggard, S. *Pathways from the Periphery: The Politics of Growth in the Newly Industrializing Countries.* Ithaca: Cornell University Press. 1991.

Hamilton, C. "Can the Rest of Asia Emulate the NICs?" *Third World Quarterly* 9, No. 4. October 1987.

Harberger, A. "Growth, Industrialization and Economic Structure: Latin America and East Asia Compared." In *Achieving Industrialization in East Asia,* edited by H. Hughes. Cambridge: Cambridge University Press. 1988: 164-194.

Harris, N. *The End of the Third World.* Harmondsworth: Penguin. 1987.

Jenkins, R. "Learning from the Gang: Are There Lessons for Latin America from East Asia?" *Bulletin of Latin American Research* 10, No. 1. 1991a: 37-54.

____. "The Political Economy of Industrialization: A Comparison of Latin American and East Asian NICs." *Development and Change* 22. 1991b: 197-231.

Kagami, Mitsuhiro. *Voices of East Asia: Development Implications for Latin America.* Tokyo: Institute of Developing Economies. 1995.

Kim Kyong-Dong, ed. *Dependency Issues in Korean Development: Comparative Perspectives.* Seoul: Seoul National University Press. 1987.

Kreye, O., J. Heinrichs, and F. Frobel. "Export Processing Zones in Developing Countries: Results of a New Survey." Paper No. 43. Geneva: International Labor Office. 1987.

Krugman, Paul. "The Myth of the Asian Miracle." *Foreign Affairs* 73, No. 6. Nov./Dec. 1994a.

____. "Competitiveness: A Dangerous Obsession." *Foreign Affairs* 73, No. 2. March/April 1994b.

____. "Is Free Trade Passé?" *Economic Perspectives* 1, No. 2. Fall 1987: 131-4.

Kuchiki Akifumi. "The Pricing Mechanism of Primary Commodities since the 1970s." In *The Present and Future of the Pacific Basin Economy: A Comparison of Asia and Latin America,* edited by Takao Fukuchi and Mitsuhiro Kagami. Tokyo: Institute of Developing Economies. 1987.

Lafay, Gerard, and Denis Unal-Kesenci. "Les trois poles geographiques des echanges internationaux. Institute of Developing Economies." In *Economie Prospective Internationale.* Paris: Centre d'Etudes Prospectives et d'Informations Internationales.

Legorreta, Omar M. *Industria, Comercio y Estado: Algunas Experiencias en La Cuenca Del Pacifico.* Mexico, D.F.: El Colegio De Mexico. 1991.

Lin, C. "East Asia and Latin America as Contrasting Models." *Economic Development and Cultural Change* 36 (3) Supplement: S153-S197. 1988.

Ludde-Neurath, R. *Import Controls and Export Oriented Development.* Boulder: Westview Press. 1986.

Lustig, Nora. *The Remaking of an Economy.* Washington, DC: The Brookings Institution. 1992.

Macomber, J. "East Asia's Lessons for Latin American Resurgence." *The World Economy* 10(4). 1987: 469-82.

Naya Seiji. "Economic Performance: NIEs and Beyond." In *The Present and Future of the Pacific Basin Economy: A Comparison of Asia and Latin America,* edited by Takao Fukuchi and Mitsuhiro Kagami. Tokyo: Institute of Developing Economies. 1989.

Ozawa, T. "Foreign Direct Investment and Structural Transformation: Japan as a Recycler of Market and Industry." *Business and the Contemporary World* 5, No. 2. Spring 1993.

Pack, H., and Westphal, L. "Industrial Strategy Technological Change: Theory vs. Reality." *Journal of Development Economics* 22. 1986: 87-128.

Ranis, G. "Employment, Income Distribution, and Growth in the East Asia Context: A Comparative Analysis." In *Export-Oriented Development Strategies,* edited by V. Corbo, A. Krueger and F. Ossa. Boulder: Westview Press. 1985: 249-74.

Ranis, G., and L. Orrock. "Latin American and East Asian NICs: Development Strategies Compared." In *Latin America and the World Recession,* edited by E. Duran. Cambridge: Cambridge University Press. 1985: 48-66.

Rodan, Garry. *The Political Economy of Singapore's Industrialization.* London: Macmillan. 1989.

Rosales, Osvaldo. "Escenarios y tendencias en el comercio internacional." In *La agenda internacional en los anos noventa,* edited by Roberto Russel. Buenos Aires: Grupo Editor Latinoamericano. 1990: 97-126.

Sachs. J. "External Debt and Macroeconomic Performance in Latin America and East Asia." *Brookings Papers* 2. 1985: 523-73.

Sheahan, J. *Patterns of Development in Latin America: Poverty, Repression and Economic Strategy.* Princeton: Princeton University Press. 1987.

____. *Conflict and Change in Mexican Economic Strategy: Implications for Mexico and for Latin America.* Monograph Series No. 34. San Diego: Center for U.S.-Mexican Studies, University of California. 1991.

Szekely, G., ed. *Manufacturing Across Borders and Oceans: Japan, The United States, and Mexico.* Monograph Series No. 36. San Diego: Center for U.S.-Mexican Studies, University of California. 1991.

Thurow, Lester. *Head to Head: The Coming Economic Battle Among Japan, Europe and America.* NY: William Morrow and Company. 1992.

Urrutia, Miguel. "Trends in Latin American Development." In *The Present and Future of the Pacific Basin Economy: A Comparison of Asia and Latin America,* edited by Takao Fukuchi and Mitsuhiro Kagami. Tokyo: Institute of Developing Economies. 1987.

Villarreal, Rene. "The Latin American Strategy of Import Substitution: Failure or Paradigm for the Region?" In *Manufacturing Miracles: Paths of Industrialization in Latin America and East Asia,* edited by Gary Gereffi and Donald Wyman. Princeton: Princeton University Press. 1990.

Wade, R. "East Asia Economic Success: Conflicting Perspectives, Partial Insights, Shaky Evidence." *World Politics* 44. 1992: 270-320.

____. *Governing the Market: Economic Theory and the Role of Government in East Asian Industrialization.* Princeton: Princeton University Press. 1990.

____. "What Can Economists Learn from East Asian Success?" *The Annals of the American Academy of Political and Social Sciences* 505. Sept. 1989: 68-79.

____. "State Intervention in 'Outward Looking' Development: Neoclassical Theory and Taiwanese Practice." In *Developmental States in East Asia,* edited by G. White. London: Macmillan. 1988: 30-67.

White, G., ed. *Developmental States in East Asia.* London: Macmillan. 1988.

Whitehead, L. "Tigers in Latin America?" *The Annals of the American Academy of Political and Social Sciences* 505. Sept. 1989: 142-51.

Wilkinson, Bruce. "Regional Trading Blocs: Fortress Europe versus Fortress North America." In *The New Era of Global Competition: State Policy and Market Power,* edited by Daniel Drache and Mercis Gertler. Montreal: McGill University Press. 1991.

World Bank. *The East Asian Miracle: Economic Growth and Public Policy.* Washington, DC: World Bank. 1993.

2

Financial Liberalization in Latin American and East Asian Countries

Antonio Gutiérrez Pérez

The 1980s witnessed profound change in international economic relations. After a period of great instability during the 1970s, the world economy experienced rapid transformation that brought about significant changes in the productive, commercial and financial sectors. The most important features of the recent process of restructuring have been: the deregulation of national economies, the regionalization of markets and the globalization of competition. Undoubtedly, the internationalization of production and financial sector operations at a time of growing interdependence among nations introduces a new set of difficult questions. There is a need to redefine the role of the state, the limits of national economic policies, and the new meaning of international borders.

These complex developments in the world economy are taking place in a context of great uncertainty and instability, in an environment of growing macroeconomic imbalances and uneven adjustment among nations. Underlying this process is a modification of the structure of power in the world economy. The new set of relationships in the global economy, regional blocs and national states is one of the most difficult problems that will have to be resolved in the coming years. The strength and proliferation of regional agreements—compared to the growing weakness of multilateral international agreements—are an expression of the real difficulties involved in trying to harmonize divergent tendencies. In this context, most developing countries have been redefining their development strategies and their new role in the world economy.

In particular, the Latin American debt crises reflected the intimate relationship between a country's sovereignty, and its financial strength. The financial strength of a country reflects its strength in international markets besides defining each country's margin of action in the world economy. The experiences of Japan and South Korea in the last decade are clear examples of how financial strength goes hand in hand with commercial success and a country's ability to promote its strategic interests in international institutions such as GATT.

The aim of this chapter is to compare the processes of financial integration and deregulation in Latin America and East Asia, by specifically addressing the experiences of Mexico, South Korea and Taiwan. In each case, the nature of financial liberalization has determined the country's role in the global financial system; this addresses the question of whether financial liberalization in these countries is the expression of a nationally articulated process of development, or alternatively, whether it is simply the expression of subordination to a foreign hegemonic financial center.

What is ultimately at stake in this process is not the question of financial liberalization per se, but the mechanisms of control of money circuits, and along with them, a country's financial stability and economic sovereignty.

In this context of greater integration and globalization of the world economy, that is redefining the concept of national sovereignty itself, the challenge for Latin American and East Asian countries is to retain their autonomy in defining monetary policy and financial stability; both necessary for macroeconomic and price stability and, therefore, for economic development.

Tendencies and Changes in the International Financial System

The 1980s was the decade of finance.[1] During those ten years, the world witnessed the erosion of the foundations upon which post-war national financial systems were built. It was a decade of sweeping innovations in financial markets involving the creation of new financial products and services. There was a significant decrease in barriers to trade, within both domestic and international markets. New ways to finance economic activity emerged.

But it was also a decade characterized by great instability, signaled by the 1982 debt crisis and the 1987 stock market crash. Great volatility and uncertainty were associated with the functioning of monetary and financial circuits.

There is a whole range of issues that cannot be understood without referring to the structural changes taking place within financial markets, including: (i) the persistence of macroeconomic instability in the world economy, (ii) the process of adjustment and structural change in Latin America, (iii) the restructuring of important economic sectors, and (iv) the rapid growth of speculative activities.

The radical transformation of financial markets in the last 15 years amounts to a truly revolutionary transformation. It has introduced radical changes to the dynamics and role of different players in financial markets. All changes taking place in the functioning of financial markets point in the same direction, namely the globalization of financial markets, with a continuous flow of resources around the world.

The development of a global financial market should be perceived as an integral part of the overall process of globalization taking place at all levels of economic activity. In turn, the tendencies towards globalization constitute a new phase of capitalist development, characterized by the geographical and functional integration of world markets. This is the expression of a new pattern of capitalist accumulation based on more open and integrated economic activities.[2]

In this context, the integration of a global financial market represents a new stage in the internationalization of monetary capital, new stage where the role of financial institutions goes beyond the traditional financing of international trade, or even the financing of direct investment in other countries. This new stage of development also differs from the struggle over markets to recycle excess world liquidity (especially petro-dollars), characteristic of the nineteen seventies.[3] What is at stake this time, is the construction of a new way to finance economic activity, and therein lies its significance. It is important to keep in mind that the financial system is the organizer and the mechanism that articulates production, both in its role as lender and in the distribution and appropriation of economic surplus. Thus, financial globalization is a condition for economic globalization.

This new phase in the internationalization of financial capital is the result of a process of innovation and deregulation of financial markets. Technological innovation has had important consequences: (i) it has eroded the national barriers to the flow of resources, (ii) it has facilitated the development of closer links between stock and credit markets, (iii) it has forced rapid changes in the structure of regulation of financial markets, and (iv) it has facilitated greater overall harmonization in the operation of financial institutions.[4]

Changes in the operations of financial markets cannot be understood without referring to the emergence of a new technological base, i.e., the development of telecommunications and the generalized use of computers, which has introduced permanent structural changes. Technological innovation is behind the growing sophistication of today's financial services.

Technological innovation has made it possible to carry out transactions around the clock. Technological changes, rapidly assimilated by the financial sector, have made key contribution to the globalization of capital markets. Decreasing costs of telecommunications has facilitated instantaneous transmission and storage of information, financial statements and transactions. Market fragmentation no longer makes sense. In recent years, we have witnessed a rapid redefinition of the concepts of time and space in the operation of financial markets. The significance of distance has been virtually eliminated, and the concept of space has broadened with the virtual elimination of national borders.

Innovation and financial deregulation are taking place in all market economies, the result of a combination of several factors.[5] Among them, macroeconomic changes (fluctuations in interest and exchange rates, inflation, etc.) and growing competition in domestic and international markets that result from the emergence of new financial institutions, and the drive to circumvent the government regulations enacted after the 1929 stock market crash.

We can distinguish two forms of financial innovation and deregulation.[6] The first originates mainly in the United States and England in the private sector. The driving forces of this type of innovation and deregulation were the growing competitive pressure and financial uncertainty generated by inflation and the subsequent decline of deposit institutions, both commercial and mortgage banks. The role of the federal government in this case was simply to provide a new legal framework to incorporate changes in the operation of markets brought about by the financial institutions themselves.

The second form of financial innovation and deregulation has been induced by the government. In Japan, France, Germany, Italy and in most developing countries, changes in legislation have created the conditions for the emergence of new financial products and markets. The objective of these changes has been to generate new non-inflationary mechanisms to finance a growing fiscal deficit. In addition, in countries like Japan and France, changes in the legal framework were enacted in order to re-assess the role of financial institutions in international markets. In developing countries, financial deregulation is associated with the cancellation of international sources of credit since 1982.

The consequences of financial innovation and deregulation are numerous. Among them are the decreasing costs of transactions, greater competition that stimulates efficiency, a wider range of financial instruments, better investment opportunities and portfolio diversification, that leads to a greater spread of risk.

To the extent that deregulation and innovation have furthered the development of capital markets, they have modified the structure of financial circuits in domestic markets and reinforced the tendency towards greater internationalization. The new emerging capital markets have provided the resources to finance the budget and trade deficits without engaging in deflationary structural adjustment. In addition, financial deregulation and innovation have seriously undermined the role of commercial banks as the main financial intermediaries.

On the other hand, however, financial markets have become more unstable. The demand schedule for money is subject to more erratic fluctuations, interest rates have increased, the ability of central banks to regulate money markets has been weakened, and financial markets have become more volatile. In addition, financial institutions—especially commercial and mortgage banks—are now more fragile. This is the result of several causes: (i) financial institutions are more exposed to bad debtors, (ii) there is a decrease of profit margins due to greater competition and (iii) they are now forced to take greater risk.

Financial innovation tends to eliminate the differences between monetary and non-monetary assets, between long-term and short-term financing, and between stocks and bonds. All these changes have led to deterioration in the quality of financial assets, and a tendency to engage in speculative and risky transactions. Both in the United States and in Mexico, there are several examples of the difficulties in maintaining a stable financial sector in the context of the changes taking place in financial markets.

Two outcomes of these changes should be discussed in greater detail. First, the phenomenon of securitization of financial assets. This involves the rise and expansion of new kinds of financing, tied to all kinds of securities backed by debt, instead of more traditional forms of bank financing.[7]

The growth of the Euromarket opened up new forms of financing to firms and governments in the 1970s. It offered funds that were not dependent upon domestic markets nor on official multilateral institutions. Securitization of financial assets has eliminated the dependency of corporations and governments on bank credit, thereby eliminating restrictions on traditional forms of financing. At the same, time it is becoming a common practice for governments and firms to raise money in international and domestic markets by issuing bonds and other financial papers, rather than by relying on traditional forms of bank lending.

The creation of this new pattern of financing, centered around financial assets, has placed the stock market at the center stage of the international financial system. These new trends have several important implications: (i) the structure of power among various types of financial institutions has changed, (ii) there is a change in the relationship between financial institutions and productive enterprises, (iii) significant changes have been introduced in the functioning of the banking system, (iv) the mechanisms determining interest rates have been modified, etc.

The second important effect of the process of financial reform discussed in this section refers to the deterioration of commercial banks. Traditionally, commercial banks were the most important financial intermediaries. Their role as financial intermediaries (for loans and deposits) has been severely disrupted by the changes taking place in the operation of financial markets. Profound changes in the financial structure associated with technical development, innovation and deregulation have intensified the competitive struggle for market shares.[8] The aggressiveness of non-bank financial institutions in the market offering the same type of services as commercial banks is a sign of greater competition.

Financial conglomerates nowadays provide a wide range of services, such as investment funds, insurance, credit cards, demand deposits, etc. Furthermore, large industrial and commercial corporations (such as automobile manufacturers and retail stores) have their own financial departments. Corporate financial departments have challenged the banks' supremacy by successfully providing their own financial services.

These changes have forced commercial banks to develop all kinds of non-traditional financial operations: exchange market operations, overnight repurchase agreements, markets for futures, loans backed by financial assets, etc.. Commercial banks have increased their investment operations in international markets. They were facing increasing pressures, especially in countries like the U.S. and Japan, to eliminate the restrictions that have prevented them from operating as universal banks or financial supermarkets in their own domestic markets. At the international level, there is an underlying tendency towards harmonizing the functions of financial institutions as universal banks.[9]

In this context, differences among financial institutions are not determined by government regulations, but rather by their own investment strategies. Differences will depend on their own drive, as megabanks, to expand on a global scale vis-à-vis the tendency to develop market niches, providing very specialized financial services in particular market segments. Worldwide, commercial banks are confronted with the challenge of developing new forms of financing within a much more competitive framework.

From Financial Repression to Market Liberalization

The importance of the financial sector lies in its unique economic role of articulating society by facilitating the circulation of national currency. Its role as an intermediary in savings and loan operations organizes and articulates production. It also facilitates the appropriation and redistribution of surplus. Not surprisingly, any change in the operation of the financial markets will have a profound impact on the economy, economic growth, and the design of economic policy.

A characteristic feature of the post-war period was significant government intervention in the financial sector. The objectives were to promote the development of the industrial sector, exports and construction (especially housing). In particular, governments played a key role in the creation of institutions which specialized in long term financing. Simultaneously, governments were responsible for the creation of institutional networks to guarantee sound financial practices, including governments' role as a lender of last resort.

Assuming different characteristics, depending on each country's own history and political system, government intervention in the financial sector was common among developing countries during the post-war period.

Control over financial sectors was one of the most important tools in the development strategies, particularly in the promotion of import-substituting industrialization.[10]

Two important policies were implemented: (i) strict control over the supply of money in order to influence the level of economic activity, and (ii) control over the allocation of credit, including interest rate determination in order to influence the composition of investment. The particular mechanisms used to implement these policies varied, from the nationalization of banks, to different forms of direct government participation in financial institutions, and direct control over the allocation of credit and determination of interest rates.

However, the crisis in the world economy during the 1970s and the economic restructuring that followed in the 1980s triggered profound structural changes in the world economy. Within developing countries, this period was associated with the exhaustion of the pattern of finance and developments of the post-war period. The development strategy in these countries was characterized by the substitution of imports, the importance of government intervention in the economy, protection of the domestic market and the availability of external sources of credit.

Trade liberalization, privatization, and the deregulation of developing countries' markets were perceived as necessary conditions for the integration of these countries into the world economy. Developing countries have been liberalizing their trade and financial markets with different degrees of success. Argentina, Chile and Uruguay experimented with radical processes of liberalization, while countries like South Korea, Taiwan and Malaysia followed more gradual models of trade and financial liberalization. Most financial reforms took place during the 1980s, although there were several attempts to liberalize financial markets in a few Latin American countries dating back to the 1970s.[11]

The results from these experiences demonstrate that financial liberalization alone does not guarantee an efficient allocation of resources, nor does it lead to a substantial reduction of financial fragility and uncertainty. Market mechanisms to allocate resources and the leading role of the private sector in capital and money markets are not synonymous with stability and efficiency. Moreover, they do not automatically solve the problems of developing countries.

As stated by the World Bank in its 1989 Annual Report, "Perhaps the most important lesson to be learned from the experience of high income countries is that financial decisions within the private sector are also imperfect—as demonstrated by the collapse of savings and loans institutions in the United States and excessive lending of commercial banks to developing countries in the 1970s."[12]

The fragility of financial markets has been evident since October 1987. The future of financial systems in developing countries should not be conceived as passive alignment to developments in the international financial system. On the contrary, financial modernization must start with a definition of domestic priorities geared towards growth and well-being. Collectively, three important lessons may be drawn from recent experiences of financial liberalization in developing countries:[13]

First, financial liberalization should be gradual and must be accompanied by macroeconomic stability (e.g., as in Korea). Otherwise, it may lead to greater instability and volatility (e.g., as in the Southern Cone in Latin America). Recent history must be kept in mind. To the extent that developing countries face limitations in their monetary sovereignty—as their currencies are not international currencies—and suffer from macroeconomic instability, they must be careful to guarantee monetary stability above all, especially given the structural fragility of their financial sectors.

Second, financial liberalization must be accompanied by a return to long-term planning horizons. For financial liberalization to be successful, it is important to ensure allocation of resources to productive activities. Increases in productivity and the competitiveness of the economy should be promoted. Developing countries must modernize their stock markets, diversify options and create new financial assets. Efforts must be made to overcome their characteristic volatility, while promoting medium and long term investment projects.

Third, the state must continue to play an important role in financial markets. Strong government regulation and supervision is a precondition for financial stability. The objectives of government intervention in financial markets should be to promote competition and to reduce instability.

Changes in the Mexican Financial System: From Adjustment to Development?

The last decade and a half has been one of the most interesting and complex periods in the history of Mexico's financial system. The 1982 financial crisis not only marked the breakdown of the accumulation model based on import substitution and the orientation towards the domestic market. It also saw the last attempts to maintain the leading role of the state in the economy.

Three distinctive periods may be distinguished, from the nationalization of banks to the present. The first, from 1983 to 1985, was a period of gradual reconstitution of the financial and monetary circuits disrupted by the 1982 debt crisis, capital flight and the interruption of external sources of credit that followed. In this period, the banking system merely survived, trying to resist the emergency conditions and defending their market share.[14] A clear indicator of this problem was the decline of their role as financial intermediaries. Demand deposits in the banking system dropped from 28.2 per cent of GNP in 1982 to 23 per cent towards the end of 1985.

The second phase began in 1985, with the introduction of a new legal framework for the operation of the Mexican financial system. During this period, there was a reclassification of banks according to their coverage, and the process of bank mergers was completed. The number of banks decreased from 64 to 20. Six of them had national coverage, seven were defined as multi-regional banks and five as regional banks. Additionally, two private banks remained: Citibank and Banco Obrero. This phase ended in mid-1988, when the process of internal deregulation began.

The Public Banking Service and Credit Law, enacted in January 1985, defined the new financial system in Mexico. The most important elements of this new legislation include: (i) setting limits to the resources the central bank may lend to the government, (ii) lowering the legal reserve requirements of commercial banks, (iii) increasing the proportion of bank liabilities subject to stock and credit investment requirements, (iv) recreating the private financial sector through separation of the functions of non-bank financial intermediaries and commercial banks, and (v) increasing private sector participation within nationalized banks by allowing up to 34 per cent private ownership of bank assets. The latter was achieved through the creation of the so-called Certificados de Aportación Patrimonial (CAPS, a sort of ownership certificate).

This phase was characterized by a gradual process of financial innovation and the amazingly rapid expansion of the non-bank financial sector, especially of stock brokers. Non-bank holdings increased from 2.9 percent of the GNP in 1985 to almost 7 percent in 1988. The rapid expansion of non-bank financial institutions was partly associated with the prevalence of legal restrictions for commercial banks to compete with stock brokerage firms.

Throughout this period, the performance of the financial sector was closely linked to the country's macroeconomic conditions. In the context of severe recession, great volatility and financial uncertainty, the development of the financial sector was subordinated to the national strategy to confront the crisis. Changes in the financial sector were, in fact, central to the resolution of the country's economic crisis.

The role of the banking system during this period was not so much to promote economic development. Instead, it primarily contributed to the restructuring of the private sector and also played a key role in financing the budget deficit. Its contribution to the restructuring of the private sector was achieved through FICORCA, which provided exchange rate risk coverage to private companies. It made an important contribution in reducing private companies' external debt, from almost US$24 billion in 1982 to a little over US$7 billion in 1988. Such a drastic reduction was achieved through the cooperation of commercial banks with the central bank, with the former providing US$12 billion in credit to private companies through 4,800 financial operations, while the latter acted as lender of last resort in such operations.[15]

The role of commercial banks in financing the budget deficit is evident when one considers the rising importance of commercial bank lending to the government in relation to the government's total requirements, which increased from 14 to 60 percent in this period. In other words, during this period, commercial banks were not financing development, but instead were financing adjustment.

The third phase began in mid-1988 and continued at least to the time of writing (June 1992). Its characteristic features include:

1. A rapid process of domestic deregulation of financial markets, including: (i) market determination of interest rates, (ii) substitution of reserve requirements for a 30 percent liquidity ratio, (iii) elimination of credit rationing policies, (iv) the elimination of the minimum liquidity ratio, and (v) deregulation of the fees charged by brokers. These last two policies concluded the process of deregulation of domestic financial markets.

2. A gradual, but profound process of financial liberalization. The most important aspects of the process of liberalization involving exposure to external markets include: the creation of neutral trusts and freely underwritten stocks, foreign investment participation in all financial assets, including CETES, and up to 30 percent foreign ownership of financial institutions. Consequently, there has been greater penetration by foreign banks in Mexico's monetary and financial circuits.

Although only Citibank has been legally established in Mexico, there are 114 other offices, representing the interests of 142 foreign banks. Most of them are U.S. banks like Bank of America, First Chicago, Morgan, Chase Manhattan, etc. together with a few European banks. In effect, foreign banks undertake all kinds of financial operations, from short-term financing to participation in long-term capital markets, but concentrating on corporate finance, where they are most innovative. The signing of NAFTA will further the process of financial integration with the United States and Canada.

3. Internationalization of the Mexican financial sector. This is reflected in the existence of 14 affiliates of foreign banks, 11 brokers, 21 representative offices and foreign banks, and Mexican holdings of stocks in 13 foreign banks. In addition, Mexican corporations are raising money once again in foreign markets, as is the case of companies such as TELMEX, CIFRA, VITRO, CEMEX, SIDEK, etc.

4. A reorganization of markets and financial institutions triggered by the re-privatization of banks and the emergence of new financial groups. These financial groups not only control the monetary circuits, but also the forms of surplus appropriation. For instance, the new owners of Mercantil and Banpaís—Probursa and Mexival—who invested 1.2 billion pesos, will manage financial resources of more than 10 billion pesos. Not participating in this process actually amounts to missing an opportunity to influence important economic decisions in the country.

The new owners of banks are buying companies reporting large profits in the last few years. As Alan Stoge has noted, these bankers are buying "not so much banks' assets, but banks' licenses" to operate in financial markets. Hence, their present value is closely linked to their future values based on expected profits.

The consolidation of the process of deregulation and financial liberalization has been determined by two factors, both of which shape the evolution and nature of the financial sector. First, domestic savings have dramatically decreased since the mid-1980s. While investment increased from 16.8 to 19.7 percent of GDP, the savings rate decreased by five percentage points from around 20 percent of GDP in the first half of the 1980s to around 15 percent since 1988. The decrease in the rate of savings is mainly the result of a decrease in private savings from around 15 percent to 8.2 percent of GDP. Second, external financial restrictions have been overcome and the flow of resources away from the domestic market has been reversed. In the short run, these two problems seem to have been resolved, although there are still serious doubts about the medium and long term.

Structural reforms of the financial sector will adapt it to the new model of capital accumulation centered around external markets. Two key elements in the reorientation of the new model of accumulation are the increase of financial resources and their re-allocation.[16] This new model also involves a major shift of real economic power from the public to the private sector.

This involves major changes in the relationship between the private sector and the state; a major restructuring of the largest corporations in Mexico and a major reorganization of government intervention in the monetary and financial circuits. Furthermore, it promotes the creation of a new generation of bankers who abandon the two traditional principles of banking, namely the idea that lending is determined by savings and that credit must be backed up by collateral. Thus, financial prudence is threatened, if not undermined, potentially disrupting growth itself.

Financial Developments in South Korea and Taiwan: From Gradual Liberalization to Internationalization of Financial Markets

The structure and functioning of the financial sectors in South Korea and Taiwan experienced drastic changes in the 1980s. Through open, direct and massive government intervention, the financial sectors in both countries became central elements in their economic "miracles" in the last three decades.

During the 1970s, there was important government intervention in both cases. Governments played a direct and key role in credit allocation, interest rate determination, maintaining high reserve requirements and the segmentation of the banking system. As opposed to Singapore and Hong Kong, where the government strategy was geared to develop as international financial centers, in South Korea and Taiwan the financial sector was, primarily, an instrument to promote rapid industrialization. At a second stage of development, the financial policies of these two countries were oriented towards the selective liberalization of external trade.[17]

In this context, the autonomy of commercial banks in South Korea and Taiwan was limited, while the development of the financial sector in these two countries was truncated. However, at the beginning of the 1980s a deep but gradual process of financial liberalization has begun. Several factors explain such changes: (i) the growth of financial markets, (ii) the significant development of unregulated, non-bank institutions, (iii) the acceleration of financial disintermediation, as restrictions in the operation of financial markets imposed limitations to competition among financial institutions, which decreased the level of financial intermediation and inhibited the development of new financial assets and services.

The objective of financial liberalization was to improve the efficiency of financial institutions by allowing markets to operate freely, thus improving the level of competition among them. However, the most important characteristic feature of the processes of financial liberalization in both countries has been its gradualism.[18]

In South Korea, we can identify two phases. First, there was a slow reform that introduced gradual changes in financial markets which occurred up to the mid-1980s. The second stage involved a process of rapid financial liberalization with growing integration in international markets.[19]

The most important features of the first phase were:

1. Privatization of financial intermediaries, especially commercial banks. This process took place in the period 1981-83, when four national banks were privatized. Simultaneously, the General Banking Law was reformed. The objective of the reform was two-fold, namely, to grant greater autonomy to bank operations and to prevent the concentration of commercial banks in the hands of a few individuals as individuals cannot hold more than 8 percent of a banks' assets.
2. A gradual process of liberalizing interest rates, that were now allowed to fluctuate within given margins. In the case of commercial paper, corporate bonds and inter-bank lending, interest rates ceilings were lifted.
3. Gradual elimination of market segmentation and the promotion of financial innovation to develop short- and long-term financial markets with an improved ability to mobilize savings.
4. Opening up new domestic and foreign financial institutions. The traditional system of permits was replaced by a simple system of

approvals, facilitating the penetration of foreign banks. From 1980 to 1985, the number of foreign banks operating in South Korea increased from 33 to 52.

This phase was the point of departure for further liberalization of financial markets. As such, the first phase did not introduce substantial changes in the operation of financial markets. It should be recalled that during this time, South Korea was running large trade deficits while its external debt was the fourth largest among developing countries.

It was not until the second half of the 1980s that South Korea recovered, its growth accelerated and it became a surplus country (in terms of its current account). This was the time when financial liberalization was also deepened. Surprisingly enough, the rapid increase in savings was larger than investment growth.[20] The policies undertaken during this second phase of financial liberalization may be summarized as follows:

1. Liberalization of interest rates and a change in the mechanisms of money supply determination from direct control over the money supply to an indirect mechanism of money supply determination through open market operations, discount transactions, etc.
2. Internationalization of capital markets in two phases. During 1989-90, there was an expansion of investment funds from foreigners (Korean Fund, European-Korean Fund), an increase in the sale of stocks in foreign markets, and the inclusion of foreign brokers in the Korean stock market. From 1991, the government allowed foreign direct investment in South Korean capital markets, the establishment of affiliates of foreign companies in Korea, and new joint-ventures between Korean and foreign financial firms.

Three aspects of the Taiwanese experience are particularly interesting here. First, the fact that financial liberalization has taken place in a context of price and exchange rate stability. However, there was a disturbing tendency for gross domestic investment to decrease, from 29 percent of GDP in the first half of the 1980s to less than 20 percent by 1989. At the same time, the rate of savings has remained constant, at around 35 percent of GDP throughout the second half of the 1980s. The combination of these factors increased speculative tendencies.

The second surprising element in the Taiwanese experience is the fact that direct government intervention in the banking system has not been reduced. Out of 16 commercial banks and 8 credit banks, 13 are government owned, in spite of the fact that starting in 1989, the government allowed the creation of new private banks as well as individual participation in the three largest state banks with up to 51 percent private ownership.

Third, the new legislation introduced in 1989 has been the most important effort to liberalize and modernize the financial sector. Such changes in legislation supplement the liberalization of interest rates introduced in mid-1985. The new legislation allowed greater flexibility in the operation of foreign bank affiliates and promoted the internationalization of the financial institutions in Taiwan. Simultaneously, there has been a gradual and selective process of liberalization in the stock market, allowing greater participation of foreign brokers as well as opportunities for non-residents to invest in the domestic market.

Financial liberalization in South Korea and Taiwan in the 1980s occurred in the context of highly dynamic stock markets.[21] In 1980, Mexico was first in terms of total valuation of its stock market among the so-called emerging markets. Chile and Brazil were third and fourth respectively. The total value of these three stock markets together with Argentina represented more than 40 percent of the total value of stocks in emerging markets.

On the other hand, South Korea, Taiwan, the Philippines and Malaysia accounted for 33 percent of emerging markets. In 1990, South Korea and Taiwan alone accounted for 45 percent of the total value of emerging stock markets, while Asian stock markets accounted for 68 percent of the total. Meanwhile, Latin American stock markets reduced their share to less than 20 percent of the total.

The reasons behind this shift and the rapid growth of Asian stock markets are to be found in the economic performance of the two areas. Asian countries displayed spectacular growth rates, at more than 8 percent a year throughout the late 1980s. They also developed the capacity to penetrate international markets. It is well known that for Latin America, on the other hand, it was a lost decade in terms of economic development. One by one, Latin American countries undertook severe deflationary policies under the structural adjustment programs imposed by external debtors. This situation resulted in drastic regressions in living standards and the well-being of the populations, with profound price and exchange rate instability.

The reasons behind the success of the East Asian countries and the decline of the Latin American countries are complex and beyond the scope of this chapter. However, it is important to bear in mind that the dynamism and strength of their markets are not primarily associated with the processes of financial liberalization and internationalization of their financial sectors. On the contrary, the strength of these countries is based on their dynamic economic growth and their ability to export. The latter explains why South Korea became a net international creditor by 1989 and Taiwan had accumulated official reserves of US$80 billion dollars by 1989, below the level of reserves accumulated by Japan, but above all other industrialized countries.

Conclusion

The period of closed national financial markets is over. Government intervention in financial markets, however, is not over, but has taken different forms. Deregulation and financial liberalization are necessary in a period of globalization of financial markets and sharper international competition. Postponing the necessary adjustments may result in profound financial disintermediation, that may be even more damaging to the stability and financial sovereignty of developing countries.

Having said this however, this does not imply that deregulation and financial liberalization in developing countries should be conceived along the same lines as in industrialized countries. The mechanical application of the same form and timing of such financial liberalization in developing countries, does not necessarily lead to a successful transition. Nor does it lead to the stability and growth of the developing countries' financial sectors.

This is perhaps the most important lesson to be drawn from the East Asian countries. Financial sectors are very different in developing, in contrast to industrialized, countries. There are important differences in their role as sources of fiscal revenue, in the degree of diversification in financial markets, and in relation to the role of national currencies in international markets. There are enough reasons to suggest that developing countries need to adopt their own strategies to liberalize financial markets to one that better respond to the risks and challenges posed by the liberalization and deregulation of financial markets.

The second lesson to be learnt relates to the fact that macroeconomic stability, long-term considerations in the operation of financial markets, and the introduction of gradual reforms and government intervention in the market, are central to the process of deregulation and liberalization of financial markets in the context of developing countries. The experience of East Asian countries shows that these are all necessary conditions to prevent the development of new cycles of instability, speculation and macroeconomic disequilibrium.

The 1980s was characterized by the growing role of financial markets. Throughout the decade, economic growth—or the lack of it—was closely associated with the rapid changes taking place in financial markets. It was especially linked to those regulations that set limits to interest rates and reserve levels, restrictions to financial institutions to diversify markets, and the separation between domestic and international markets. At first it was tied to public debt financing and later on to the generation of liquidity and new forms of financing for the private sector, characterized by stagnation of GDP, declining real wages, contraction of employment, consumption, and gross capital formation, defined by high rates of interest and inflation, exchange rate disequilibrium, capital flight, etc. This was a process that was unequal in depth, evolution and results in the different countries of the region. In the case of industrialized countries, their domestic currencies become international currencies, whereas the domestic currencies of developing countries play a subordinated role in international capital markets.

Notes

1. M. Aglietta. *Globalisation financière.* Paris: CEPII-Economica. 1990.

2. Antonio Gutiérrez Pérez. "La Globalización económica: alcances y limites." *Revista de la Universidad.* December 1991.

3. Dominique de Laubier. "L'internationalisation des services financiers." *Economie Prospective Internationale* No. 16. 1986.

4. E. Versluysen. "Financial Deregulation and the Globalisation of Capital Markets." Federal Reserve Board. 1988.

5. W. Silver. "The Process of Financial Innovation." *American Economic Review.* May 1983.

6. Christian Boisseu. "Quelques réflexions sur l'analyse économique des innovations financières." *Economie Appliqué* No. 3. 1986.

7. Morgan Guaranty Trust. "Global Financial Change." *World Financial Markets* (December 1986); Herbert Baer and Ch. Pavel. "Does Regulation Drive Innovation?" *Economic Perspectives.* Federal Reserve Bank of Chicago. 1988.

8. R. Levich. "Financial Innovations in International Financial Markets." In *The United States in the World Economy,* edited by M. Feldstein. 1988.

9. Gerald Corrigan. "Reforming the U.S. Financial System: An International Perspective." *FRBNY Quarterly Review.* Spring 1990.

10. F. Morris et al. *Latin America's Banking System in the 1990s.* World Bank Discussion Paper No. 81. Washington, DC. 1990.

11. OECD. "Financial Systems and Financial Regulations in Dynamic Asian Economies." *Financial Market Trends* No. 47. October 1990.

12. World Bank. *World Development Report 1989.* Oxford University Press. 1989.

13. Cho Yoon-Je & D. Khatkhate. *Lessons of Financial Liberalization in Asia.* World Bank Discussion Paper No. 50. Washington, DC. 1989.

14. Javier Márquez. *La Banca Mexicana.* México: CEMLA. 1987.

15. Secretaría de Hacienda y Crédito Público. *Reestructuración del Sistema Financiero.* Cuadernos de Renovación Nacional, Fondo de Cultura Económica, México. 1988.

16. Celso Garrido et al. "La evolución de los mercados bursátiles en los ochenta. Una perspectiva internacional." In *Mercado de valores, crisis y neuvos circuitos financieros en México, 1970-90,* Coord. Celso Garrido. UAM, Mexico. 1991.

17. Wanda Tseng et al. *Financial Liberalization, Money Demand, and Monetary Policy in Asian Countries.* IMF Occasional Paper No. 84. IMF. July 1991.

18. OECD. "Financial Systems and Financial Regulations in Dynamic Asian Economies." *Financial Market Trends* No. 47. October 1990.

19. Park Soon Poong. *Financial Repression and Liberalization in Korea.* KEBMR. 1989.

20. Cho Yoon-Je & D. Khatkhate. *Lessons of Financial Liberalization in Asia.* World Bank Discussion Paper No. 50. Washington, DC. 1989.

21. International Finance Corp. *Emerging Stock Markets Factbook, 1991.* Washington: International Finance Corporation. 1991; Euromoney Publications PLC. *The Guide to World Equity Markets 1991.* London. 1991.

3

Globalization and Technology Acquisition by the Developing Countries of East Asia

Anuwar Ali

Since the early 1980s, the world has witnessed many fundamental economic and political changes affecting the relationships between countries, regions and economic blocs. These changes are increasingly reinforced by a new phenomenon referred to as economic globalization, symbolizing a movement towards greater economic integration among countries. This chapter begins with a discussion on this globalization process in the world economy and its impact on the developing countries, with particular emphasis on changing trends in investment flows among countries of the East Asian region, with Japan playing a major role as the newly industrialized East Asian economies (NIEs) provide the back-up role. The changing investment flows will invariably have important repercussions on the industrialization process itself as well as the technology acquisition capabilities of developing countries to the region.

While the next section will examine the extent of technological dependence of developing countries, technology transfer issues are examined in greater depth in the following section, highlighting the numerous constraints faced by the developing countries in their search for appropriate policies to upgrade their domestic technological capabilities. These constraints are both internally and externally induced, the latter largely emanating both from the role of direct foreign investment (DFI) and multinational companies (MNCs) from the industrial countries. The final section will outline the major policy areas which must be given emphasis by developing countries of the East Asian region if they were to become technologically competent in an ever changing global economic scenario.

Globalization Trends and the Industrialization Process

The rapidly changing world economic scenario, particularly since the mid-1980s, will certainly have many policy implications for the developing countries in the region. While these changes are likely to affect the industrialization process of the developing countries, not all these countries can respond in a similar manner to such changes. For many of the poorer countries, their response is so weak that they are unable to cope with the changing environment, thus leaving them further behind. In the East Asian region, two principal changes since the mid-1980s seem to have had a tremendous influence on the industrial development of the region; firstly, the increasing pace of globalization of production, mainly by Japanese firms and secondly, the increasingly important role of the Asian newly industrialized economies (NIEs) in international trade and investment flows.

At the same time, the developing countries are strongly competing with one another for the same direct foreign investment (DFI). During the past three decades, many developing countries especially in the socialist bloc and Latin America, were particularly against foreign participation in their economies. But since then, the anti-DFI rhetoric has toned down, and many developing countries are eager to obtain some benefits from the participation of multinational companies (MNCs). In fact, since the mid-1980s, more and more developing countries are encouraging more private sector participation; and measures such as privatization have expanded the scope for DFI participation apart from other deregulation and liberalization measures which may improve the investment climate (Chee Peng Lim, 1990).

Since the early 1970s, the MNCs of the advanced industrial countries, including those of Japan, backed by their respective government policies, have successfully "globalized" their production structures via the development of off-shore facilities. The establishment of export processing zones (EPZs) in many countries of the region is one distinct manifestation of this process. The massive spread of these facilities adds a new dimension to the relationship between the industrial countries and the developing countries, involving a division of labor in the world economy through the imposition of an intra-firm division of labor within the MNCs.

The intra-firm transfers of inputs and outputs of these MNCs and their intra-firm trade now constitute a significant proportion of the import-export trade of many developing countries. In fact, it has even been argued that the most important contribution by MNCs in host countries is the formation of both "internal and external networks which meant the creation of an input and output relationship between industries at home and the creation of an external trade network through intra-firm and/or inter-firm trade. The linchpin of these developments is Japan or Japanese affiliates which have been established on foreign soil" (Aoki, 1992).

Thus, there has been a large number of cases of induced investments where the presence of Japanese manufacturers in developing countries (e.g., in ASEAN) has necessitated investments by their affiliates and subcontractors in Japan. Such a shift of production activities overseas from Japan continuously induces changes in industrial structure and the international division of labor. As a consequence, the procurement and sales behavior of Japanese affiliates overseas is reflected in high trade ratios with companies in the same group. Japanese subsidiaries abroad therefore play a crucial role in the increased exports of manufactured goods from ASEAN, especially after the mid-1980s.

According to Urata (1992), as a result of substantial increases in Japanese investments, notably in Asia, in order to minimize manufacturing costs in Japan following the rising value of the yen after the 1985 Plaza Accord, some of the products they manufacture are exported to Japan, often referred to as "reverse imports." More than 50 percent of reverse imports were in the form of intra-firm trade. For MNCs, this internal division of labor strongly implies that particularly for manufacturing activities, they will inevitably control technology and innovation, while the routine and standardized production and marketing of products for domestic markets are located in developing countries.

The increasing integration of national economies, standardized manufacturing techniques and perfected systems of coordination among dispersed production units, together with a worldwide marketing system, have in fact accentuated the dominance of the MNCs. This allows them to not only widen their market shares, but more importantly, to indirectly stifle the entry of newcomers through product differentiation. Their strength in R&D activities, driven by the desire to remain competitive and the need to be at the frontiers of technology development, has consolidated their oligopolistic positions. The manner in which the MNCs dominate world trade tends to make export-led industrialization a difficult task for most developing countries without the partnership of the MNCs, at least in the initial stages. Very few countries have been able to do this on their own.

A number of external factors also have a bearing on competition and technology transfer by Japanese and other MNCs in the East Asian region. The opening of economies such as China, Indochina and perhaps later, Eastern Europe and the Commonwealth of Independent States (CIS), have caused new expectations of liberalization and the resurgence of market forces. In Asia, growth triangles and economic zones have sprouted. These include the **baht** economic zone, covering Thailand and Southern Vietnam, the Yellow Sea (Huang Hai) Economic Zone, covering the west coast of South Korea, Shantung and Liaotung in China, and Kyushu and Yamaguchi in Japan, the Hong Kong-Guangdong Economic Zone, the Taiwan-Fujian Economic Zone covering the areas on both sides of the Formosa Straits extending to Shanghai in China, and finally, the Tumen Jiang Economic

Zone covering the cities of Vladivostok and Yenchi in China near the mouth of Tumen Jiang River. Within ASEAN, there is also the proposal to establish the ASEAN Free Trade Area (AFTA) in ten to fifteen years as enunciated at the last ASEAN Summit Meeting in Singapore in early 1992.

An equally significant development during the 1980s was the emergence of new forms of foreign investment in the developing countries. Following a period of slow world economic growth and rising debt, there was a shift in attitudes towards the role of foreign investment, not only among policy makers in developing countries, but also among the MNCs themselves. The economic difficulties of the 1980s persuaded many developing countries to liberalize their investment policies to attract more direct foreign investment (DFI). Policy measures in developing countries have increasingly focused on ways to raise capital inflows and to encourage collaboration between domestic and foreign firms.

However, the willingness of developing countries to accept DFI occurred at a time when transnational capital was moving away from traditional DFI, employing a diverse range of non-traditional forms of investment. In part, MNCs had adapted to the restrictions by most countries by substituting DFI with a range of contractual agreements not involving equity. The changing character of foreign investment, with the new forms of collaborative agreements and joint ventures was equally determined by the needs of increasingly global corporate strategies. The expansion of new forms of investment can therefore be seen as part of ongoing strategic business responses to changes in the global economy and to the rapid pace of technological change in the 1980s; this trend is likely to grow in the 1990s.

In response to oligopolistic competitive pressures, non-equity collaborations have been used by firms as a means of gaining entry to markets already dominated by major MNCs. For similar reasons, small MNCs—including many from the NIEs, which lack either the international marketing knowledge or the technological capacity of the market leaders—have been more willing to enter into joint ventures and licensing arrangements as a means of securing their position in national markets.

The role of MNCs in trade and investments in the region has further strengthened the globalization of production in the Asia-Pacific region. The importance of technology, finance and marketing channels has been increasingly demonstrated by MNC activities. It remains for developing countries to ensure that effective technology transfer does take place besides enhancing the spin-off effects of DFI in the host countries. The need for rapid technological diffusion within a developing economy becomes more decisive in the light of global macroeconomic adjustments, technological changes and breakthroughs, especially since the early 1980s. These may be seen in terms of macroeconomic policies by the more advanced industrial countries, either individually or as economic blocs, affecting international trade as well as technology flows.

The continued restructuring of the industrial countries and the prevailing mood of protectionism add to instability and uncertainty in the world economy. Such complexities become all the more disconcerting for developing economies given the rapidity of the development of new emerging technologies in areas such as microelectronics, biotechnology and advanced materials, which are primarily driven by intensifying competition and shifting competitive advantages among Japanese, American and European MNCs.

At the same time, major changes have taken place in international investment patterns since the mid-1970s, with significant implications for international technology diffusion. For instance, there was a relative decline, followed by a severe reduction, in the flow of DFI into developing countries with two exceptions, i.e., China and the Asian NIEs. However, since the mid-1980s, there has been a number of changes in the pattern of DFI. First, industrial countries increased their significance, both as suppliers as well as recipients of DFI. Among these countries, Japan has gained an important position as it became the world's largest DFI supplier while the U.S. is the world's largest recipient. Second, in recent years, Asian countries particularly ASEAN, have been increasingly important as hosts to DFI (Tran Van Tho & Urata, 1991).

The flow of DFI within industrial countries has experienced a radical restructuring. As European and later Japanese MNCs have developed their investments in the U.S. market, the U.S. economy has become as much a "host" as a "source" country for MNCs. For example, in the case of motor production, all the major Japanese car makers have established production facilities in the United States together with their own parts suppliers who have gone abroad with them (do Rosario, 1992: 56-58). Equally importantly, Japan has emerged as a major "home" country for MNCs and a major source of DFI to the United States, East Asia, including ASEAN, and the European Community. While ample empirical evidence of what this implies for international technology diffusion is still lacking, it is useful to note that with the exception of the Asian NIEs, ASEAN and China, the dissemination of technologies to developing countries has declined relatively.

During the last decade, Japan has basically changed world trends in DFI. While the world economy used to be a bipolar system dominated by the United States and the European Community, it is now a tripolar one, with Japan emerging as an equally important player. These three now account for a substantial proportion of total world DFI and world trade. Other rapidly developing countries are important extensions to this triangle since most of their exports are destined for these three markets.

The strong international competitiveness of Japanese products have usually been attributed to their MNC management styles. The long-term employer-employee relationship facilitates the upgrading of human capital, as well as the development and diffusion of technologies. In addition, lifetime employment and company unions facilitate the introduction of new technologies, even if labor-saving (Tran Van Tho, 1992). Japanese MNCs have moved to locate their R&D activities overseas in order to consolidate their global strategies. There is little doubt that Japanese firms constitute the leading edge as far as the globalization of East Asian technologies is concerned.

Along with the internationalization of Japanese investment and manufacturing activities since the mid-1980s, the establishment of overseas bases for R&D has also rapidly increased. Japanese companies have expanded both the number of overseas R&D bases as well as the scale of R&D operations conducted outside Japan. As of mid-1991, approximately ten percent of manufacturing companies listed on the Tokyo Stock Exchange (with capitalization of over one billion yen) had established some form of R&D facilities abroad, mainly in the U.S. and the EC.

In many cases, Japanese firms have transformed what were basically "information collection bases" in the 1970s into "development and design bases" from the mid-1980s and "research bases" from the late 1980s. The former are closely tied to Japanese factories to assist with market responsiveness; in the case of the latter, the establishment of independent technology centers and basic research operations are given priority. These multiple activities will eventually be linked together within a broadly based global technology network, thus allowing for both horizontal and vertical movement of information and technical knowledge within specific Japanese MNCs across the globe.

Japanese MNCs are equally determined to identify appropriate partners for coordinating R&D and related activities in a systematic fashion. In this respect, Japanese MNCs recognize the critical need to share technological assets as the only way to gain access to U.S. and European know-how. To these Japanese firms, such a linkage is deemed vital in an economic environment of intense competition. The increasing costs and risks associated with R&D activities make it imperative for Japanese MNCs to approach these ventures in a more collaborative fashion if they want such opportunities to expand.

Even more significantly, Japanese MNCs have begun to develop R&D facilities overseas in Asia for the first time as part of their shift away from reliance on regional locations just for cheap labor and marketing outlets. Today, there is increased interest in the establishment of local R&D facilities as a means to respond more quickly to shifts in the regional and global marketplace. With the new emphasis on time, flexibility and responsiveness as sources of competitiveness, these facilities are expected to yield substantial dividends for the MNCs.

At the same time, there are growing "synergies" between MNCs of industrial countries. For instance, Motorola and Toshiba formed an alliance by establishing a joint chip-making venture in 1987, in which Toshiba provided Motorola with marketing help, especially in Japan. This link has been found to be invaluable for both parties. While the American firm is strongest in micro-processors and custom-designed chips, Toshiba is better as a supplier of memory chips. Motorola is also exploring links with two Korean chip makers, Lucky Goldstar and Samsung (*The Economist*, 1992: 75-76).

In a wider context, globalization is also being driven by technological change and the rising costs and risks involved in large scale R&D activities. As indicated above, such activities have also become globalized as the potential success of processes of technological discovery and commercialization are becoming more dependent on the pooling of specialized resources and the sharing of costs. Some have argued that there is growing technological interdependence, albeit among the industrial countries especially the U.S. and Japan via the exchange of scientists and exports among firms and universities (Simon, 1991).

There has thus been an increase in the globalization of R&D activities. During the early period, such activities tended to be primarily conducted in Japan, with activities outside Japan playing a minor role, mainly utilizing local skilled manpower. However, during the 1980s, an increasing number of the firms have established R&D centers mainly in the United States and the EC; and since 1987, an increasing number of centers have been conducting advanced R&D activities and basic research, rather than merely collecting information on advanced technologies and giving support to local production, as before (Baba & Suzuki, 1991).

The emergence of the Asian NIEs—including South Korea, Taiwan, Hong Kong and Singapore—as major exporters of more mature consumer products to the industrial countries has also had a significant influence on international trading patterns. In fact, in certain industries, such as electrical and electronic appliances, batteries and radio receivers, the technological gap between the NIEs and Japan has narrowed substantially in the last decade (Yamazawa & Watanabe, 1988: 203-26). This phenomenon has become the focus of a new international division of labor, especially with the expansion of the NIEs' multinationals and their successful export performance.

Industrial relocation by the NIEs has become increasingly important as part of their overseas investment policies in the East Asian region. The opening up of China with respect to DFI is also a significant factor influencing investment flows from the NIEs. In the case of South Korean DFI, for instance, China seems to offer distinct advantages compared to other countries in the region; these include proximity and the availability of a large number of ethnic Koreans, mostly in northeastern China, to provide a supply of mid-level managerial manpower (Shim Jae Hoon, 1992: 37-8).

What is perhaps more significant as far as the Asian NIEs are concerned is their clear policy response to the rapidly changing economic and technological environment within which they have to operate internationally. This is made possible by clearly defined strategies enhancing export-led growth. South Korea and Taiwan, in particular, have both managed to have focused programs to encourage new high technology industries designed to draw their economies further into the high-end sphere of global competition. Both countries, for example, have begun highly ambitious aerospace programs, primarily designed to help local companies qualify as key components suppliers to leading aerospace companies in the world. It must also be emphasized that once they put their economies on an export footing, the pressures to catch up technologically intensified. With higher export shares, sustaining economic growth comes to depend increasingly on maintaining international competitiveness.

With all the above mentioned changes, one would expect technology diffusion to expand its geographic spread; but, in reality, its dissemination has become even more unequal than before. Today, a growing number of developing countries are, at best, marginally integrated into international technology flows. The need for rapid technological changes becomes more crucial in the light of global adjustments, especially since the early 1980s. New innovations in microelectronics and information technology, robotics, biotechnology and new materials in recent years have gradually entered industrial production processes and are beginning to affect relative factor costs and comparative advantage among countries. In a sense, developing countries are thus confronted with the possibility that their efforts to expand their manufactured exports may be inhibited by the diffusion of new electronic technologies in the industrial countries as well as the convergence of computer and telecommunications technology, or "information technology."

Increasing the Technological Dependence of the Developing Countries

The industrialization process in developing countries has been extensively influenced by the economic development of the industrial countries as well as the extent of DFI and technology flows into the developing countries. Most of these countries have relied on both DFI and technology imports, while some have relied on the latter and less on direct foreign equity participation. Ever since the developing countries embarked on industrialization in the early 1960s, imported technologies from the industrial countries have been relatively dominant. During the early period, "search" activities for new products and processes were significant, with the DFI component playing a major role in this respect.

During the second stage, when the industrial base was expanded and export promotion was encouraged, the importation of technologies was still important, as in the preceding phase, but on a more selective basis, depending on the needs of the industrial sectors promoted, while a very limited number of indigenous technologies appeared in established industry sub-sectors. At this stage, much of the production activities would also relate to product and process adaptation, especially within domestically-oriented industries. During this initial export orientation phase, export processing zones were established to encourage the location of MNC activities in the electronics and textile sub-sectors.

During these phases, "learning by doing" and "learning by adapting" are important components of technology transfer and acquisition. An important prerequisite for learning is the availability of an industrial labor force fully equipped with the necessary technical skills and experience, implying that shop floor technicians, engineers and technically trained managers are needed in increasing numbers such that secondary, technical and vocational education, and in-service training must be emphasized. With increasing industrialization, "learning by design" becomes more critical so that design engineers play a more dominant role and advanced technical and engineering education is required, while in-service training for technical personnel becomes a significant component of technology upgrading.

As suggested by the experiences of the Asian NIEs, during the last two decades, the increasing technological competence of these countries suggests that they are better positioned to acquire and adapt the technical components of imported technologies compared to other developing countries. They are currently in a technological phase in which they have increasingly mastered production technologies to run sophisticated manufacturing operations ranging from food processing to electronics. While these technologies are generally associated with the initial steps in technology acquisition, consisting primarily of the ability to acquire operational skills to run a production facility efficiently, other more complex stages of technological advancement (including innovative technology, design, engineering and technology consultancy services) are being developed in these countries.

Moving to a higher phase of industrial development would inevitably require the promotion of high-technology industries. But their development must be accompanied not only by an increasing supply of highly-skilled labor, but also by a substantial increase in R&D and technical training expenditure. In both the areas of R&D and in-service training, it is equally important to stress the role of locally-owned enterprises. In all these areas, human resource planning should focus attention on attempting to develop both the critical skills needed by industry and, more importantly for labor's capacity to innovate. As indicated by the experience of most industrial countries or newly industrialized economies, there is little doubt that innovative capacities will determine a nation's competitiveness.

In many developing economies, existing human resource development efforts do not really emphasize the capacity to innovate. The lack of funds for R&D purposes may be important in this respect while local manufacturing enterprises are too reluctant to allocate substantial funds for such activities. But equally important, the existing industrial structure, partly arising from DFI and existing investment incentives, encourages the adoption and importation of highly capital-intensive equipment from industrial countries. This not only discourages the adoption of appropriate technologies in domestic industries, but also negates the capacity to innovate as the dependence on imported technologies is allowed to continue.

Foreign direct investment in general seems to discourage meaningful transfer of technology and the development of domestic innovative capacity. If there is any transfer at all, it is normally between the principal licenser or investor and its subsidiary or affiliate established in the developing country. It is thus internalized within its global production structure. There is a reluctance to allocate funds for R&D activities since most of these activities are controlled by the head offices in the industrial countries where extensive R&D facilities have already been established (see Anuwar Ali & Muhd Anuar Adnan, 1990: 151-71; Ozawa, 1982: 7-53).

The shortage of qualified and technically experienced scientists and engineers is an added impediment to the establishment of R&D facilities. Consequently, the top management of foreign MNCs mostly tends to perform management and organizational, rather than innovative functions, unlike their counterparts in the industrial countries. These factors tend to have a stifling effect on the development of domestic entrepreneurship. Nevertheless, in an industrializing economy, domestic entrepreneurship must play a more prominent role in taking initiatives to direct domestic capital into manufacturing concerns.

Technology transfer basically implies purchasing a technology from another country based on the mutuality of interests. This means that in the case of the importing country, there is a price to be paid for the technology import. In theory, developing countries need to assess whether the technology transferred is suitable in the context of their own technological capabilities and the various inputs available at their disposal. Likewise, they have to assess whether they have the capacity to bear the costs of such a transfer, including the direct and indirect costs imposed by technology suppliers. In practice, however, these are complex questions because any technology import will have numerous repercussions within the domestic economy.

Technology Acquisition: Major Issues

Despite the rapid pace of technological advancement and its commercialization in the last two decades, the actual choices of applied technologies open to developing countries are rather limited. The bulk of the technologies has origins in a relatively small number of industrial countries which confer proprietary rights and can thus impose obligations/restrictions upon those permitted by the owners to make use of such technologies.

This concentration of technology generating capacity arises because most R&D activities are being done in the industrial countries. Although the international patent system was intended to protect and encourage innovations, the system seems to work against the interests of developing countries (see World Bank, 1979: 65-6). In such a situation, manufacturing enterprises of the developing countries are in no position to reduce the technological gap. In practice, therefore, most firms in developing countries become increasingly dependent upon the technology licensers of the industrial countries for the supply of technical know-how. The choice of technologies is therefore largely determined by either large industrial country MNCs or technology suppliers, although recently, technology transfers by the NIEs provide a new option open to developing countries. Technology acquisition can also be viewed as transactions which take place under very imperfect market conditions, generally favoring the industrial countries. This is even more true in cases where the transactions take place between the principal MNC or technology supplier and its subsidiary or joint-venture partner. Furthermore, DFI occupies a commanding position in the economies of developing countries, especially the smaller ones. From the point of view of the developing countries, the international flow of capital and technology is an important index of dependence on the industrial countries. The interdependence between the industrial countries and the developing countries is asymmetrical. While there is a two-way flow of capital and technology among the former, i.e., the United States, the European Community and Japan, there are only one way flows from the industrial countries to the developing countries (Nurul Islam, 1988: 399-420).

Given their generally limited pool of highly skilled personnel, firms in developing countries often lack sufficient knowledge and expertise about the technologies they hope to acquire from their potential suppliers. Technology suppliers are reluctant to disclose full information about their products to potential buyers until all transactions are completed to protect the proprietary value of the product. As such, valuable technological knowledge is not readily given away, but has to be purchased at a cost. Thus, buyers lacking technical expertise will generally agree to purchase technology without sufficient knowledge of its eventual functional performance and hence value.

The price paid to obtain any particular technology may also reflect the lack of technical, financial, legal and commercial expertise required to acquire information on the technology and for evaluating the various options which may exist. This disadvantage is felt particularly by countries whose technological base is small. The relatively more industrialized countries, on the other hand, tend to have greater access, either because of their better organizational ability or because they have established linkages with the MNCs of the industrial countries.

The terms and conditions attached to technology transfer are generally restrictive to local licensees on questions such as export outlets, purchasing and pricing policies, technology diffusion and in-house R&D. One of the most common restrictions is the prohibition of exports of goods produced under licensing or technical assistance agreements. There are also cases in which licensees are prohibited from producing competitive products; they are normally required to secure prior approval from their technology licensers before they can sell intermediate products also covered under such agreements. Licensees are also required to sell their products through local agents or marketing firms appointed by the licensers. Another common constraint faced by developing countries is the tied purchases of materials from the licensers. These consequently will have significant implications for the need to broaden the country's industrial base.

In view of the above, the supplier-buyer relationship in international technology purchases can be viewed as a "bilateral monopoly" where the price tends to be determined through a series of negotiations between two parties. If both sides are equally strong in the negotiating process, the final negotiated price would be reflective of a price determined in a competitive market. However, if one party is in a weaker bargaining position, the final negotiated price would deviate from the competitive one. Thus, where buyers have less than sufficient mastery and knowledge of the technology, suppliers are able to extract larger economic rents from the technology transactions.

When licensees in developing countries lack technical, financial and commercial expertise in technology transfer negotiations, they often get very disadvantageous terms or may have to pay unreasonably high prices. This appears to be the case among many small and medium-scale firms known to be paying royalties for expired patents. The situation is reinforced by other factors such as industrial country MNCs' inherent strengths and their considerable negotiating and bargaining skills often built up through extensive experience in transferring technology. On the other hand, manufacturing firms of developing countries generally lack any significant expertise in acquiring technology and thus incur substantial costs in acquiring advanced technology even at the negotiations stage.

It must also be noted that equity ownership by local capital in companies where DFI participates does not necessarily mean management control. With some exceptions, most DFI operations appear to be effectively controlled by expatriate personnel from the foreign parent companies. This is particularly apparent in companies dependent on foreign partners to provide technical know-how and market access. It is in this sense that the extent of foreign equity participation may underestimate the full impact of its control and influence in the domestic economies of developing countries.

The above can also be related to the extent of local decision-making autonomy versus the global strategic framework of DFI operations in many developing countries. This issue has a crucial bearing on DFI operations and behavior. Obviously, DFI with relatively centralized systems of decision making will be less susceptible to leverage by local factors than DFI with more decentralized styles of management.

In this respect, the different approaches to technology development by American and Japanese MNCs have often been cited. It has been argued that the latter have been able to internationalize because of their competitive edge in their internal and external production management systems based on business groups or subcontracting. According to Nakagawa (1991: 73-86), "Japanese companies started to produce locally, but only on a knock-down basis: they import the necessary parts and raw materials from Japan. Moreover, they import Japanese equipment and machinery because they preferred quality parts, raw materials and equipment produced in Japan to those made locally or in Third World countries." In terms of technology identification and the sourcing of capital equipment and machinery, parent companies generally make the decisions or give technical advice to local operations on these matters. It is certainly in the interest of parent companies to maintain this type of relationship, as the parent companies are also the technology suppliers in many cases. This situation may also apply to local subsidiaries at the initial stage when they still lack the expertise to determine their needs for technology, capital equipment and machinery.

A very significant proportion of international trade is intra-firm, where the costs of technology acquisition can be inflated through transfer pricing manipulations. Vertically integrated firms (i.e., where the various stages of production from raw materials into finished goods are undertaken by the same firm or its subsidiaries) relocate their profits internationally by using transfer pricing, i.e., under-pricing goods for export while selling them at market prices within foreign markets. Thus, they can minimize global tax burdens and reduce political risks. In such a situation, the pricing of technology or its components may not reflect competitive market values, but may instead be dictated by transfer pricing considerations to minimize taxation on overall corporate income.

The bargaining position of developing countries vis-à-vis technology suppliers has tended to weaken in recent years due to intensifying competition among developing countries for DFI in general and "high-tech" investments in particular (also see Djeflat, 1988: 149-165). In addition, in "sun-rise" industries characterized by rapid technological change, they are unable to catch up, and as such, are much more vulnerable to and dependent upon the large industrial country MNCs to provide the latest improvements.

Technology suppliers are undoubtedly in a better position to dictate the terms and conditions of technology transfer. High rates of return obtained by them may take the form of profits earned on equity, as well as from provision of intermediate goods, capital equipment, spare parts and technical services, not to mention transfer pricing. Thus, although technology may be transferable to a developing country, the costs can be very substantial; and such costs will, to a large extent, be determined by the technological gap between the foreign technology supplier and the recipient firm in the developing country.

One view often expressed is that technology imports reduce the urgency to develop indigenous technologies as such imports become substitutes for indigenous technological capacity. This observation may well apply to many developing countries. They have few options to do otherwise because the development of domestic technologies requires economies of scale; currently, local firms are unable to take the risks of utilizing untested domestic technologies even if they are available.

Policy Options: Emphasizing Technology Acquisition

Role of the State: Managing Technological Change

A critical issue that developing countries face in quickening the pace of industrialization is managing technological development. International adjustment to globalization trends will make it more complicated for smaller developing nations, given their relatively nascent industrial base. This is further constrained by the fact that some of these countries are locked-in with DFI, which implicitly determines the nature of their industrial structure. The rapid economic changes at the international level and the widening technological gap between the industrial countries and the developing countries make it imperative that the state intervenes to ease the necessary technological change.

Managing this change has become more vital, given the increasing complexity of technology advancement as well as innovations principally emanating from the industrial countries. The notions of "technological leapfrogging"—i.e., bypassing certain stages of historical technological progress—and of "catching up" with and "overtaking" the more industrial countries pose substantial challenges and problems for aspiring developing countries, e.g., since they must aim at moving targets. It may prove futile for developing countries to simply import currently available technologies from the industrial countries, for by the time such technologies are adopted and assimilated, the industrial countries would have progressed further and the relative position of the developing countries may be unchanged or may even worsen (Freeman, 1988: 67-84).

The failure of market mechanisms to ensure concerted and sustained efforts towards such progress makes it all the more important that the state be involved. The government's role becomes crucial since technological development requires substantial infrastructural support of all kinds, including education and training, technical extension services, development of public-private sector linkages, and a legal framework (i.e., patent laws) to enforce property rights and to maintain secrecy.

For developing countries, it is even more difficult to manage this technological change in view of the increasing pace of technology development and innovations which require shorter response times to move from product development to commercialization. There has also been increasing specialization and complexity of systems, bringing about the need for proper interfacing of manpower and disciplines, and integrating critical skills from various sources.

The state's role in providing the leadership to enhance technological change must also be complemented by mechanisms to increase public sector-private industry collaboration. The experiences of Japan and, to a lesser extent, South Korea bear testimony to the necessity for such collaboration (see Yoo Seong-min, 1989: 80-104). But more significantly, in both Japan and South Korea, state intervention in the economy has been extensive and more readily visible than in most western industrial economies. The planning agencies of both Japan and South Korea initiated economic plans which were somewhere between indicative and command planning, stipulating government priorities and indicating to the private sector the directions in which the governments wanted their economies to develop.

In Hong Kong, where state intervention has been kept low, in recent years, government policy has shifted from a posture of non-involvement to increased intervention as the promotion of skill-intensive, high-technology industries are considered as crucial for enhancing technology acquisition, innovation and productivity improvement (Ng, 1987: 467-78). Even in the United States, state governments have been taking an active part in promoting university research to facilitate innovation; this is also done with the formulation of long-range policies for the utilization of S&T resources, and by fostering greater university-industry research interaction (Lindsey, 1985: 85-90).

The state can therefore play a rather explicit role and may be involved in both advancing and directing technological change. State agencies can certainly affect technical innovation; some of the most important ways for doing so include demand creation, subsidies to firms, regulation, technical and scientific infrastructure, support for small and medium-scale manufacturing firms and through a banking system well adapted to the needs of innovative industries.

The most important role of the state is thus to establish an environment that stimulates firms and specialized technological agents such as engineering firms, intermediate goods producers and capital goods suppliers to engage in ongoing technological development and to enhance technological capabilities. The state can also intervene directly to influence choices of techniques deemed socially most appropriate, foster imports of technology on the best possible terms, and stimulate the development of specialized technological agents (also see Lall, 1992: 165-86).

Acquiring Technologies via Human Resource Development

The technological development of any country wishing to industrialize invariably begins with imported foreign (industrialized country) technologies, and progresses through the development of domestic variants of these imported technologies, ostensibly to the final goal of technological self-reliance. However, nothing substantial can be expected from imported technologies in the absence of domestic capacities to modify and improve them for local utilization. Therefore, substantial efforts must be made to assimilate and adapt imported technologies in the technology acquisition process. This depends on human resource development, including the upgrading of engineering and technical skills through formal education, in the long run. However, in the short and medium term, skill enhancement at the firm-level via in-house training and apprenticeship schemes ought to be rapidly increased (Anuwar Ali, 1991: 59-64).

Harnessing MNC Technologies

The effective "localization" of imported technologies can also generate conflicts between the MNCs and the recipient countries. For the latter, the effective transfer of technology must eventually result in the localization of human-embodied technology. This means that the local firm or local personnel should not only be able to handle, understand and modify production technology, but also to manage factory operations. It would thus be beneficial for an economy to harness MNC technology. If the activities of the MNCs are "kept under reasonable control and the host country economies are sufficiently viable to integrate their domestic sector with the MNC sector, then MNC activities can be a blessing rather than an evil to the development process of developing countries" (Chen, 1987: 617-42).

The Asian NIEs have been relatively successful in utilizing trade to enhance technological capability. High volumes of production for export have helped them to reap substantial benefits from economies of scale and the learning process. The sort of learning involved, however, has largely been localized to a limited number of activities associated with low cost manufacturing of standardized products. Continued dependence on such products to sustain export expansion is becoming increasingly difficult, thus eroding their competitive edge.

To move to different sorts of competitive advantages based on product or quality enhancement requires new skills which involves additional investments in imported technologies as well as in complementary R&D activities. Even then, there is no guarantee of success as the international environment is presently less favorable to continued export expansion than in the 1960s and 1970s, when the East Asian NIEs first embarked on export-led growth.

Strengthening Industry's Role

The state must take the lead in promoting private sector R&D using inducements such as fiscal incentives, establishing effective delivery and information systems and creating special R&D funds. Market forces alone are not sufficient to generate rapid technological advancement and industrial growth. This has been recognized in countries such as Japan and South Korea, where state interventionism has strongly influenced technological development.

However, once a high level of technological development has been achieved, as in the industrial countries, research institutes are no longer the only source of new production process and product technologies. In fact, private industry should play a leading role in research as well as in developing technological applications. Resources required for effective R&D are often substantial and beyond the reach of individual research institutes or universities. Furthermore, the gestation period from research to commercialization has become shorter. This implies that technological advances ought to be driven by industrial requirements and thus rapidly incorporated into business strategies.

In developing countries, locally-owned firms do not seem to have a tradition in industrial technology development, although there are some exceptions. Both import-substitution and export-led industrialization generally failed to create this kind of tradition as they were usually dependent on direct foreign investments and thus, foreign technology. Since the private sector responds to market signals, and since its planning horizon is relatively short in pursuing its interests, the private sector does not necessarily have the incentive to undertake projects in industrial technology development whose returns may not be immediate. The market therefore fails to work as a sufficiently adequate mechanism for allocating resources to R&D efforts because decision making at the firm level is principally based on the profit motive.

In essence, especially in countries seeking to industrialize themselves, the state has to provide policy direction and be directly involved in S&T development. Technology acquisition has more frequently resulted from planning and state intervention than simply in response to market forces (see Tuma, 1987: 403-7). Equally importantly, there is a need for a well-defined industrial strategy integrating technological development with economic planning. This is an important condition for the successful preparation of meaningful technology development strategies.

Concluding Remarks

The East Asian region will undoubtedly experience profound changes with the increasing importance of Japan as a global economic superpower, the opening up of China to DFI and the increasing industrialization of the other countries of the region. While one would expect a higher degree of regional integration in terms of trade, investment and technology flows, the performance of the countries, especially those wishing to expand their industrial foundations will not only depend on external factors but also on their respective policy responses to the new challenges facing them.

While this chapter has highlighted the major issues relating to technology acquisition by the developing countries, and how such acquisition can be affected by globalization, these issues are largely controlled by the technology exporting countries. There is little doubt that after spending substantial effort and investment on R&D and technology improvements, MNCs expect to more than recover these costs, by gaining extra profits or economic rents from their technology.

While it is crucial for developing countries to try to reduce the constraints to technology acquisition with appropriate strategies and the right mix of responses, the industrial countries are generally unsympathetic to developing countries' desire for technological enhancement. While the amount of DFI may be important to induce economic growth in the short term, for long term development, the quality or type of foreign investments are more critical. This means that investments made by MNCs and in the NIEs, for instance, must be viewed in terms of their impact on the development of domestic technological capabilities as well as inter-industry linkages that could be developed by locally-owned enterprises.

If developing countries were to broaden their industrial base, they inevitably have to ensure not only an increasing supply of highly-skilled labor but also a substantial increase in R&D and technical training expenditure. In both the areas of R&D and in-service training, it is important to stress the role of locally-owned enterprises rather than foreign enterprises. All this would require that human resource planning focus attention on the development of the critical skills needed by industry and domestic capacity to innovate (Anuwar Ali, 1984).

There is little doubt, as indicated by the experiences of industrial countries and the NIEs, that innovative capacities will ultimately determine an economy's competitiveness. In all these activities, the appropriate role of the state must be duly emphasized so that a developing economy wishing to industrialize rapidly can benefit from the correct mix of incentives and price signals, infrastructure for human resource development, and institutional framework for science and technology enhancement.

References

Anuwar Ali. "In-service Training: The Malaysian Experience and Policy Implications." In *Pacific Cooperation in Science and Technology,* edited by Karen Minden. Honolulu: East-West Center. 1991.

____. "The Need for Technical Skills and Innovative Capacity: The Case of Manufacturing Industries in Malaysia." *Akademika* No. 25. 1984.

Anuwar Ali, and Muhd Anuar Adnan. "Technological Acquisition and Absorption Via Multinational Companies: The Malaysian Experience. *Jurnal Fakulti Ekonomi* 21-22. 1990.

Aoki, T. "Japanese Direct Investment in Asia and Its Impact on Trade." Paper presented at "The Third Joint Research Conference on Asia Pacific Relations." Kuala Lumpur. 5-7 July, 1992.

Baba, Y., Suzuki, T. "Japan's Evolving Strategies for Science and Technology Toward the 21st Century." Paper presented at the International Conference on "The Emerging Technological Trajectory of the Pacific Rim." Medford, USA. 4-6 October, 1991.

Chee Peng Lim. "International Capital Flows and Economic Development in the Asia Pacific Region." Paper presented at the International Conference on "Financial Institutions and Investment Opportunities in the Asia-Pacific Region in the 1990s." Kuala Lumpur. 11-12 May, 1990.

Chen, Edward K. Y. "The Role of Transnational Corporations in the Economic Development of the Asia-Pacific Region." In *Asian and Pacific Economy Towards the Year 2000*, edited by Fu-Chen Lo. Kuala Lumpur: Asia Pacific Development Centre. 1987.

Djeflat, A. "The Management of Technology Transfer: Views and Experiences of Developing Countries." *International Journal of Technology Development* 3, No. 2-3. 1988.

do Rosario, L. "Multinationals: The Not Always Welcome Guests." *Far Eastern Economic Review.* 18 June, 1992.

Freeman, C. "Technology Gaps, International Trade and the Problems of Smaller and Less Developed Economies." In *Small Countries Facing the Technological Revolution*, edited by C. Freeman and B. A. Lundvall. London: Pinter. 1988.

Lall, S. "Technological Capabilities and Industrialization." *World Development* 2, No. 2. February 1992.

Lindsey, Q. W. "Industry-University Research Cooperation: The State Government Role." *Journal of the Society of Research Administrators* 17, No. 2. 1985.

Nakagawa, T. "Internationalization of Japanese Production Management." *Thai Japanese Studies Journal* No. 2534. December 1991.

Ng, Sek-Hong. "Training Problems and Challenges in a Newly Industrializing Economy: The Case of Hong Kong." *International Labour Review* 126, No. 4. 1987.

Nurul Islam. "Economic Interdependence Between Rich and Poor Nations." In *Crisis & Response: The Challenge to South-South Economic Co-operation*, edited by Noordin Sopiee, B.A. Hamzah, and Leong Choon Heng. Kuala Lumpur: Institute of Strategic and International Studies (ISIS). 1988.

Ozawa, T. "The Role of Transnational Corporations in the Economic Development of the ESCAP Region: Some Available Evidence from Recent Experience." ESCAP/UNCTC Publication Series B, No. 2. Bangkok: United Nations. 1982.

Shim Jae Hoon. "Overseas Investment: Looking Ahead, Looking Abroad." *Far Eastern Economic Review.* 13 August 1992.

Simon, D. F. "Globalization and Regionalization of the Pacific Rim: The Technological Dimensions." Paper presented at the International Conference on "The

Emerging Technological Trajectory of the Pacific Rim." Medford, USA. 4-6 October, 1991.

The Economist. "Asia Beckons." Vol. 323, No. 7761. 30 May-5 June 1992.

Tran Van Tho. "Status of Technology Transfer in the ASEAN Region." Paper presented at the International Seminar on "Japan's Role in the Transfer of Technology in ASEAN Countries." Bangkok. 26-27 June, 1992.

Tran Van Tho, and S. Urata. "Emerging Technology Transfer Patterns in the Pacific Asia." Paper presented at the International Conference on "The Emerging Technological Trajectory of the Pacific Rim." Medford, USA. 4-6 October, 1991.

Tuma, E. H. "Technology Transfer and Economic Development: Lessons of History." *Journal of Developing Areas* 21, No. 4. 1987.

Urata, S. "Export Increase of Developing Countries in Asia and Japanese Imports." Paper presented at "The Third Joint Research Conference on Asia Pacific Relations." Kuala Lumpur. 5-7 July, 1992.

World Bank. "International Technology Transfer: Issues and Policy Options." Staff Working Paper No. 344. Washington DC. July 1979.

Yamazawa, I., and T. Watanabe. "Industrial Restructuring and Technology Transfer." In *Challenge of Asian Developing Countries: Issues and Analyses*, edited by S. Ichimura. Tokyo: Asian Productivity Organization. 1988.

Yoo Seong-min. "Investment Priorities and Government Support Policies in Korea's Economic Growth." In *Strategies for Industrial Development: Concept and Policy Issues*, edited by Suh Jang-Won. Kuala Lumpur: Asian and Pacific Development Centre. 1989.

4

Trade Liberalization and Income Distribution: Lessons for Mexico from East Asia

Diana Alarcón-González

This chapter argues that the impact of trade liberalization on the distribution of income depends largely on the structural linkages of the exporting sectors to the rest of the economy and on institutional factors which include the structure of ownership of the means of production and the role of the government in promoting human development. This argument thus suggests that there is no unique or a priori relationship between the liberalization of trade and the distribution of income. Whether trade liberalization has an equalizing or disequalizing impact on income distribution depends on how it is refracted through the governing institutional framework of the economy.

A few examples may help to clarify this point. The promotion of exports from an agricultural sector based on large farms will improve the income of large landholders, whereas a substantial increase of exports from small agricultural producers is more likely to equalize the distribution of income by raising the incomes of the poorer sectors of society. Similarly, an export strategy based on capital-intensive manufactured goods will tend to concentrate income among those receiving income from capital with much less effect in raising the incomes of broad segments of wage earners. On the other hand, a strategy based on labor-intensive manufactured products will result in significant employment creation and is more likely to lead to a more equal distribution of income.

East Asian countries were among the first developing countries to undertake thoroughgoing policies of trade liberalization. Their development experience is thus a valuable point of reference for framing discussion on the effect of free trade on the development of countries such as Mexico, that have only recently followed a similar strategy. The focus of this chapter is an analysis of the impact of the foreign trade regimes of these countries on their income distribution patterns.

The next section presents some measures of the spread effects of exporting sectors on the economies of six East Asian countries. The argument in this section is that exporting sectors can play an important role in promoting greater equality in the distribution of income if they have large multiplier effects on the rest of the economy. The following section discusses the importance of institutional factors as determinants of how trade liberalization affects the distribution of income. It focuses on the particular institutional framework of countries such as Taiwan and South Korea that were successful in equalizing the distribution of income within the context of trade liberalization. The next section presents a brief review of the way Mexico has attempted to liberalize trade in the 1980s, contrasting its experience with that of Taiwan and South Korea. The final section summarizes the main arguments of the chapter and underlines the lessons that can be drawn from the experience of countries carrying out trade liberalization about the possible complementarities of promoting both greater efficiency and equity.

The Effects of Trade on the Structure of Production

In order to explore the production linkages of exporting sectors with the rest of the economy, we utilize the work of Linnemann et al. (1987), which constitutes, we believe, a very helpful point of reference. The Linnemann study was conducted for seven countries: Indonesia, South Korea, Taiwan, Philippines, Thailand, Malaysia and Singapore.[1]

By examining the sectoral interdependencies of the economy, Linnemann was able to analyze the spread effects of exporting sectors on the rest of the economy. Following the methodology of Rasmussen (1956), the study relies on the calculation of two effects: first, the power of dispersion of exporting sectors, which indicates the backward linkages of these sectors with the rest of the economy, i.e., the extent of their use of domestic inputs and thus their ability to generate demand for the output of other sectors of the economy, and second, the direct and indirect employment effects of exporting sectors. The latter represents a particularly important way to evaluate the income distribution effects of exporting sectors because it can measure the extent to which exports are able to generate employment throughout the economy. This measurement includes not only employment directly generated in the production of exports, but also indirect employment creation in the sectors of the economy that supply inputs to exporting sectors. (For an explanation of the methodology, refer to the appendix.)

The study of the structure of the economy in these six countries was conducted for the years 1974 through 1976, depending on the availability of input-output tables for the different countries. For the purpose of comparison between the trade regimes[2] of the East Asian experience and the more recent experience of other developing countries initiating liberalization, this is a relevant period of analysis because it captures the structure of production of these Asian countries at an earlier stage of trade liberalization. This is especially the case for Indonesia, Philippines, Thailand, and Malaysia. Examination of these particular countries in the 1980s would no doubt reveal that some of them have progressed rather rapidly beyond this early stage. In 1974-6, both South Korea and Taiwan, by contrast, were already well on their way to implementing a more liberalized trade regime, and their more advanced stage is of particular interest.

By the nature of their trade regimes in 1974-6, the East Asian countries can be classified into three distinctive groups. The first group is represented by Indonesia, which at that time was following an import substitution strategy of industrialization. The second group includes South Korea and Taiwan, characterized by a relatively open trade regime (although some industrial sectors were protected at earlier stages of development) and small contributions from free trade or export processing zones (EPZs). The third group includes Philippines, Thailand and Malaysia, which were following a dualistic strategy of industrialization where the import-substituting industrial sector has been protected from international competition, but exports have been promoted through subsidies and/or the operation of EPZs. In Malaysia, EPZs have been used as the main instrument to promote export orientation.

A detailed analysis of the structure of production of these three groups of countries reveals the salient features which we discuss below. Indonesia, which consistently followed import substitution industrialization during this period, shows a pattern of specialization based on capital-intensive products. The average total employment effects of Indonesia's exporting sectors are lower than the effects of total manufacturing production for both natural resource based and non-natural resource based exports. The overall spread effects of manufactured exports from both exporting sectors are also lower than those for total manufacturing production. Because of the relatively weak linkages of Indonesia's exporting sectors with the rest of its economy, trade was not a dynamic source of growth. To the extent that export growth promoted the capital intensity of industrial production it had a diminished impact on the generation of employment.

The opposite is true for countries such as South Korea and Taiwan that pursued a comprehensive policy of export promotion that relied on their comparative advantage. In the early stages of development of these countries, labor was their abundant resource. These two countries showed a consistent pattern of specialization in the export of labor-intensive manufactures. By all measures of factor intensity (direct and indirect employment effects), the sectors exporting manufactures make a more significant contribution to employment creation than manufactures produced for domestic demand. The same is true when account is taken of the spread effects of exports. The direct and indirect backward linkages of manufactured exports are larger than those for all manufactures.

Contrary to the commonly held belief, based mostly on the experience of developed countries, that capital-intensive sectors have more spread effects than labor-intensive sectors, the study of sectoral interdependence conducted by Linnemann shows just the opposite for developing countries. "Apparently, at lower levels of economic development it is easier to supply labor-intensive production processes with domestically produced intermediates than capital-intensive processes" (Linnemann, 1987: 427). This finding has an important implication. It means that systematic export orientation by developing countries based on comparative advantage helps to promote the integration of their domestic structures of production and decreases the reliance on imported inputs. In addition, it stimulates the production of domestic suppliers of inputs by giving them a larger market for which to produce. An exception to this conclusion must be made with regard to EPZs. Although it is empirically difficult to isolate the performance of EPZs, because they are usually not reported in input-output tables as distinct sectors, several studies have indicated that EPZs are characterized by their relative isolation from the rest of the economy and their heavy reliance on imports. Their effects are thus basically limited to the direct creation of employment with very small multiplier effects on other domestic sectors.

The third group of countries—Philippines, Thailand and Malaysia—followed a policy combining import substitution with special provisions to promote exports. In the case of Malaysia, exports were mainly promoted through the creation of EPZs. On average, these countries show that non-natural resource-based exports of manufactures are relatively labor intensive when compared to total domestic production, but the spread effects of their exporting sectors are not particularly large. The average spread effects of manufactured exports in the Philippines and Thailand are slightly above the average for all manufacturing.

Malaysia is in an intermediate position, with the average value of spread effects for exports being the same as those for total manufactured production. The value of this parameter indicates that the export of manufactures from Malaysia does not have a particularly positive impact on the rest of the economy. This result can be explained by the prevalence of EPZs as the main instrument of export promotion.

The conclusion that can be drawn from this brief review of the experience of East Asian countries is that the role of trade liberalization as a dynamic mechanism of development and its effect on the distribution of income depends to a great extent on the structure of the economy, i.e., the manner in which exporting sectors are intertwined with the rest of productive activity. What the experience of these countries shows is that exporting sectors have had the greatest impact on the rest of the economy, both in terms of stimulating other sectors and creating employment in countries that have implemented the most comprehensive policies of trade liberalization based on comparative advantage. In South Korea and Taiwan, the implementation of export orientation promoted the development of a very distinctive structure of production characterized by a high export-output ratio in manufacturing and a pattern of specialization in labor-intensive export goods. It is precisely in these countries where both the spread effects of manufactured exports and the creation of employment throughout the economy are the largest.

Institutional Determinants of Income Distribution

Interdependence among exporting sectors and the rest of the domestic economy explains only part of the relationship between trade and the distribution of income. The potentially equalizing effect of the backward linkages and employment multipliers of exporting sectors can be magnified or restricted by the distribution of productive assets and government policy with regard to human capital formation and social expenditures. We regard this as the institutional framework through which changes in the trade regime have their effect. Trade liberalization can reduce income inequality to the extent that it raises the income going to those factors of production that are more equally distributed. Since labor power is the most equally distributed factor of production, a trade policy that promotes the export of labor-intensive products will help to reduce inequality by increasing the wage share in national income relative to the share of capital. By contrast, a policy that promotes the export of capital-intensive products would lower income inequality only in those cases where the ownership of capital is equally distributed.

Government policy can play a critical role in equalizing the distribution of income by broad-based measures to improve human capital. Not only is this objective a valuable end in itself, but it serves to make a country more competitive internationally. Substantial investment in education and health care, particularly in primary and vocational education and in preventive health care, benefits large segments of the population, improves economic efficiency, and can equalize the distribution of income by improving the human capital of the sectors of the labor force with lower incomes.

The experience of South Korea and Taiwan is interesting, not only because they were among the first developing countries to adopt a comprehensive policy of trade liberalization, but also because in both cases, trade liberalization was accompanied by an impressive improvement in the distribution of income. Gini coefficients in both countries are among the lowest for developing countries, but they also compare favorably with those for developed countries.[3] Thus, it is important to examine the experience of these two countries in order to determine the general conditions under which a more open trade regime can lead to a more equal distribution of income.

One of the most interesting lessons from their experience is that free trade with equity was not the result of trade liberalization and the promotion of labor-intensive exports alone, but was accompanied by two other key policies: first, the redistribution of productive assets, in the form of a major land reform in both countries and the additional redistribution of industrial assets in Taiwan, and second, large government expenditures on human development.

The redistribution of assets in these two countries proved to be key to the reduction of inequality. The rapid expansion of labor-intensive exports led relatively quickly to a condition of full employment and a subsequent rise in industrial wages. But this served to improve the distribution of income only to the extent that land reform had raised the living conditions of rural workers and thereby raised the reservation wage of urban workers.[4] The land reform slowed migration to urban areas and this led to full employment being reached at a relatively early stage of export oriented development. Not only did industrial wages rise, but the combination of restricted supply of labor because of land reform and the increased demand for labor from export production raised the wages of the lowest-paid workers. Even in the case of Korea, where industrial assets remained highly concentrated, land reform alone was able to provide sufficient impetus for a more equal distribution of income.

Governments in both countries made a concerted effort to increase investment in human capital, i.e., basic health and education. Illiteracy was almost eradicated with the provision of 9 years of compulsory education in Taiwan and 6 years in South Korea. By the time these countries reached full employment and their rising wages started to threaten the competitiveness of their light manufactures, the Taiwanese and South Korean exporting sectors were in the enviable position of being able to make the transition to the export of more sophisticated manufactures based on skilled labor. Too often, countries undergoing structural adjustment have combined trade liberalization with dramatic reductions in government financing of health and education, and thereby undermined their long-term international competitiveness.

As a result of the above factors, the distribution of income in both countries has become remarkably equal. Taiwan started with a Gini coefficient of .56 in 1953 and by 1964, it had been lowered to .32. In 1978, it had become as low as .28. In South Korea, Gini coefficients have remained low, but there has been no clear trend. As argued before, concentration of assets in the industrial sector has kept non-wage incomes high. In 1965 the Gini coefficient in Korea was .34 and remained relatively stable thereafter. In 1982, it was .36. However, this stable pattern of income distribution accompanied a major improvement in the standards of living and the quality of life of the population.

Trade Liberalization in Mexico

Industrialization in Mexico was promoted by a policy of import substitution which protected the domestic market from international competition. But the resultant heterogeneous structure of protection of the manufacturing sector and the concentration of ownership of industrial enterprises reinforced inequality in the distribution of income.[5] Gini coefficients for the period of most rapid industrialization fluctuated around a value of 0.5, which is very high by international standards.[6]

Beginning in 1982, the Mexican government introduced a major shift in the direction of its economic policy. It adopted a program of major trade liberalization which removed the protection which had traditionally been accorded to the domestic market. Sharp devaluations in the exchange rate were followed by a drastic reduction of import tariffs and the virtual elimination of non-tariff import restrictions. Within a few years Mexico became a relatively open economy. But there are major differences between the way trade liberalization has been taking place in Mexico and the manner in which it was carried out in the East Asian countries:

1. Contrary to the experience of Taiwan and South Korea, trade liberalization in Mexico was accompanied by a drastic contraction of the government's role in the economy. Not only was direct involvement of the government in production undercut by the sale of most **parastatal** companies, but basic social expenditures on education and public health were also substantially reduced. Expenditures on education dropped from 16 per cent of total government expenditures in 1979 to 6.4 per cent in 1989. Expenditures on public health were reduced from 2.6 per cent of total government expenditure to 0.9 per cent during the same period of time. Primary schools were severely affected. Whereas there was a 55 per cent increase in the number of elementary schools from 1970 to 1979, the increase for the period 1980 to 1989 dropped to only 8.4 per cent. While the number of students in elementary school increased by about 53 per cent during the 1970s, there was no real increase for the 1980s.

2. Although the new export orientation has been relatively successful in promoting exports, especially of manufactures, its overall impact on development, and in particular on the distribution of income, remains unclear. One of the most dynamic exporting sectors during the 1980s were the EPZ-type of operations that go beyond maquiladora production to include other special tax break arrangements to exporters.[7] A recent study calculates that the proportion of EPZs' manufacturing exports to total

manufacturing exports is as high as 78 per cent (González-Arechiga, 1991).[8] However, maquiladora operations are known for their low utilization of domestic inputs: only 2 per cent of total inputs used by maquiladoras are produced in Mexico. The other 98 per cent are imported. Thus, while the direct employment effects have been significant as a result of the rapid growth of exports from EPZs, their relative isolation from the rest of the economy has limited their indirect multiplier effects. The point is that this type of operation may have a once-and-for-all equalizing influence on the distribution of income by providing direct employment, but may not represent a dynamic source of development and equity for the whole economy.

3. The third major difference between the experience of Mexico and those of Taiwan and South Korea relates to the broad question of the operation of labor markets. As suggested above, the liberalization of trade in Taiwan and South Korea was implemented after a major land reform had distributed land equitably among the rural population. In this context, labor-intensive manufactured exports had the effect of generating full employment encompassing even relatively unskilled workers, and this pushed wages up and thus improved the distribution of income. Full employment in Mexico is a more difficult target. With a much larger population than Taiwan and South Korea, Mexico would have to create enough new jobs to provide employment not only to the new workers entering the labor market every year, but also to those disguised unemployed or underemployed workers in the informal sector. Possibly militating against this and contrary to the experience of Taiwan and South Korea is the current danger in Mexico of greater concentration of landholdings. New reforms to the Mexican Constitution instituted in 1992 by the Salinas administration may open up a new process of land concentration by allowing the sale and rental of *ejido* land. This may increase rural migration to urban areas, aggravate the problem of unemployment and underemployment, and maintain downward pressure on wages.

This brief review of Mexico's trade reforms during the 1980s indicates that unless important changes are introduced in the economic policy that accompanies trade liberalization, the equalizing effects of free trade on the distribution of income may be very limited. Without a deliberate policy to promote the export of labor-intensive manufactures, the growth of exports will only have a limited impact on the expansion of employment. And unless an explicit policy of industrial integration is instituted, the free trade export processing zones will remain relatively isolated and have very small multiplier effects on the rest of the economy. Finally, unless there is a major effort to invest in human development, trade liberalization alone will prove insufficient to reverse the gross inequalities in the distribution of income inherited from the period of import substitution industrialization. The primary equalizing impact of free trade on the distribution of income may remain a once and for all direct employment effect.

Conclusions: Trade with Equity

A comparative study of the experience of East Asian countries during the early period of their trade liberalization reveals that countries can reduce protectionist distortions in trade that adversely affect economic efficiency while promoting a more egalitarian pattern of income distribution. Trade liberalization which involves major structural changes in the economy is compatible with greater equality when accompanied by policies oriented to promote human development, thus raising the incomes of broad sectors of the working population.

From the experience of these countries, one can draw some important lessons:

1. Exporting sectors have the greatest effect on the development of an economy when comprehensive policies of trade liberalization are adopted. A trade strategy based on exporting according to a country's comparative advantage has been shown to have the largest spread effects on the rest of the economy, both in terms of direct and indirect employment effects and backward linkages in general.
2. Trade liberalization is most likely to have an equalizing impact on the distribution of income when productive assets in agriculture and industry are equally distributed. This ensures that the additional income generated by exporting sectors is more equally distributed throughout the economy.
3. Contrary to some of the most publicized misconceptions about the experiences of East Asia, the egalitarian effects of trade liberalization were achieved through active government intervention. The cases of South Korea and Taiwan illustrate that the transition to freer trade with equity requires substantial government investment in education and health services directed to broad segments of the population. Such investment in human capital not only raises the income of the working population, but also helps to develop a country's dynamic comparative advantage that can enable it to achieve higher stages of industrialization.

In a classification of countries with respect to economic efficiency and the egalitarianism of their societies, Khan (1992) argues that in countries where inefficiency and inegalitarianism prevail, there are broad complementarities between policies designed to improve the efficiency of their productive structure and policies to reduce poverty and improve the distribution of income. Dismantling the old productive structure can be complemented with the dismantling of the old system of privileges, but this requires an explicit commitment of the government to these objectives. "The distribution of access to productive assets, human capital and public services should be improved to complement the structural adjustment measures" (Khan, 1992: 22). Particular attention must be paid to the implementation of complementary measures that offset the unfavorable costs of structural adjustment that adversely affect the poor.

One of the most important lessons that can be drawn from the experience of trade liberalization in East Asia is the recognition of significant complementarities that can be developed between economic efficiency and equity. Dismantling the old system of protectionism that breeds inefficiency can be achieved within a context of equity, but as is the case in any country undergoing radical structural changes, there has to be the political will to proceed in that direction. "The potential convergence of efficiency and equity in the adjustment process in a country with inefficiently inegalitarian initial conditions does not necessarily mean that it would in practice be possible to combine adjustment with equity. Groups benefiting from the initial policies and institutions would oppose adjustment policies that would promote equity by eliminating their benefits. The success of adjustment with equity in this case would require both a substantial autonomy on the part of the state and an ability on the part of the state to forge a sufficiently broad political coalition in favor of the adjustment package" (Khan, 1992:54).

Addendum

The concept of the power of dispersion refers to a standardized measure of backward linkages derived from input-output tables. In the framework of intersectoral analysis, backward linkages represent the average intermediate input requirements per unit of output. Sectors with large backward linkages are said to have large spread effects on the rest of the economy in the sense that output in that sector requires a large amount of inputs from all other sectors of production. In order to facilitate international intersectoral comparisons, Rasmussen (1956) developed a standardized measure of the total sectoral spread effects by using elements of the Leontief inverse matrix. The power of dispersion for sector j becomes:

$$P_j = \frac{\frac{1}{n} \sum_{i=1}^{n} r_{ij}}{\frac{1}{n^2} \sum_{i=1}^{n} \sum_{j=1}^{n} r_{ij}}$$

where Pj is the power of dispersion for sector j and r_{ij} are the elements in the Leontief inverse matrix.

The numerator of the ratio P_j denotes the average increase in output of a sector induced by a unit increase of the final demand for products of sector j. In making international comparisons of sectoral linkage patterns, the average degree of sectoral interdependence must be taken into account. Hence the standardizing of P_j by the average r_{ij} in the denominator. The value of the power of dispersion for an imaginary sector that equals exactly the average value of backward linkages in an economy is 1. Consequently, if $P_j > 1$, it implies that sector j has above-average backward linkage effects, whereas if $P_j < 1$, it can be stated that sector j is operating in relative isolation from other sectors." (Linnemann et al., 1987:214-215)

Power of dispersion employment measures can be calculated in a similar fashion. By denoting P_j^E as the power of dispersion of sector j in terms of employment,

$$P_j^E = \frac{\frac{1}{n} \sum_{i=1}^{n} l_i \; r_{ij}}{\frac{1}{n^2} \sum_{i=1}^{n} \sum_{j=1}^{n} l_i \; r_{ij}}$$

where li denotes the direct labor coefficient for sector i, and r_{ij} are again the elements of the Leontief inverse matrix. Thus, the power of dispersion in terms of employment includes the direct and indirect employment effects of sectoral output throughout the economy.

In the chapter, power of dispersion measures are interchangeably referred to as power of dispersion, backward linkages or spread effects. A sector's employment effects refer to the second measure, the power of dispersion in terms of employment.

Notes

1. We exclude Singapore from consideration in this paper because of its special characteristics as a City-State, which makes its case less applicable to other countries.

2. The concept of trade regime refers to all the rules, legislation, government policies and institutional constraints that regulate external trade.

3. The Gini coefficient measures inequality in the distribution of income, with 0 representing perfect equality and 1 representing perfect inequality.

4. The reservation wage is the minimum wage that will motivate a worker to accept a job because it is at least equal to the income from his next best alternative.

5. For a discussion of the difference in the rates of protection of various industrial sectors, see Ten Kate and Wallace (1980). The effects of import substitution policies on income distribution are well documented in the literature on trade and economic development. A classic reference is Little et al. (1970).

6. A comprehensive discussion of the different methodologies used to calculate income inequality in Mexico and the different Gini coefficient values can be

found in Oscar Altimir (1982). This study reveals that despite differences in the calculated values of Gini coefficients, all studies concur that the highest coefficients coincided with the period of rapid industrialization.

7. Maquiladora is the Mexican name for production in a free trade export processing zone (EPZ) located along the country's northern border with the United States. During the 1980s, similar provisions were extended to domestic producers throughout the country who wanted to export under the name of PITEX and ALTEX.

8. This proportion results from adding together the exports from PITEX and maquiladoras and comparing it to total manufacturing exports plus the value added in maquiladoras.

References

Alvarez Bejar, Alejandro, and Gabriel Mendoza Pichardo. *México 1988-1991: un ajuste económico exitoso?* Mexico: UNAM. 1991.

Altimir, Oscar. "La Distribucion del Ingreso en Mexico 1950-1977." In *Distribucion del Ingreso en Mexico, Ensayos. Analisis Estructural.* Cuaderno 2, Tomo I. Mexico: Banco de Mexico. 1982.

Bourguignon, Francois, and Christian Morrison. *External Trade and Income Distribution.* Paris: OECD. 1989.

Cortés, Fernando, and Rosa María Rubalcava. *Autoexplotación Forzada y Equidad por Empobrecimiento.* Mexico: El Colegio de México. 1991.

Griffin, Keith. *Alternative Strategies for Economic Development.* London: Macmillan. 1989.

Griffin, Keith, and Khan, Azizur. *Growth and Inequality in Pakistan.* London: Macmillan. 1972.

Khan, Azizur Rahman. *Structural Adjustment and Income Distribution: A Review of Issues and Experiences.* Working Paper No. 31. Geneva: International Labour Organization. 1992.

Linnemann, Hans, ed. *Export-Oriented Industrialization in Developing Countries.* Singapore: Singapore University Press. 1987.

Little, Ian, Tibor Scitovsky, and Maurice Scott. *Industry and Trade in Some Developing Countries.* Oxford: Oxford University Press. 1970.

Lustig, Nora. "Economic Crisis, Adjustment and Living Standards in Mexico, 1982-85." *World Development* 18. 1990: 1325-1342.

Ten Kate, Adrian, and Fernando De Mateo Venturini. "Apertura Comercial y Estructura de la protección en México un análisis de la relación entre ambas." *Comercio Exterior* 39, Núm. 6. 1989: 497-511.

____. "Apertura Comercial y Estructura de la protección en México: Estimaciones cuantitativas de los ochenta." *Comercio Exterior* 38, Núm. 5. 1989.

USITC (U.S. International Trade Commission). *Review of Trade and Investment Liberalization Measures by Mexico and Prospectivs for Future United States Mexican Relations.* Phases I and II. Washington, DC: USITC. 1989.

5

The Idea of National Economic Integration and the Experience of Korean Development

Dae-Hwan Kim

The purpose of this chapter is two-fold: theoretically, it advances the concept of national economic integration (NEI) as an appropriate structural perspective on economic development and, practically, it analyzes the Korean experience since the early 1960s from this perspective. This may contradict current thinking on economic development in general and on the Korean experience in particular; the former emphasizes global integration beyond national boundaries, whereas the latter tends to portray South Korea as a successful example of such international economic integration.

International economic integration may be synonymous with development in advanced countries, particularly in Europe, where integration at the international level is accelerating. But in underdeveloped countries, economic integration at the national level is first required, even for international economic integration. Most such countries have in fact pursued national economic integration since their independence from colonial rule,[1] although they have also been forced by the world capitalist system to accept international integration. Korea is no exception. Not only in terms of objectives or goals of economic development, but also strategies pursued, even for export, policy-making has been strongly inspired by nationalism. Korea's economic success also needs to be seen in this context, while recognizing that more and more international integration has been accompanied by export-oriented industrialization. This perspective has tended to be neglected, however, by the presumption that the concept of economic integration should be exclusively identified with international integration.

The following discussion, therefore, begins by criticizing this way of thinking, and instead proposes the concept of national economic integration, emphasizing its significance for the economic development of underdeveloped countries. To render this concept analytically operative, four elements are proposed: balance, linkages, interrelationships, and equality. The next section analyzes the Korean experience in the last three decades, following a brief look at nationalism in the country's economic development. Then, an overall assessment from the perspective of national economic integration is based on this analysis, leading to some considerations on the relevance of the idea of national economic integration as well as the Korean experience to underdeveloped countries today.

Development as National Economic Integration

National Economic Integration: Concept

The concept of "integration"—meaning "bringing or combining parts into a whole"[2]—has long been used in economics. But, strangely enough, the concept—originally adopted in order to discuss the combination or merger of business firms (Machlup, 1977: 3)—subsequently seems to have bypassed the national and moved directly to the international level. Thus, the concept of "economic integration" is usually identified with "international economic integration," often to the exclusion of the national level (Balassa, 1961: 1-4).

However, this mainstream presumption is not agreeable to all. The concept of integration itself is ambiguous and abstract, and remains so unless the reality of "a whole" into which parts are brought together can be made clear. "International integration" is not logically more coherent than "national integration," as the "whole" for the latter has the nation state as its reference point and is analytically operative. The national economy is generally accepted as a basic unit of economic analysis, and even international economic analysis regards national economies as units of analysis.

The advocates of the exclusive use of the concept of economic integration for the international level actually presuppose that national economies, even in underdeveloped countries, are already integrated units. However, G. Amin (1976: 393):

> refuse[s] to accept the legal or geographical borders of a country as an adequate frame of reference in drawing a development strategy. For, if we are concerned with real and not fictitious societies, we cannot fail to notice that in almost every underdeveloped country there is more than one "society," each having its own per capita income, values, and aspirations.

National economic integration thus satisfies two essential components of the concept of integration—"parts" and a "whole"—more properly than international integration. We can rightly maintain, therefore, that the concept of economic integration is more applicable at the national level than at the international level.

We can therefore define the concept of national economic integration as the process by which various economic sectors in a country are organically and self-correctingly brought together into an independent national economy. This process is not merely a mechanical aggregation, but rather a process of increasing organic relations among economic sectors, such that the whole is "always more than the sum of its parts" (Markovits & Oliver, 1981: 66), in that their relations establish the structure of the national economy.[3] This concept is thus particularly concerned with the interconnectedness of domestic economic sectors and functions. This does not mean that external transactions or the differentiation of economic sectors and activities should be excluded from consideration. Our NEI concept suggests a dynamic process including these, in which the parts are, at the same time, being organically integrated within a national economy. Through such adjustments, economic sectors and activities are brought into a higher degree of interdependence.

National Economic Integration: Significance for Development

The significance of national economic integration for economic development in general is drawn by rejecting the assumption that the existence of nation states automatically brings internal integration within a national economy, which in turn obstructs international economic integration, and therefore development. Although it cannot be denied that the existence of the nation state is an important factor in national economic integration, it does not necessarily guarantee national economic integration among sectors, industries, classes, regions and so on. Rather, the economic policies of the nation state can not only create barriers to external economic intercourse, but also to domestic integration, e.g., by accepting "growth poles" or even "economic polarization."

Further, the argument that national economic integration leads to international disintegration (e.g., Balassa, 1961: 3) is an inaccurate oversimplification; in reality, international integration usually takes the form of cooperation among national states and economies. Hence, the national integration of these economies can contribute to international integration rather than disintegration. Conversely, international integration does not necessarily help national integration. In contrast to Balassa, whose argument is based on a harmonious Euro-centric world-view, in the real world, national disintegration can occur precisely because of international integration, particularly in underdeveloped countries (Griffin, 1978: 2).

The fundamental rationale of national economic integration for the economic development of underdeveloped countries lies in the fact that their basic initial conditions are characterized by national economic disintegration. Domestic economies are generally unbalanced, lacking linkages among industries, lacking close interrelations among economic activities, and characterized by marked inequalities in income distribution and economic power (Kim, 1986). This "structural disarticulation" underscores the need for and the significance of national economic integration in these countries. Here, national economic integration must come before, and even for, international integration (Myrdal, 1956: 3-4; S. Amin, 1974: 28; Duvall et al., 1981: 330), clearly because "removal of these disintegrating roadrocks . . . deserve the highest priority on the nation's . . . agenda" (Machlup, 1977: 95).

Elements of National Economic Integration

National economic integration can be studied through the interconnectedness among economic sectors and activities. For analytical purposes, four elements of national economic integration can be distinguished: (i) balance among economic sectors, (ii) linkages among industries, (iii) interrelationships among economic activities, and (iv) equality.[4] The first refers to balance among different economic sectors, particularly domestic sectors. The second focuses on backward and forward domestic linkages and the gap between domestic and world linkages. The third element refers to the relations among domestic production, exports, imports, and the generation of value-added. The element of equality centers upon relations among classes, regions, and firms. These four elements represent the major elements in national economic integration for which data availability permits quantitative analysis. The higher the degree of these four relationships, the higher the level of national economic integration.

Balance: National economic integration requires balanced development of the national economy, i.e., balance among domestic economic sectors. As is well known, the debate over balanced versus unbalanced growth eventually led to a general agreement to regard balance as an objective of development.[5] In the process, limited temporary imbalances may be needed to further this goal, but excessive imbalance is harmful to national economic integration. A corrective process thus requires deliberate policy efforts to ensure balance. This objective was endorsed long ago by List (1841: 5), who described it as a process whereby "a nation achieves a proper ratio in its national production, where agriculture, industry, [and their subsectors] . . . are harmoniously developed."

Linkages: Mere balance among economic sectors does not necessarily guarantee national economic integration—this also requires forward and backward linkages, particularly among various industries. Such linkages are the record of structural integration of the economy, indicating "the relation of parts to the whole (and between parts)" (Yotopoulos & Nugent, 1976: 286); the greater the linkages among sectors or industries, the more integrated the economy.[6] Linkages are closely related to balance among sectors (Duvall et al., 1981: 327). In particular, greater domestic linkages are important for national economic integration because they involve a simultaneous dynamization of industries—through the "multiplier effect"—as the foundation for sound structural development of the national economy.

Interrelationships: National economic integration also requires close interrelationships among and within economic activities, resulting in functional interdependence within the national economy. These interrelations again involve the dynamics of the system: the interactions of economic sectors and the structural integration of the economy as a whole. The closer the interrelations among domestic economic activities, such as production, demand, exports, and the generation of value-added, the higher the level of national economic integration. This is particularly important for export-oriented underdeveloped economies, where the economic structure is strongly influenced by the international division of labor. This, in turn, inhibits balanced development among industries and reduces domestic linkage effects.

Equality: Equality among people and regions is the fourth essential element of national economic integration. This element is, in fact, a basic value premise of integration. Based on the belief that the advanced countries' experiences of national economic integration have entailed realization of greater equality, Myrdal (1956: 4, 37; 1974: 41-2, 104) suggested equality—rather than growth—as a primary condition for the rapid and steady development of underdeveloped countries. More equal distribution of economic power contributes to an increase in products for mass consumption and the development of domestic markets, besides reducing luxury imports. This element of distributional equality is additive to our other three elements of national economic integration.

Needless to say, these four elements are closely interrelated. In the case of great concentration of economic power in a few big business groups, which have closer links to foreign sectors, enhancement of the relative position of small and medium firms has the effect of increasing the degree of domestic balance, linkages, and interrelationships. At the same time, the other three interrelated elements, in turn, contribute to equality: e.g., balance, through adjustments of "entitlements" and "exchange";[7] linkages, through increase in employment; and interrelationships, through the expansion of the domestic market.

The Korean Experience from the Perspective of National Economic Integration

Nationalist Stance in Development

Before going on to an economic analysis of the South Korean experience during the last three decades from the perspective of national economic integration (NEI), let us briefly discuss the nationalist current underpinning and actually encouraging rapid economic growth, particularly its relationship with the idea of national economic integration.

Korea's rapid growth has largely been inspired and borne by nationalism, besides the desire and will to get out of the economic misery prevailing until the early 1960s. Although the nationalist tendency is found in almost all underdeveloped countries that experienced colonial rule, it was probably strongest in Korea. The Koreans had incessantly fought against Japanese colonial rule, and have retained a spirit of competition particularly with Japan. This strong nationalist sentiment has, at least until recently, boosted national economic development led by the government. Despite its lack of political legitimacy, the military regime could gain people's cooperation by directing the nationalist current to economic development, with such slogans as "Let's try to live well" and "We too can do it." It is not a coincidence at all that at the early stage of their rule, the military junta proposed "nationalistic democracy" as their ideology, even though this—together with "Koreanistic democracy" during the repressive *Yushin* regime (1972-79)—was, in fact, a camouflage for authoritarianism.

Crude and "petty bourgeois" as it may have been (Sohn, 1991: 187), it cannot be denied that the military regime also had a nationalist stance. This was reflected in its definition of the goal of economic development as "self-reliance" and "balanced development of the national economy," from the outset of the five-year economic development plans. In introducing foreign capital, unlike Taiwan and many Latin American countries, Korea preferred borrowing to direct foreign investment (DFI). In the case of DFI, joint ventures were preferred to total foreign ownership. As is well known, the Korean government imposed strict regulations and controls on imports, while promoting exports. Through these policies, the government supported the formation and development of Korean capital and locally-owned industries.

By equating economic growth with national pride, the regime made people work hard and long, repressing the rights of workers. Along with this, huge projects—which then seemed to be leaps into the dark, such as highways as well as heavy and chemical industries—were undertaken "risking the national fate." In the case of the development of heavy and chemical industries in the 1970s, the government got the big business groups (*jaebul*) to assume responsibility by invoking nationalism. Financial and other policy support was also given to them, as before. Even the promotion of *jaebul* for rapid economic growth and industrialization was justified in terms of economic nationalism (Cheng, 1990: 159).

Thus, it can be said that strong nationalism among the people and its utilization by the regime was an important factor underlying Korea's economic performance in the last few decades, especially when compared with Latin America in particular.[8] Without strong nationalism among the people and the nationalist stance underlying development policies, such rapid growth and industrialization would probably not have occurred in the Korean economy; and even if it did, the outcome might not have been very different from the Latin American experience.

This does not mean that I endorse the regime's idea of nationalism *per se*. Nor has the government consistently maintained its nationalist stance, as it were. Their idea of nationalism was not well-grounded, but arbitrarily applied, and therefore faded away in the process of rapid economic growth, especially with export orientation. The official goal of self-reliance has mainly been a legitimating slogan. Instead, the government quickly conceded to technological dependence abroad, particularly on Japan. The other idea of "balanced development of the national economy" has been replaced by an unbalanced growth strategy, exacerbated by policy neglect of distributional equality.

This implies that the idea of nationalism held by the regime was far from coherent and consistent, in contrast to our concept of national economic integration, and soon lost its significance. Nevertheless, the interconnected ideas of self-reliance and balanced development can be interpreted as being similar to our concept. Although the government has diluted its nationalism, the strong nationalist sentiments among the people remain to check the government. Thus, at least until the 1970s, streaks of nationalism remained in development policies, which were in turn reflected in the structure of the Korean economy as will be revealed by the following analysis.

National Economic Integration: Analysis of the Korean Economy

Here, the Korean experience of economic development is analyzed from the perspective of national economic integration, in terms of the four elements of national economic integration discussed above.

Balance. For a quantitative analysis of the extent to which economic growth has been accompanied by balance among economic sectors, I have computed the imbalance indices for every year[9] and then averaged them over the period studied. This was first done for three sectors (primary, secondary, and tertiary), and then for 12 subsectors. The results are presented in Table 5.1. Note that the 12 sector classification is not consistent over the periods,[10] owing to the nature of the data used. In addition, the unavailability of time series data at consistent constant prices for the whole period means that the table has to be comprised of two parts.

As can be seen from the table, balance among economic sectors worsened in the period 1967-72, and then greatly improved in the next period. Although it worsened again during 1977-81, it improved again in the period 1982-86. After that, an increase in imbalance was recorded, but this was not worse than during the period 1972-76. This implies that Korea's

TABLE 5.1. South Korea: Indices of Sectoral Growth Imbalance

Period	3 Sectors	12 Sectors
1963-66	0.522	0.757
1967-71	0.820	1.071
1972-76	0.461	0.618
1977-81	0.966	1.457
1972-76	0.444	0.666
1977-81	1.219	1.593
1982-86	0.292	0.636
1987-90	0.450	0.607

Sources: Bank of Korea, *National Income in Korea*, 1982 (for the first part, at 1975 constant prices); *National Accounts*, 1990 and *1990 National Accounts*, 1992 (for the second part, at 1985 constant prices).

growth has been moving unsteadily towards greater sectoral balance. However, our imbalance indicators by sector (not presented here) clearly show that agricultural stagnation has been the most important factor generating greater imbalances during the whole period, pointing to a serious structural problem in the Korean economy.

Linkages. For the analysis of linkages among industries, aggregate backward and forward direct linkages have been calculated based on Korea's input-output tables. As indirect linkages are derived from direct ones, the consideration of total (i.e., direct plus indirect) linkages does not involve a big difference. Rather, special attention is paid here to the distinction between domestic linkages and world linkages, by excluding imports from the latter.[11] Thus, the gap between both are also displayed in Table 5.2.

This table shows an increasing trend for all linkages until 1980. The increases in both domestic and world linkages, as well as the increases in the gap between the two, should be mentioned. This reflects the increasingly export-oriented economy, involving processing and assembly. The fact that domestic industrial linkages increased despite widening gaps with world linkages points to greater structural integration of the national economy. At least on this macro-level, the argument of growing industrial dependency can be refuted for the Korean economy. Although all linkages decreased between 1985 and 1987, the gap between world and domestic linkages remained the same. But, compared with 1980, the decreases in the gap since the mid-1980s are observed.

Relatively good performance in enhancing linkages among domestic sectors has resulted from two policies: (i) advancing the industrial structure by moving from light (in the 1960s and early 1970s) to heavy and chemi-

TABLE 5.2. South Korea: Industrial Linkages

	World (A)		Domestic (B)		Gap (A-B)	
	Backward	Forward	Backward	Forward	Backward	Forward
1963	0.406	0.364	0.326	0.288	0.080	0.076
1970	0.457	0.402	0.364	0.320	0.093	0.082
1978	0.534	0.450	0.401	0.338	0.133	0.112
1980	0.604	0.514	0.462	0.392	0.142	0.122
1985	0.586	0.509	0.457	0.397	0.129	0.112
1987	0.580	0.501	0.451	0.390	0.129	0.111
1990	0.572	0.503	0.464	0.408	0.108	0.095

Sources: Bank of Korea, *The Input-Output Tables of Korea*, various years (at producers' current market prices).

cal (until the mid-1980s) and then to high-tech (since the mid-1980s) industrialization; (ii) protecting and developing domestic industries through import controls and government subsidies. However, these developments have not reached the point where the gap between world and domestic linkages has closed, while domestic linkages in some important sectors (e.g., machinery, electronics and chemicals) are still low. It is also a problem that both effects began to decrease in 1985 due to increases in consumption.

Interrelationships. To examine functional interrelationships among economic activities, we focus on the effects of generating (i) domestic production, (ii) value-added, and (iii) imports, by a unit of consumption, investment and exports (see Table 5.3).[12]

The production generation coefficients (the volume of domestic production generated by a unit of each factor) showed increases until 1980, except in the case of investment in 1978, when over-investment in heavy and chemical industries was apparent. This means that the Korean economy, as a whole, experienced increasing production efficiency. The greatest production generation effect of exports, among them, indicates not only that economic growth has largely been led by exports, but also that the country's exports have been closely related to and have encouraged domestic production. But production generated by investment and exports both recorded decreases in 1987, whereas the production generation coefficient of consumption remained high, implying that a structural change is going on.

The value-added generation coefficient, showing the efficiency of each component in generating income, generally decreased until 1980, though an increase was recorded since the mid-1980s, thanks to wage increases and relative stabilization of import prices. This trend was the result of in-

TABLE 5.3. South Korea: Generation Coefficients

	Consumption	Investment	Exports
Production			
1963	1.36	1.25	1.64
1970	1.44	1.43	1.70
1978	1.50	1.32	1.84
1980	1.72	1.64	1.96
1985	1.69	1.75	1.95
1987	1.67	1.61	1.89
1990	1.68	1.74	1.98
Value-added			
1963	0.91	0.57	0.80
1970	0.87	0.61	0.74
1978	0.83	0.52	0.64
1980	0.77	0.58	0.62
1985	0.81	0.66	0.63
1987	0.82	0.62	0.65
1990	0.82	0.72	0.67
Imports			
1963	0.10	0.41	0.22
1970	0.13	0.39	0.26
1978	0.17	0.48	0.36
1980	0.23	0.42	0.38
1985	0.19	0.34	0.37
1987	0.18	0.38	0.35
1990	0.18	0.28	0.33

Sources: Bank of Korea, *The Input-Output Tables of Korea*, various years (at producers' current market prices).

creases in the degree of processing in production and changes in the degree of national income leakages through imports. With industrialization, the Korean economy has increased the degree of processing; but the nature of its assembly and processing involved increasing import requirements. This trend is reflected in the reversal of the earlier upward trend in import generating coefficients, as can be seen in the table.

Equality. The Korean experience has been described as a case of "growth with equity." However, its "success" in securing equality in income distribution, an argument initiated by Adelman (1973) and followed by many others, is neither the result of egalitarian policies nor relevant any more to the present time. Insofar as it was the case, it was primarily due to historical conditions at the outset, including the land reform and civil war in the 1950s which provided it with a leveled-out base. The government policy since the 1960s has been "growth first, distribution later," and effectively remains so. This has resulted in an increase in inequality in the distribution of income, particularly during the 1980s.[13]

Korea's distributional problems are also pronounced and serious in other respects: (i) the low economic position of the working class, (ii) "excessive" concentration in the few hands of big business groups (the *jaebul*), and (iii) regional disparities.[14] These are all by-products of government policies for rapid growth and industrialization, i.e., discriminating against labor in favor of capital; in favor of conglomerates among businesses; and supporting manufacturing at the expense of agriculture.

Despite an enormous increase in the number of employees (60.2 percent of all employed in 1990), their share of national income was 59.1 percent, whereas in 1970, 38.6 percent had 50.5 percent, clearly pointing to a relative deterioration in the income share of the working class. This policy discrimination against labor has been closely related to the low price policy for agricultural products, which has contributed to low wages. This, in turn, led to regional economic disparities between industrial and agricultural areas. Korea's industrialization is characterized by a "bipolar" regional pattern, concentrated in the Metropolitan (northwest) and Youngnam (southeast) areas. As of 1990, these two poles accounted for 85.6 percent of industrial employment, 86.2 percent of the number of firms, and 83.0 percent of value-added. Meanwhile, the main agricultural area's (Honam, southwest) economic condition has worsened.

The concentration of economic power in the *jaebul* can be seen as the result of government support for their expansion like "the legs of an octopus." This seems true in the light of the top 30 companies' dominance of the Korean economy (some indicators of which are shown in Table 5.4), and their speculation on real estate. In fact, these family-owned, monopolistic big business groups are seen as the symbols of inequality and immorality in Korean society.

This means that Korea's rapid economic growth and structural changes through industrialization have been achieved at the expense of distributional equality. Distribution was subordinated to growth until the mid-1980s, when this proved to be no longer possible. This problem also affects the efficiency of the economy as a whole. Without resolving this problem, production efficiency (not to mention allocative efficiency) will not be secured.

Conclusion

The analysis in the previous section provides an overall assessment of Korea's experience. At the macro-level, the Korean economy has not only achieved rapid growth, but also structural integration. It is believed that the nationalist thrust of government policies has made a contribution to

TABLE 5.4. South Korea: The Top 30 *Jaebuls'* Ranking

	Percent	Year/Period
Share in total sales[a]	38.6	1987
Share in shipments[a]	37.3	1987
Share in employment[a]	17.6	1987
Share in financial loans	23.3 (bank)	1988
	41.3 (others)	1988
Stock holdings	16.1 (family)	1988
	49.5 (internal)	1988
Increase in net assets	80.0	1987-89

[a]Confined to manufacturing.
Source: Lee and Lee (1990) and Kang et al.(1991).

this "success." The nationalist idea, however, was generally not well organized, and particularly did not take distributional equality into account. Thus, despite relative equality at the outset, Korea has seen deepening distributional inequality, which, in turn, now threatens national development.

Many students of the Korean experience have either misunderstood its distributional impact or regarded distributional considerations as obstructions to national economic development. But the benefits of latecomer industrialization can only be reaped by paying attention to the recent situation in Korea, where intensifying social conflicts over distribution threaten to impede further development. The implication is that sustained development can only be secured when distributional equality is combined with close interconnectedness among economic sectors, underscoring the idea of national economic integration.

Lastly, but fundamentally, there arises the question of the applicability of the concept of national economic integration to underdeveloped countries today. It may seem to be impractical or irrelevant in the present world system, which has increasingly restricted the policy options for underdeveloped countries. But the world system is not monolithically static, and the abandonment of the idea of national economic integration will further restrict the options available. National economic integration remains relevant to national development efforts pursued by underdeveloped countries.

Notes

1. This implies that national economic integration has a strong political connotation. But this does not overshadow its economic significance as well as analytical operativeness. This will be dealt with in the next section, where the definition of this concept is discussed.

2. Myrdal (1956: 9); Balassa (1961: 1), on the basis of the *Oxford English Dictionary*.

3. Balassa (1961: 1) distinguished integration as a process from integration as a state of affairs, while Orantes (1981: 148-9) emphasized it as a process. That the concept of economic integration should be used as a process is also argued, though on the international level, by Keohane and Nye (1975). On the other hand, Ghantus (1982: 18) implies both dimensions—national and international—in the case of process, while confining the concept only to the international dimension in the case of state of affairs.

4. This is based on my previous studies: on the review of literature on the ideas, something like our concept of national economic integration (1985: 66-76) and on the initial conditions in underdeveloped countries (1986). Beside these four elements, many others can also be picked up. Among them, political factors deserve attention. But they are excluded here just for the reason of the scope of our discussion.

5. The agreement has been made by Streeten's retreat (1963: 66; more clearly in 1979: 284) from his previous position advocating unbalanced growth (1959). Concerning this, Bhatt (1965: 94) concluded: "the objective to be attained through a deliberate policy of creating imbalance is to induce a *movement* towards a balance . . . it would be necessary to ensure . . . to generate a corrective process." (Emphasis in the original.)

6. Related to this, the linkage analysis needs to separate domestic linkages from Yotopoulos and Nugent's (1973) "total" linkages, in order to distinguish those from world linkages. For this, see Jones (1976).

7. Sen (1980: 52), seeing equality as determined by "entitlement" of ownership and "exchange" of products, pays attention to the effects of balance mainly on entitlement. But, balance among sectors also has impact on exchange conditions, by affecting price relations between products.

8. This paper does not go deep into this subject. Suffice it to refer to some excellent comparative works showing the details, within my knowledge: Evans (1987), Gereffi (1989a, 1989b), Gereffi and Wyman (1987), Sachs (1985) and several chapters in Gereffi and Wyman (eds.) (1990).

9. The measure of this is written as

$$V = \sqrt{\frac{\sum w_i (g_i - G)^2}{G^2}}$$

where V denotes imbalance index; G, the overall growth rate of GDP in a given year; w_i, the share of sector i in the total GDP in the end of the previous year (or the beginning of the year); and g_i denotes the growth rate of sector i.

10. In the first part (1963-81): 1) agriculture, 2) forestry and fishing, 3) mining and quarrying, 4) manufacturing, 5) electricity, gas and water, 6) construction, 7) wholesale and retail trade, restaurants and hotels, 8) transport, storage and communication, 9) finance, insurance, real estate and business services, 10) residence, 11) public administration and defense, and 12) social and private services.

In the second part (1972-90): 1) agriculture, forestry and fishing, 2) mining and quarrying, 3) manufacturing, 4) electricity, gas and water, 5) construction, 6) wholesale and retail trade, restaurants and hotels, 7) transport, storage and communication, 8) finance, insurance, real estate and business services, 9) community, social and personal services, 10) government services, 11) private non-profit services, and 12) import duties.

11. For various concepts of industrial linkage and their measures, please see Kim (1985: 139-44).

12. The methodology employed, by the Bank of Korea, for these computations is an extension of the applied input-output analysis, which is comprehensively treated by, among others, Bulmer-Thomas (1982).

13. According to a recent estimate (Ahn & Kang, 1990), which is thought to be more reliable than others, the Gini coefficient increased from 0.3137 in 1970 to 0.4029 in 1988. It also reports continuous increases since 1983 (0.3674).

14. The details of these aspects have been dealt with in my previous paper (1992), on which our discussion below relies. An updated version of the paper is to be published in Kim and Kong (eds.).

References

Adelman, I. *Redistribution with Growth: the Case of Korea*. Washington, DC: The World Bank. 1973.

Ahn, K., and S. Kang. "Hankuk ui Kyecheong-byul Soduk Bunbae Chui wa geo Kyuljung Yoin" [The Trend of Korea's Personal Income Distribution and Its Determinants]. *Kyungje Nonmoon-jip [Review of Economics]*. The Institute of Economic Research, Chung-Ang University. Vol. 4. 1990.

Amin, G. "Dependent Development." *Alternatives* 2, No. 4. 1976.

Amin, S. *Accumulation on a World Scale: A Critique of the Theory of Underdevelopment*, 2 vols. New York: Monthly Review Press. 1974.

Balassa, B. "Towards a Theory of Economic Integration." *Kyklos* 14, No. 1. 1961.

Bhatt, V. "Some Notes on Balanced and Unbalanced Growth." *Economic Journal* 75. March 1965.

Bulmer-Thomas, V. *Input - Output Analysis in Developing Countries*. New York: Wiley and Sons. 1982.

Cheng, T. "Political Regimes and Development Strategies: South Korea and Taiwan." In *Manufacturing Miracles: Paths of Industrialization in Latin America and East Asia*, edited by G. Gereffi and D. Wyman. Princeton: Princeton University Press. 1990.

Cumings, B. "The Origins and Development of the Northeast Asian Political Economy: Industrial Sectors, Product Cycles, and Political Consequences." *International Organization* 38, No. 1. 1984.

Duvall, R. et al. "A Formal Model of 'Dependencia Theory': Structure and Measurement." In *From National Development to Global Community*, edited by R. Merritt and B. Russett. London: Allen and Unwin. 1981.

Evans, P. "Class, State, and the Dependence in East Asia: Lessons for Latin Americanists." In *The Political Economy of the New Asian Industrialism*, edited by F. Deyo. Ithaca: Cornell University Press. 1987.

Gereffi, G. "Development Strategies and Global Factory: Latin America and East Asia." *Annals of the American Academy of Political and Social Science* No. 505. 1989a.

____. " Industrial Restructuring and National Development Strategies: A Comparison of Taiwan, South Korea, Brazil and Mexico." In *Taiwan: A Newly Industrial-*

ized State, edited by H. Hisao, W. Chen, and H. Chan. Taipei: National Taiwan University. 1989b.

Gereffi, G., and Wyman, D., eds. *Manufacturing Miracles: Paths of Industrialization in Latin America and East Asia*. Princeton: Princeton University Press. 1990.

____. " Determinants of Development Strategies in Latin America and East Asia." *Pacific Focus* 1, No. 2. 1987.

Ghantus, E. *Arab Industrial Integration: A Strategy for Development*. London: Croom Helm. 1982.

Griffin, K. *International Inequality and National Poverty*. London: Macmillan. 1978.

Jones, L. "The Measurement of Hirschman Linkages." *Quarterly Journal of Economics* 90, No. 3. 1976.

Kang, C., J. Choi, and J. Chang. *Jaebul* [*The Jaebul*]. Seoul: Beebong. 1991.

Keohane, R. and J. Nye. "International Interdependence and Integration." In *Handbook of Political Science*, edited by F. Greenstein and N. Polsby, Vol. 8. Reading: Addison Wiley. 1975.

Kim, D.-H. "Economic Concentration and Disparities: Class, Region and the Jaebul in Korean Politics." Paper presented at the Political Economy of Korean Development Seminars. St. Antony's College and Asian Studies Centre, The University of Oxford. 13 March 1992.

____. "Korean Economic Performance and Problems: A Structuralist View." *Inha University Economic Review* 1. 1988.

____. "The Initial Condition of Economic Development in the Third World." *Pacific Focus* 1, No. 1. 1986.

____. "Rapid Economic Growth and National Economic Integration in Korea, 1963 - 78." D. Phil. Thesis, The University of Oxford. (Unpublished.) 1985.

Kim, D.-H., and Y. Kong, eds. *The Korean Peninsula in Transition*. Oxford: Macmillan. Forthcoming.

Lee, K., and J. Lee. Kiup Jipdan gwa Kyungjeryuk Jipjung [The Business Group and the Concentration of Economic Power]. *Seoul: Korea Development Institute. 1990.*

List, F. *National System der Politischen Oekonomie*. Berlin: Reimer Hobbing. 1841.

Machlup, F. *A History of Thought on Economic Integration*. London: Macmillan. 1977.

Markovits, A., and W. Oliver III. "The Political Sociology of Integration and Social Development," In *From National Development to Global Community*, edited by R. Merritt and B. Russett. London: Allen and Unwin. 1981.

Myrdal, G. *Against the Stream: Critical Essays on Economics*. London: Macmillan. 1974.

____. *An International Economy: Problems and Prospects*. London: Routledge and Kegan Paul. 1956.

Orantes, I. "The Concept of Integration." *CEPAL Review* 15. 1981.

Sachs, J. "External Debt and Macroeconomic Performance in Latin America and East Asia." *Brookings Papers on Economic Activity*. 1985.

Sen, A. "Levels of Poverty: Policy and Change." World Bank Staff Working Paper No. 401. Washington, DC: The World Bank. 1980.

Sohn, H. *Hankuk Jeongchihak ui Sae Kusang [The New Conception of Korean Politics]*. Seoul: Pulbit. 1991.

Streeten, P. "Self-Reliant Industrialization." In *The Political Economy of Development and Underdevelopment*, edited by C. Wilber, 2nd edition. New York: Random House. 1979.

____. "Unbalanced Growth: A Reply." Oxford Economic Papers 15, No. 3. 1963.

____. "Unbalanced Growth." *Oxford Economic Papers* 11, No. 2. 1959.

Yotopoulos, P., and J. Nugent. *Economics of Development: Empirical Investigations.* New York: Harper and Row. 1976.

____. "A Balanced Growth Version of the Linkage Hypothesis: A Test." *Quarterly Journal of Economics* 87, No. 2. 1973.

6

Agricultural Reforms in Taiwan and South Korea

Hsin-Huang Michael Hsiao

This chapter will explore the relationship between government agricultural strategies in Taiwan and South Korea and three of their broader settings—agrarian conditions, as well as the national and international situations. Two major government strategies for agriculture during the postwar period in both Taiwan and South Korea are identified, namely the land reforms in the early 1950s and the post-reform agriculture "squeezing" policies in the 1950s and 1960s.

Land Reform

Decisions on land reform in Taiwan and South Korea are explained in terms of the relations between the governments on the one hand and tenants (sharecroppers), landlords and the U.S. government on the other.

Government-Tenant Relations

In both Taiwan and South Korea, it appears that how the regimes perceived the connection between tenants and political instability—and not what actually happened—is crucial for understanding the governments' policy initiatives. In other words, as the regimes believed that the failure to solve tenant problems threatened their political legitimacy, they initiated land reforms, almost regardless of whether or not political revolt and instability actually existed in the countryside.

In the case of Taiwan, the tenants were not even demanding reforms of any sort. There was very little political unrest in the Taiwanese countryside before reform. The 1947 violence was largely an urban phenomenon without any significant participation by the rural population. In short, rural tenants were not the source of socio-political instability in post-war Taiwan. But the Guomindang (KMT) or Nationalist regime perceived things differently upon arriving in Taiwan. Their embarrassing defeat on the mainland made the Nationalists realize that the countryside was the crucial battlefield they had lost to the Communists. Therefore, immediate rural reforms in Taiwan were perceived to be necessary to safeguard their political future on the island, even though the Taiwanese countryside was not the main source of resistance. To the Nationalists, the tenants in Taiwan were perceived as potential forces of socio-political revolution, already successfully mobilized by the Communists on the mainland.

Also, the Nationalist government feared grave consequences if they failed to significantly reform the land tenure system on Taiwan. In other words, the decision to launch land reform in Taiwan was because of the fear and perception by the Nationalist government of potential rural instability that could threaten its political survival. By doing so, the Nationalists believed that they could avoid political crisis.

In contrast, the case of South Korea involved a real threat. The decisions of the American Military Government (AMG) (1945-1948) on land sale (1948), and later of the Rhee regime on land redistribution (1950), were basically due to their realization of actual rural unrest and conflict in the Korean countryside. The de facto post-war Korean government, the leftist-dominated People's Republic, had raised tenants' hopes of land reform. Actions against local landlords often took place with the Republic's encouragement. In these circumstances, delay and inaction on land policy by the AMG caused growing rural unrest and riots. Even the AMG admitted that the rural political situation was more precarious after the occupation began. Finally, despite the reluctance of the Korean Interim Assembly, the AMG was forced to sell Japanese owned land to Korean tenants in March 1948. Between the completion of the land sales and the inauguration of the Rhee government in August 1948, the Korean countryside was more stable than before.

However, the expectation of further redistribution of Korean landlord-owned lands was not realized in Rhee's first two years in power. During this period, frustration in the rural areas built up again. Social and political instability throughout the country was very visible and serious, particularly in the countryside. Some armed revolts occurred. Communist guerrillas were a major force in the countryside. Like its predecessor, the Rhee regime believed a connection existed between the Communist threat and rural unrest. In March 1950, President Rhee finally signed the land reform bill, hoping to thus end the rural political threat to his regime. Korean tenants thus forced the regime to try to "buy" political stability with the land reform.

This is one of the major differences in the relations between tenants and the regimes in South Korea and Taiwan. Taiwanese tenants were not actually participating in forceful actions like demonstrations, violence and armed rebellion, but the outcomes were similar. Legitimacy and political stability for the regimes were "bought" by granting land ownership and improving tenant socio-economic well-being and status. In short, from the available evidence for Taiwan and South Korea, it is clear that the American Military Government, the Rhee regime and the Nationalist government all considered land reform to be an effective "counter-revolutionary" weapon to gain political stability and the political support of the rural populations.

Government-Landlord Relations

It is important to note that even though reciprocal relations between the regimes and the sharecroppers constituted a significant "pre-condition" to land reform in both Taiwan and South Korea, actual political decision-making on land reform mainly involved the regime and the landed class. When the landed class does not control the regime or when it has moved its political and economic interests to the urban-industrial centers, a regime is more likely to carry out land reform.

In the cases of KMT's Taiwan and the AMG's South Korea, the regimes were non-indigenous to the polities they ruled. The Nationalist and the American Military Governments were both quite distinct from the local landed classes. Relations between the regimes and the landlord classes were unequal, even competitive. The Nationalist regime moved to Taiwan from the mainland after its defeat by the Communists in 1949. The new Nationalist elite had no vested interests in the land of Taiwan and were free of related pressures from the landlords. Besides, Taiwanese landlords were not politically powerful, especially after over half a century of Japanese colonialism from the late 18th century. Only 66 landlords on the entire island, or .01 percent of all landlords, had farms of more than 100 *chia* (97 hectares), while large land owners possessed only 2.09 percent of all private farm land. Hence, the landlords could not have become a rallying point for opposition. The Provincial Assembly, in which local landlords were relatively influential, lacked strong ties with the central government, completely controlled by the Nationalist Party. Fearing that the rural sector would become a revolutionary force, the Nationalist government decided to cut off its traditional ties with the landed class. The Nationalists' focus thus shifted to the tenants and in order to assure their political future in Taiwan, a redistributive land reform was enacted.

A similar situation can be observed in South Korea under the American occupation. The American Military Government, like the Nationalist government in Taiwan, was unconnected to the Korean landlords. The only influential forum available to the landlord class was the American-established Interim Assembly, and its indifference to land reform was clear. However, since the American occupation force was the *de facto* ruler of South Korea, the opposition of the Assembly to land sales was not enough to prevent the reform. This crucial separation from the landed class gave the American Military Government a free hand to carry out land sales in South Korea.

The American-initiated land sales generated much support and enthusiasm among the Korean farming population for further redistribution of Korean-owned lands, which influenced elected officials and the Assembly. The political climate for the seemingly inevitable land reform was right. In anticipation of the reform, many landlords sold a great deal of land to tenants prior to the reform. In fact, only 56 percent of 1949 tenant farm land was actually redistributed in the reform. Landlords' economic interests were already changing. Politically, the National Assembly still had fairly strong landed interests among its members, but they recognized that sectoral support from the countryside was shifting to the rural masses. Meanwhile, they also attempted to shift their political base to the urban-industrial sector in view of the strong sentiment for land reform among the population.

Land reform also became a major issue in the power struggles between landed and non-landed interests in the Assembly, as well as between the Assembly and the president to define who should be the ultimate decision-maker in Korean politics. Therefore, much more was involved in the final decision on land reform in 1950 than the fact that the landlord sector had moved its economic and political interests from the rural areas to the urban-industrial centers. Nevertheless, this factor certainly helped lessen resistance from potential landlord opposition.

Legitimacy and stability for the regimes were thus achieved, while the landlords incurred some costs but also gained some rewards. Both Taiwanese and Korean landlords lost the ability to expand and assert their social, economic and political interests and influence. But both sets of landlords thus avoided the confiscation of their land without compensation, as had taken place in mainland China and North Korea under communism. For Taiwanese landlords, particularly, a peaceful transformation of their economic interests was another important advantage.

U.S. Influences

The preceding analysis highlights domestic factors affecting the land reform undertaken in post-war Taiwan and South Korea. Both Taiwan and South Korea emerged at the end of the 1940s as client states of the United States of America, involving dependent relations between the regimes in Taiwan and South Korea and the American government. After World War Two, the U.S. had a foreign policy to "defend" the U.S.-led capitalist "free world" against Soviet-led communism. One U.S. foreign policy emphasis in Northeast Asia was on agrarian reform to establish stable and reliable allies. Land reform along liberal lines was considered to be an effective weapon to counter communist appeal in the Third World countryside. Simply stated, it was in the U.S. interest to keep potential allies stable politically by gaining rural loyalty and support.

The U.S. was involved from the outset in the land reforms in Taiwan and South Korea. The U.S. government had put pressure on the Nationalist regime to carry out an ambitious agrarian reform on the mainland during and after the Second World War to counter deteriorating rural conditions and to win support from the Chinese Communists. But the Nationalists were then unwilling to undermine their traditional ties with the landlords, on which their power had long been based.

An American-financed Joint Commission of Rural Reconstruction (JCRR) was set up in Nanking on the eve of the KMT collapse on the mainland in 1948. The JCRR was immediately given powers to initiate an appropriate land reform program in China. After the JCRR moved to Taiwan, U.S. foreign policy favored land reform in Taiwan even more. Much evidence suggests that had the Nationalist government been tardy, a forceful U.S. initiative on land reform would nevertheless have followed in Taiwan. In fact, at that time, total agreement on the necessity of land reform in Taiwan was reached without any debate between the Nationalist and the American governments.

Compared with Taiwan, the degree of U.S. involvement in South Korean land reform was much greater and more direct. Under direct American occupation, the quick sale of Japanese-owned lands was possible. More importantly, the American Military Government determined what type of land reform was to be adopted and who would do the job. The Americans did not want any leftists to play any role in the land reform, in order to block the Korean communists. Only politically reliable or "safe" Koreans, favored by the American authority, were allowed to implement the land reform. The Interim Legislative Assembly was established by the American Military Government in the hope that it would assume responsibility for the reform. But the Assembly was indifferent to reform due to the strong landlord presence. The American Military Government finally realized that since the Assembly was too conservative, it had to carry out the land reform itself, which it did in 1948.

The degree of U.S. involvement in the 1950 land reform act under the Rhee government is not clear. However, since American aid supported the Rhee regime, it seems reasonable to suggest that there must have been significant input from the U.S. on the Korean land reform decisions in 1950. The regimes in Taiwan and South Korea both gained strength from American support on land reform while the U.S. consolidated two reliable anti-communist allies for containment of communism in Asia besides maintaining its prestige as a major power in post-war world politics. Meanwhile, the sharecroppers and tenants also gained the status of independent landowners and improved their social standing in both countries.

One may be tempted to generalize that when a regime perceives a political treat from the rural sector related to the existing land tenure system, reform in the system may become possible. But this condition alone cannot guarantee implementation of a land reform unless at least one of the following three additional criteria is met:

- the regime should not be dominated by the landlord class;
- the landlords should have alternative means to achieve and exercise economic, social, and political power, allowing them to shift their interests from rural land to other sectors;
- a strong and powerful state (e.g., the U.S.) should back the regime's land reform efforts.

Post-Reform Agriculture "Squeezing" Strategy

With the completion of land reform, a policy of "squeezing" the agricultural sector was adopted by both regimes to further general economic growth. In both countries, two aspects of this squeezing were apparent: a "production squeeze," transferring increments in farm production to the non-agricultural sector, made possible by a policy of low farm prices; and an "expenditure squeeze," by means of taxes, forced savings and high prices for agricultural inputs. For various reasons, this squeeze strategy had a greater impact on national development in Taiwan than in South Korea. (See Chapters 2, 3, 4 and 6 of Hsiao, 1981, which also indicates some reasons why this agriculture squeezing strategy was preferred by the regimes following land reform, and why this strategy was maintained without being challenged by the rural-agricultural sector.)

The squeezing policy was more complicated than land reform since it involved more sectors: small landowner-farmers, ruling elites, urban-industrial class, urban-working class and the U.S. Not only had the number of sectors involved increased, but the nature of the relations had also become more complex.

Government-Small Landowners-Farmer Relations

Land reform in both Taiwan and South Korea created a mass of small landowner-farmers who had benefited from the land reform. Samuel Huntington has noted the politically conservative character of small land holding farmers. Land reform can thus transform the social character of the rural sector from a potentially revolutionary into a fundamentally conservative force. Though no systematic evidence exists to prove that independent small landowners are more conservative than their tenant counterparts, it is commonly believed that the former are more likely to be concerned with minor changes in commodity markets than with any major change in the institution of property. Indirect supporting evidence is provided by Paige's cross-national study of agrarian social movements in the Third World after WWII (Paige, 1976), which concluded that very few significant social movements emerged under small-holding systems in the Third World.

The same also holds true for both Taiwan and South Korea. No rural social movements have been observed since the reforms. One plausible explanation for the conservatism of small landowners in the post-reform era is that as long as land ownership is equitable and living conditions are bearable, any disruptive collective movement would not be welcomed by them. Since the agricultural sector had recently experienced much worse "exploitation" under Japanese colonial dominance, small farm owners were satisfied with what they had after the land reform. Consequently, they found any further radical change in government policy both unattractive and costly.

Rural political support for the regimes was manifested in post-reform electoral results. In South Korea, Rhee's Liberty Party dominated the rural areas after the reform, while opposition came solely from the cities. For example, in the 1956 presidential election and the 1958 National Assembly election, Rhee's candidates won the rural areas, but the opposition party carried the urban areas. After the coup and a temporary policy favoring agriculture, Park Chung-Hee won 50 percent of the rural vote against 41 percent for his rival. Even when the agriculture squeezing policy was in effect, which cost some rural votes, the rural southeast still supported the Park regime in the 1967 election.

A similar trend also prevailed in the Taiwanese countryside. For more than 30 years, the Nationalist Party has consistently won votes for the provincial assembly and other elections in the rural areas, while challenges have primarily come from the large industrial cities. Election results also provide some clues as to why the post-land reform regimes were compelled to meet the growing demands of the urban-industrial sector rather than help the rural-agricultural sector. The squeezing of agriculture in the 1950s and 1960s moved resources from the agricultural sector to the non-agricultural sectors as the gap between the two sectors widened. The politically conservative character of the small farmers held them back from engaging in any movement to challenge the government's squeezing policy.

Government-Urban-Industrial Class Relations

Both regimes advocated ideologies of national modernization involving industrialization of their economies. The persistence of an unbalanced agriculture squeezing strategy for two decades can be accounted for by the new coalitions between the regimes and the emergent urban-industrial classes which emerged after the land reform.

The KMT had long been criticized for its urban-industrial bias in development efforts on the mainland. While this may be explained by the base of the Nationalist Party on the mainland, where it was supported by urban commercial-financial-industrial interests, there is also an ideological explanation. This is reflected in President Chiang Kai-Shek's book, *China's Destiny*, in which he viewed industrialization as the basis for China's modernization. He interpreted Dr. Sun Yat-sen's *International Development of China* in a way so as to support his pro-industrial view. Chiang's pro-industry writing should be interpreted against China's reality. When Chiang wrote his book in 1942, China had already been facing very serious agrarian problems for years, but he devoted very little attention to the deteriorating rural sector in the book. After the Nationalists withdrew to Taiwan, this industrialization ideology was still the leading guidance for the regime's subsequent economic development strategies.

On the other hand, the South Korean elite's modernization ideology differed between the Rhee and Park regimes. The concept of national modernization was overridden by concerns with nation-building and internal political struggle during the period of President Rhee Syngman. After the Korean War, Rhee did put more stress on economic modernization than before, but still opposed any long-range economic development planning. An ideology of modernization in terms of socio-economic development was not apparent in the Rhee era. However, for political reasons, the Korean industrial sector was favored by the regime in the 1950s when the government and the economy were dominated by American foreign aid. Consequently, the rural-agricultural sector was largely ignored.

In contrast, in the 1960s, President Park Chung-hee advocated an ideology of national economic modernization through industrialization. In his book, *Our Nation's Path*, for example, Park justified his military coup as a means to meet the challenge of modernization. An unbalanced growth doctrine was already apparent in his writing on the eve of his election as president. He saw an instrumental role for the agricultural sector in Korean development. Though "agriculture first" was his campaign slogan in the 1963 election, Park betrayed that promise after 1961 by refusing an ambitious agricultural loan program. This changed orientation in favor of unbalanced growth was officially reflected in subsequent five-year economic development plans in South Korea under Park.

There appears to be a pattern in the emergence of private industrial interests as a result of the pro-industrial development policies. Especially in the 1960s, this urban-industrial sector emerged as a strong, growing social and political force on the national scene. In Taiwan, the urban-industrial sector grew rapidly with industrial growth from the 1950s. This was reflected in their shares in both Taiwan's domestic product and employment. More importantly, both the private industrialist class and the urban working class increased in size and in significance.

Evidence suggests that coalitions existed between the regimes and the urban-industrial sectors. As a result of growth, the industrial sectors demanded more resource allocations from the regimes in excess of their contributions through representation at various levels of political and economic decision-making. It is important to note that representatives with business, industrial and professional origins have always been over-represented at various levels of government. In contrast, the agricultural sectors have been consistently under-represented in proportion to their population (see Hsiao, 1981: Tables 4-5 and 4-6). In these circumstances, the ruling coalitions have maintained the pro-industrial squeezing effects on their agricultural sectors. It also explains why there has been no resistance or challenge to the agriculture squeezing policy from the rural-agricultural sector in Taiwan.

As indicated earlier, though major industrialization efforts were not initiated in South Korea until the 1960s, the origins of the industrial sector can be traced to the political economy of the 1950s. Under the Rhee regime, a coalition between the Liberty Party and the domestic industrial-commercial class was established by both legal and illegal means of allocating foreign aid and capital. This trend of coalition building has been even more evident since national economic plans were adopted during the Park period. Some private entrepreneurs established themselves as *jaebol* (monopolistic conglomerates) similar to Japanese *zaibatsu*. Economically, industry became the leading sector in the Korean economy, in terms of both production and employment. Like its Taiwanese counterpart, the Korean urban-industrial sector emerged as a politically influential sector through its direct and indirect involvement at various levels of political and economic decision making. At the national level, the secondary as well as tertiary sectors were always over-represented in the National Assembly after the Korean War. Agricultural interests, on the other hand, have long been suppressed and poorly represented in the National Assembly (see Hsiao, 1981: Table 4-7). As a consequence, the non-agricultural interests in this key decision-making body have effectively maintained the agriculture squeezing policy.

Three important cautionary remarks should be made regarding the evidence presented from Taiwan and South Korea. First, in discussing the influences of the non-agricultural sectors on the political-economic decision making process, only the provincial and local levels are relevant for Taiwan due to the current political structure in Taiwan. Under the Republic of China (ROC) constitution, the highest legislative body in Taiwan is the Legislative Yuan, in which the overwhelming majority are Nationalist Mainlanders, whose interests coincide with those of the Nationalist central government. Therefore, only the provincial and local levels are politically relevant.

Second, it is not being suggested that the unequal distribution of sectoral interests at various levels of decision-making have caused the agriculture squeezing policy, but rather that the consistent over-representation of industrial-commercial interests, as well as the under-representation of the agricultural sector have helped support the *status quo*, pursuing further industrial growth at the expense of agriculture. Only with this perspective in mind can agricultural policy modifications in both Taiwan and South Korea in the early 1970s be comprehended. They involved tactical shifts in sectoral alliances attempted by the regimes without harming the established coalition with the industrial sector.

Third, the governments were in no way neutral in allocating resources to different sectors for economic development. However, the regimes in Taiwan and South Korea have skillfully succeeded in minimally satisfying the agricultural sector, thus avoiding any tendency to political revolt. They also successfully prevented any significant sectoral clashes between the urban-industrial and the rural-agricultural sectors. It requires a relatively strong government to achieve this, and both the Nationalist and Park governments have demonstrated their character as "hard" states (Myrdal, 1969).

U.S. Influences

Taiwan and South Korea were strongly linked to the U.S. sphere of influence after WWII (see Hsiao, 1981: Chapters 5 and 6). Americans were involved in many aspects of the internal affairs of these countries, so it is reasonable to look for evidence of involvement in domestic agricultural policies.

U.S. aid strategy—favoring private enterprise for building industrial capitalism in recipient nations—influenced the governments, recommended import substitution and then export oriented industrial growth policies, the creation of "native" private industrial-urban sector through coalitions of the private industrial sector with the government sector requiring the agriculture squeezing policy.

U.S. pressure, via aid, on the Chinese Nationalist government in Taiwan thus helped to develop the private industrial sector. In 1960, under American pressure, the Nationalist government issued a nineteen point program for accelerating private industrial growth through improvement of the investment environment for both indigenous and foreign entrepreneurs. Also, in its third four year plan for 1961-1964, an export-oriented industrial growth policy was officially established and has been in effect ever since. U.S. aid-financed technical assistance was provided to improve the quality of both production and trade skills.

A similar phenomenon can be observed in South Korea. Though U.S. pressure on the Rhee government was not effective, American aid did rehabilitate and expand many private industries. After Park took power in South Korea, American involvement in Korean industrial growth was much more direct and effective. A statute for inducement of foreign capital was enacted in 1962, and the U.S. aid mission directed its activities to assist the Park government to induce private Korean entrepreneurs by furnishing capital, management and technical know-how to the Korean industrial sector.

Why was the U.S. so interested in influencing both governments to develop their industrial sectors? First, there was the belief that capitalism was the better model for Third World countries to follow for national development. Since Taiwan and South Korea were considered client states in the U.S.-dominated world system, the inclination to advance capitalism by fostering a strong private industrial sector seems predictable.

Second, the U.S. government feared that the large amount of American aid flowing to Taiwan and South Korea might strengthen the state sectors there. Therefore, vigorous efforts were focused on limiting state enterprises and nourishing the private sector. Third, the U.S. had an economic interest in creating manufacturing industries in Taiwan and South Korea, as part of a new international division of labor within the capitalist world economy.

Finally, the U.S. shared the view that industrialization was the best path for national development, one for which they had the most experience and were best able to give advice. As a result, the growing private industrial sector started to establish external connections through foreign trade. In a broader sense, there existed a coalition among the three—the U.S., the regimes, and the private industrial classes—which clashed with the interests of the domestic agricultural sectors.

Another reason for American involvement in the post-land reform agriculture squeezing policy in Taiwan and South Korea was U.S. Public Law 480 agricultural surplus sales from 1954. PL 480 served American interests through surplus disposal and creation of foreign markets for American agricultural products. PL 480 was an effective political and economic instrument to meet its domestic grain needs without engaging in costly agricultural development programs. Providing a large amount of cheap foreign grain also lowered market prices in the cities. While the domestic agricultural sector suffered losses, the urban-industrialists as well as the working classes enjoyed cheap food prices.

The disincentive effects on domestic agriculture caused by such grain surplus sales were evident in both Taiwan and South Korea during the PL 480 sale periods. Relations between the regimes and American aid worked against the interests of the rural agricultural sectors, helping the regimes to effectively implement their agriculture squeezing strategies for years, especially in the case of South Korea (see Hsiao, 1981: Chapter 6).

Prospects and Policy Implications

The foregoing highlights the relationship between two major government agricultural policies in Taiwan and South Korea: land reform and post-reform agriculture squeezing policies during the 1950s, 1960s and 1970s.

In this final section, some policy implications will be suggested. Three issues will be particularly emphasized. First, what are the implications of "development" for the agricultural sector? What has the agricultural sector gained from "development"?

Second, what can we say about government performance in Taiwan and South Korea? How well have the two governments performed in satisfying various sectoral demands, while trying to modernize and industrialize the countries? Were any better options available for the governments other than squeezing agriculture for national growth?

Third, what will be the future of agriculture in both Taiwan and South Korea? If the answer to the first question is negative, then what can be done? Can we expect the rural-agricultural sector itself to initiate any drastic change in the future? What has caused subsequent modifications of government agriculture policy? How significant are these changes? Do they imply basic strategic shifts in either government's development ideology and policy?

Development or Exploitation for Agriculture?

Let us assess the position of small farmers under the agriculture squeezing policies during the past decades. Upon the completion of land reform, the benefits and rewards received by small farmers had exceeded what they had expected. Hence, they supported the regimes in power and also legitimized their authority. To some extent, the perceived gains for the tenants-turned-landowners contributed to maintenance of the *status quo* in the post-reform period, even when the agriculture squeezing policies were in effect. As long as net gains despite the squeezing policy still met the expectations of the farmers, support for the regimes was not threatened. After all, the farming sectors did not experience absolute deteriorations in living standards, even during the squeezing periods. They could also show their dissatisfaction with the squeezing strategy through their voting behavior; this was more obvious in South Korea than in Taiwan.

Does this mean that the reciprocal relations established between the farming sector and the regime and other sectors have been fair and just, simply because no conflict is apparent? What can we say about agricultural "development" in human terms? The fact that the small farmers accepted the relations should not blind us to the possibility that they may also have had little or no choice. The centralized control over the rural sector that was established by the central governments certainly helps account for the compliance of small farmers. The role of U.S. aid, which favored pro-industry growth, also exacerbated the unequal exchange relations for the agricultural sector. Agriculture has been squeezed and exploited in the name of national modernization, which leads us to the issue of how effectively the regimes in the two countries have used their unbalanced paths to economic progress, having squeezed agriculture.

A Successful Government Strategy?

Was there any other agricultural policy alternative available for the regimes, given the conditions which existed? How well have the regimes performed in terms of overall national economic modernization? First, let us review their growth records briefly. According to the World Bank, from 1950 to 1975, GNP per capita of developing countries (including the People's Republic of China) as a group grew at an average rate of 3.4 percent a year. Both Taiwan and South Korea were among the six economies that had the highest growth rates, averaging over five percent a year. In a World Bank study, the ranking of eighty developing nations by GNP per capita remained remarkably stable between 1950 and 1975. Only Taiwan, South Korea and Iraq rose remarkably in terms of relative rank (Taiwan from 43 to 17; South Korea from 54 to 35) (Morawetz, 1977: 20). All in all, both Taiwan and South Korea have undeniably been two of the fastest growing Third World nations. The success of overall economic growth in Taiwan and South Korea in the three decades was, to a great degree, the result of the regimes' management of their relations with other sectors involved. More specifically, the two phases of the unbalanced growth strategy were the direct consequence of the urban-industrial bias of the regimes' governing elites.

Can the urban-industrial bias be justified in terms of national development? There exists a considerable economic literature advocating the necessity of unbalanced growth for the Third World (e.g. Hirschman, 1958). As in so much reasoning of this type, the socio-political miseries involved are ignored, the rationale being that "in time," the ends will justify the means. The squeezing and exploitation of agriculture is not, however, explainable in terms of national development. It can only be explained by political decisions on the part of regimes.

There was one further common characteristic shared by both regimes in the 1960s, when the agriculture squeezing strategy prevailed. Both the Nationalist and the Park governments can be classified as "reformist or developmentalist states," in that social and economic progress took place without fundamental changes associated with "revolutionary states." There has been no intention of bringing about rapid, complete and violent change in values, social structure, political institutions and leadership (Hirschman, 1968).

A reformist regime must not pursue an exhaustive range of reforms, but should minimize potential opposition by pursuing a very limited set of reforms. In other words, if it is to be successful, a reformist regime requires a higher order of political skills than does a revolutionary one (Huntington, 1968: 345). It has to engage in two-front or even multi-front negotiation and bargaining with a multiplicity of sectors. It also requires that the regime be able to shift sectoral affiliations at the right time. In both Taiwan and South Korea, the regimes have managed to set "correct" priorities in meeting competing demands in the post-war period. For example, in the early 1950s, the Nationalist and Rhee regimes gave up landlord support in order to gain tenant loyalty, while in the 1960s, the Nationalist and Park governments shifted their sectoral identification to the urban-industrialist class, leaving the rural-agricultural sector behind. Throughout, however, their affiliations with the U.S. were always significant, close and unchanged.

In this respect, until the 1960s, both the Nationalist and Park governments were successful in balancing changes in economic structure against changes in political institutions in such a way that neither were hampered. They were pretty much in command of the direction of socio-economic change by means of government policy. In conclusion, given the limited alternatives open to the regimes, the government strategies undertaken so far for economic growth and social change have been effective and "politically feasible."

What Can Be Done?

If the foregoing analyses of the nature of government strategy and its impacts on the agricultural sector are correct, there is a dilemma in facing the conflict between the means and ends of national development. It is generally agreed that the end products of overall economic growth in both countries have been impressive, and the regimes have managed their growth quite well. They have also demonstrated the characteristics of "hard states" in embarking on economic development efforts.

However, our analysis of the means that have been used to reach these ends suggests that the agricultural sector has not shared equally in the fruits of national growth. In Taiwan, the agricultural sector fulfilled its "historical mission" during the unbalanced growth phase, while in the case of South Korea, the story is different. Compared with Taiwan, South Korean agriculture has remained relatively backward.

Throughout the import substitution period under the Rhee regime, much of agriculture's potential for further growth was not fully realized. Accordingly, after export orientation began, a tremendous burden fell upon the industrial sector, assisted by foreign capital, to continue to "pull" the agricultural sector along with it, despite the continuous drain of agricultural workers. This inevitably led to a certain distortion in the industrial sector. The simple reason was that without an agricultural push, industrial exports had to "run" even faster, requiring a "premature" backward linkage type of import substitution (Fei & Ranis, 1975: 25-27). The developmental problems confronted by South Korea were thus much more complicated than those in Taiwan.

Nevertheless, Taiwan was already facing a deteriorating agricultural situation by the 1970s as a result of the squeeze. Agriculture was no longer able to generate significant net exports and help maintain food self-sufficiency. In fact, from the late 1960s, Taiwan had already become a net importer of food, a trend which subsequently grew. The question, therefore, was whether both governments were determined to "save" the agriculture sector from total "collapse" and to keep it from being detrimental to overall growth.

Since the land reform, the agricultural sector has been in a rather weak position, economically poor and politically powerless. It is doubtful that changes in the regimes' agricultural strategies were caused by pressure from the agricultural sector. Besides, the nature of both countries' political and economic decision makers further suggests that the agricultural sector will probably never be in a position to press for any significant change in government strategy.

The policy changes in the late 1970s are best seen as temporary tactical shifts in the regimes' sectoral interests due to the deterioration of agriculture. As long as the regimes' tactical considerations do not jeopardize the established coalition with the industrial sector, opposition to halt the change will not be great. Once again, we see how reformist states have managed to shift affiliations among sectors to improve their own positions.

If the agricultural sector itself is, indeed, powerless to improve its position through social movements or politics, can there be any alternative other than depending on the government's realization of the importance of agriculture? One possibility would be a coalition between the agricultural sector and the urban-working class. As indicated earlier, the urban-working class has collaborated against their rural cousins during both import substitution and export orientation phases. However, such inter-sectoral income differentials in Taiwan and South Korea are not so large that coalitions are inconceivable. As the numbers of the urban working class increase with rural migration to the cities, increases in real wages may slow down, which could lead to a further decline of sectoral income differentials. Then, the possibility of an inter-sectoral class coalition is likely to increase, and can lead to further decreases in income gaps between sectors (Mamalakis, 1972: 111). Economic equality can then lead to political equality.

The possibility of such an inter-sectoral front will also depend on another condition. As Lipton points out, it depends on whether urban trade union leaders take an "expansionist" view of their interests. They should not build a wall around privileged urban employees and keep villagers from unionized urban jobs, thus relegating them to the informal sector. In an expansionist strategy, union leaders would seek to increase their membership with slowly growing wages, an expanding army rather than a walled garrison (Lipton, 1977: 334). As more villagers take jobs, remittance flows to the rural sector would become positive on balance. Most significantly, as class consciousness increases, the political pressure of the coalition would be strong enough to influence government development policy in a more equitable direction. However, the validity of this suggestion remains to be seen.

References

Fei, John C., and Gustav Ranis. "Agriculture in Two Types of Open Economies." In *Agriculture in Development Theory,* edited by L. Reynolds. New Haven: Yale University Press. 1975.

Hirschman, Albert O. *The Strategy of Economic Development.* New Haven: Yale University Press. 1958.

Hsiao, H. H. Michael. *Government Agricultural Strategies in Taiwan and South Korea: A Macrosociological Assessment.* Taipei, Taiwan: Institute of Ethnology, Academia Sinica, Nankang. 1981.

Huntington, Samuel. *Political Order in Changing Societies.* New Haven: Yale University Press. 1968,

Lipton, Michael. *Why Poor People Stay Poor.* Cambridge: Harvard University Press. 1977.

Mamalakis, M. J. "The Theory of Sector Clashes and Coalitions Revisited." *Latin American Research Review.* 1972: 89-126.

Morametz, David. *Twenty-five Years of Economic Development, 1950-1975).* Baltimore: John Hopkins University Press. 1977.

Myrdal, Gunnar. *Asian Drama: An Inquiry into the Poverty of Nations,* 3 Vol. New York: Pantheon. 1968.

Paige, J. M. *Agrarian Revolution: Social Movements and Export Agriculture in the Underdeveloped World.* New York: Free Press. 1976.

7

The Political Economy of Industrial Policy in South Korea and Taiwan

Tan Kock Wah

The resurgence of neo-classical thought in economics, which characterized the 1980s, can be understood in part as a reaction against earlier Keynesian and other more radical economic influences, which tended to favor government intervention to achieve economic policy objectives. This resurgence—culminating in supply side economics in the New Classical Macroeconomics and the Rational Expectations school—extends *laissez-faire* claims to macroeconomic theory and policy, undermining the case for monetary and fiscal stabilization policies that most economists, even those opposed to microeconomic interventions, had previously come to accept (Tobin, 1990).

In Africa, Asia, and Latin America, structural adjustment loans from the World Bank, with IMF endorsement, have had far-reaching consequences for the Third World. Approval of loans became conditional on economies conforming to requirements set by the World Bank (and IMF). Some of these requirements included removal of government subsidies and price controls, devaluation of currencies, wage cuts, public expenditure cuts, privatization, relaxation of foreign exchange controls, interest rate increases and other measures to promote investments.

Calls have been made for economic liberalization, and the emphasis is on getting prices right, i.e., market-determined with minimal distortions due to state intervention. Development economics is seen as misleading and harmful: it is said to be "the invention of a set of theoretical curiosities by the dirigistes to supplant the market," and it is claimed that "the demise of development economics is likely to be conducive to the health of both the economics and the economies of developing countries" (Lal, 1983). The emergence of the newly industrializing countries

(NICs) is attributed to free market forces, while stagnation is identified with countries with market failures as well as distortions and strong government intervention.

But how well founded are the theories underpinning the neoclassical view, and how well do these propositions explain and fit the facts and evidence from the East Asian NICs? Amsden (n.d.), for one, has argued that to explain the failure to industrialize as "market failure" is a tautology, such that "the market mechanism can never be working properly and fail to generate industrial development; the theory can never be wrong." This chapter aims to address these issues by looking more critically at the theories and evidence underlying the neoclassical *laissez-faire* paradigm; it also seeks to incorporate the findings of another growing stream of literature which emphasizes the developmentalist role of the state in East Asia.

Contrary to the dominant economic policy approach in the 1950s and 1960s, which assigned the state a substantial role in developing the economy and emphasized capital formation as the main engine of growth, the neoclassicists have underlined efficient allocation of resources as the primary source of growth. They have emphasized the importance of getting prices right and of promoting relatively undistorted and competitive markets. The bedrock of the free trade doctrine seems to lie in the concept of comparative advantage.

The neoclassical approach to international trade theory, i.e., the static Heckscher-Ohlin-Samuelson model, shows that any two nations will be better off, in the sense of enjoying more, if they concentrate on those activities in which their costs are relatively, though not absolutely cheapest—i.e., by concentrating on producing goods for which the country is relatively well endowed or abundant in terms of comparative costs. Resources will be thus allocated provided that international market forces are allowed to determine the relative prices of internationally tradable goods in the domestic economy. That requirement, in turn, calls for free trade, or a close approximation to it, with few or no impediments to imports, and with relative prices that give no more incentive to sell on the domestic market than to sell abroad. In the neoclassical view, the essential economic function of government should only be to (Wade, 1990):

1. maintain macroeconomic stability;
2. provide physical infrastructure, especially that which has high fixed costs in relation to variable costs;
3. supply public goods, including defense and national security, education, the legal system, etc.;
4. contribute to the development of institutions for improving markets for labor, finance, technology, etc.;
5. offset or eliminate price distortions which arise in cases of demonstrable market failure.

Government is generally seen as inefficient and corrupt, distorting more than promoting the smooth functioning of the market. Indeed, some economists think that there are few inherent market failures and that existing market imperfections are often due to government actions which distort markets. Thus, Deepak Lal (1983), for instance, argued that "[t]here are few, if any, instruments of government policy which are non-distortionary, in the sense of not inducing economic agents to behave less efficiently in some respects. . . . The best that can be expected is second best." He claims to have given reasons rooted in "second best theory," ". . . why, of the only feasible alternatives—a necessarily imperfect planning mechanism and a necessarily imperfect market mechanism—the latter is likely to perform better in practice," thus justifying free trade. However, there is nothing in welfare economics to support Lal's contention (Toye, 1987).

In practice, however, the requirements of "second best" optimal conditions are notoriously complicated, requiring considerable information, thus raising information costs. The theory also states that the removal of some, but not all distortions does not guarantee that the economy achieves greater allocative efficiency; the net welfare effect of piecemeal reform cannot be known *a priori*. Thus, "[i]f there is net loss, it may be second best to do nothing" (Lal, 1983), but if there is net gain, it may be second best for the government to intervene. Welfare economics does not seem to oppose government intervention for this reason.

With respect to the "dynamic comparative advantage" of government, Anne Krueger (1990) argued that government—being a non-market organization—should not concentrate on those areas of activity in which it has no comparative advantage (e.g., manufacturing, credit regulation and foreign exchange markets, etc.), as this would divert scarce government resources from those areas of activity (e.g., maintenance of law and order, provision of infrastructure and large-scale public services) which it has an advantage in undertaking. Krueger, like most other neoclassical economists, also assumes that government intervention in developing countries is predominantly rent-seeking-oriented, corrupt and inefficient.

While it is true that government failure has been significant in many countries, their policy conclusion calling for deregulation and a minimal government role in the economy does not necessarily follow. Besides, the experiences of the NICs have underlined the crucial role of government in late industrialization and highlighted distinct areas in which the government may have a definite comparative advantage in intervening.[1]

In light of the crucial state role in the NICs, it may be more useful to inquire into the nature and purpose of government interventions, as suggested by Amsden (n.d.): "instead of viewing rent-seeking as unbounded, it seems more reasonable to argue that . . . a development process . . . [can] emerge wherein rent-seeking is present, but not to the point where it miscarries industrialization." As is well known, rent-seeking activities are by no means alien to the history of politics and business in South Korea and Taiwan, but crucially, this has not been an obstacle to, and may even have facilitated, growth. Thus, what needs to be developed is a more sophisticated theory of government intervention which embraces this point, rather than dismissing *a priori* and *in toto* any possibility of a positive government role in late industrialization.

At variance with the orthodox interpretation of government intervention in East Asia, Bhagwati (1988b) recognized considerable government intervention in the East Asian economies. But according to Bhagwati, the positive roles of government are only limited to those which increase producers' confidence in the government commitment to export-led growth, thus inducing firms to undertake costly investments and programs as part of a national export-promotion strategy. He argued that the superior economic performance of the NICs is largely attributable to governments which issue "prescriptions" (one which identifies a number of "do's"), rather than "proscription" (one which identifies a number of "don'ts"). Such prescriptive intervention is said to explain the rapid growth of the NICs because "a proscriptive government will tend to stifle initiative, whereas a prescriptive government will tend to leave open areas where initiative can be exercised."[2]

However, the distinction between a prescriptive and proscriptive government is problematic and ambiguous. When a government prescribes something, it is indirectly—and sometimes directly—proscribing something else (the converse is true as well). There seems to be a problem of sophistry in Bhagwati's definition. At another level, it is also unclear why "although a prescriptive government may prescribe as badly as a proscriptive government proscribe," a proscriptive government "will tend to stifle initiatives, whereas a prescriptive government will tend to leave open areas where initiative can be exercised" (Bhagwati, 1988b). Presumably, a proscriptive government may proscribe little and leave much room for initiative. Conversely, a prescriptive government may stifle initiative "since it can make private enterprises do so many things against their will that they are left with little resources to do what they want, even if these activities are not explicitly forbidden" (Chang, 1994).

If, contrary to the neoclassical account, the role of government has been significant, even crucial, in late industrialization, what then is the impact of the liberalization efforts of the World Bank and the IMF in promoting growth? Krueger, for instance, has noted that "in its present state, trade theory provides little guidance as to the role of trade policy and trade strategy in promoting growth. . . . There is nothing in theory to indicate why a deviation from the optimum should affect the rate of economic growth" (Krueger, 1980). Moreover, the theoretical benefits of liberalization are of a static nature and involve once and for all changes in national income. There is no argument that liberalization can raise the rate of growth over the medium to long run (Stewart, 1985; Rodrik, 1990). Stein (1992) has argued that the structural adjustment program in Africa is likely to lead to de-industrialization.[3]

Indeed, the prescription of economic liberalization to realize comparative advantage is a static proposition, more concerned with present options, rather than with future change. It does not give enough weight to the possibility of dynamic gains from short-term distortions, and the possibility of creating comparative advantage through rapid structural change in countries concerned with long-run development. Neoclassical economics, being more prescriptive rather than descriptive, "downplay the social, political and historical dimension of the concept of comparative advantage, error is invited in both the attribution of causality of comparative advantage and in more narrowly prescribing the limits within which developmental choices can be made" (Evans & Alizadeh, 1984).

In contrast, on the theoretical level, the Sraffian or neo-Ricardian trade theorists have shown that net losses can result from unmanaged trade, and the adjustments needed to translate comparative advantage into competitive advantage may not be smooth and automatic, and "there is always a physiological or political limit beyond which real wages cannot be reduced" (Amsden, n.d.). Thus, so-called comparative advantage may remain hidden and unrealized for a long time.

More importantly, the "capital debate"—which threw the very foundation of neoclassical economics into question—also has disastrous implications for the internal logic of the Heckscher-Ohlin-Samuelson theory (Steedman, 1979). For, if factor abundance cannot be defined independently of factor prices, then, this building block of the theory is put into serious question. The observation that relatively low wages, leading to comparative advantage in labor-intensive commodities, is favorable to export-led growth no longer holds (Evans and Alizadeh, 1984). The neo-Ricardian critique has also shown that comparative advantage does not arise naturally, but is governed by differences in technology, consumer preferences and determinants of wages and profits, i.e., it can be deliberately created by economic policy.

Yet, although the causal mechanism linking liberalization to growth is unclear, neoclassical proponents claim that the record supports such a connection. Two kinds of evidence are invoked. First, cross-sectional studies of the relationship between "inward" and "outward" orientation and growth (see Balassa, 1981) and the World Bank's *1987 World Development Report*, which claimed to provide evidence demonstrating the virtues of "outward" orientation and the World Bank's *1983 World Development Report*, which claimed to show the adverse effects of price distortions on economic growth.

Toye (1987) and Evans and Alizadeh (1984) have provided useful critiques of the *1983 World Development Report*. Wade (1990) has also provided useful reviews of criticisms made of cross-sectional studies. One particularly important shortcoming common to these studies is their lack of theoretical and empirical discussion on the role of non-economic determinants (e.g., the relevance of interventionist policies of governments in promoting trade) and the importance of initial institutional and international settings (e.g., the significance of historical, social and political circumstances peculiar to the NICs prior to rapid growth) in determining growth. However, it may suffice here to point out that the studies are by no means unambiguous and cannot be invoked to justify unrestricted reliance on market forces and unambiguous opposition to government intervention in the economy (Toye, 1987), but can "... only support a cautious assessment of what a free trade approach can be expected to achieve. ..." (Wade, 1990).

We now turn to evidence from the East Asian NICs, often cited by most neoclassical economists as excellent examples of the free market economies. Wade has distinguished between the free market and the simulated market versions of the neoclassical account of East Asian success. According to the free market version, East Asian economies have done better than other countries because the East Asian states have hardly interfered in the workings of the market. On the other hand, it contends, other countries have been held back from the development they would otherwise have achieved in the "normal" course of events by excessive state intervention, especially in foreign trade.

Some neoclassical economists, however, concede that the governments of East Asia have done more than just liberalize markets and lower distortions. In their view, the governments also intervene more positively to offset other distortions, both those caused by other policies (e.g., import controls) and those remaining due to government failure to directly change distorted institutions (e.g., segmented financial markets). This view, which attributes a greater role to government in simulating the market, is called the simulated free market theory.

The simulated free market theory differs from the free market theory by distinguishing between a free trade regime and a neutral trade regime. The former is one with no or few impediments to imports, while in the latter, any incentive for domestic producers to sell on the domestic market rather than to export because of protection, is offset by export subsidies.

To take the neoclassical arguments seriously, we would need to know to what extent free market and/or simulated market conditions have been present over time, and to what extent they have been important in accounting for the achievements of the NICs, particularly South Korea and Taiwan. Robert Wade has contended that South Korea and Taiwan have met neoclassical economic conditions unusually well, but also that the government's role has been much more prominent than suggested by either the free market or the simulated market theory, a fact completely overlooked in the neoclassical economic literature. In her recent endeavor to provide a theory of government intervention for late industrialization,

Amsden (n.d.) has argued that the inability of poorer countries to industrialize is due to the workings, and not to the failure of the market:

> [As] late industrializers must grow exclusively by borrowing technology [and hence are] denied a competitive advantage from new products and processes, they initially have to rely only on their low wages to wrest market shares. . . . Low wages, however, are an inadequate basis of industrialization. . . . State intervention is necessary even in the most plausible cases of comparative advantage, because the chief asset of backwardness—low wages—is counterbalanced by heavy liabilities . . . the level of international competition, the technology gap, the investment barriers and savings deficiencies, are all so problematic, that without government intervention, little ever gets done to address these hurdles.

Hence, for a backward economy, the mere workings of the market are inadequate for achieving late industrialization. The presence of neoclassical conditions—in the sense of augmenting market competition and enhancing productivity—were at best necessary, but certainly not sufficient to stimulate the industrialization which characterized the rapid growth of South Korea and Taiwan.

Instead, Wade's governed market theory argues that the superiority of East Asian economic performance has been due, in large measure, to the effectiveness of industrial policy in developing or retrenching various industries in a national economy in order to maintain global competitiveness. Various trade incentives and control instruments, coupled with mechanisms to spread risk, have allowed the governments to guide market processes of resource allocation, producing different investment and production outcomes than would have occurred with either free or simulated market policies.

In other words, industrial policy is concerned with creating comparative advantage, as opposed to the static notion of comparative advantage which underlines geographical natural endowment or price differences to produce a global division of labor (Johnson, 1984). Thus, industrial targeting, or "dynamic anticipation of the economically efficient allocation of resources for the future" (Johnson, 1984), became an important tool in the East Asian economies. The governments explicitly identified and promoted certain industries and technologies that they anticipated would be important for the sustained growth and competitiveness of their economy in the future, i.e., they picked "winners."

Johnson has also distinguished between positive (explicit) and negative (implicit) industrial policy. Negative industrial policy is uncoordinated public action that causes distortions, disincentives and inequities which restrain one segment of the economy at the expense of another. This provides important insights into the causes of the generally inefficient interventions of many governments, so frequently emphasized by the neoclassical economists. By contrast, the positive—or explicit—industrial policy characterizing the NICs refers to the infusion of coordinated "goal oriented strategic thinking into public economic policy [which] seeks to leverage upward the productivity and competitiveness of the whole economy and of particular industries" (Johnson, 1984).

Industrial Policy in South Korea

The main pretext for state intervention in South Korea has been to build an "independent economy" (see the various five year plan documents and the various South Korean Economic Planning Board (EPB) white papers cited by Chang) and for industrial upgrading by "a transfer of labor from low productivity sectors to high productivity sectors," e.g., as realized through the heavy chemical industries drive in the late 1970s. Since "the market mechanism cannot be entirely trusted to increase the competitive advantage of industries," "custom-designed" financial, technical and administrative support has been given to sectors with high productivity growth potential, identified and designated by the state as "promising strategic industries" (Chang, 1994).

A more recent effort of the government in this respect was the integration of various industrial promotion laws into the Industrial Development Law in 1986, emphasizing rationalization programs "custom designed to the needs of industries (which) aim to provide temporary boosts for industries which need import substitution, capacity upgrading, and improvements in international competitiveness, and temporary protection to declining industries which need a smooth phasing-out" (Chang, 1994). Since its enactment, various industries—e.g., automobiles, coal mining, dyeing, ferro-alloys, fertilizers, heavy construction machinery, heavy electrical equipment, naval diesel engines and textile industries—have benefited from the program.

In return for massive support (e.g., priority in acquiring rationed credits and foreign exchange, state investment funds, preferential tax treatments, import protection and entry restriction) given to priority sectors, the firms became subject to state controls on technology, entry, capacity expansion and prices. One particularly interesting aspect of South Korean state intervention has been the evidence of "excessive competition"—as opposed to the common neoclassical preference for trying to increase efficiency through competition—which can result in "social waste" owing to "the lack of scale economies due to the participation of too many firms in each industry" (Chang, 1994).

This view is exemplified by the Sixth Five Year Plan, which stated that collusive behavior is allowed, and even encouraged, in "promising industries" which need to "increase R&D, improve quality, attain efficient production scale" and to "declining industries" which need to "scale down their activities" (Chang, 1994). This has resulted in industrial reorganization programs (e.g., the mergers of two automobile producers in 1965, of five PVC firms in 1969, and of the fertilizer, shipping, and overseas construction industries in the 1980s) and attempts to restrict entry and to regulate capacity expansion in such industries.

State-led industrialization, with its emphasis on the importance of scale economies in the economy and its various "industrial reorganizing" programs, has involved the emergence of *chaebols*, or big business conglomerates in South Korea (e.g., Samsung, Hyundai, Lucky-Goldstar and Daewoo), accounting for 60 percent of South Korean GNP in 1988. The uneasy alliance between the *chaebols* and the state has been an important plank of South Korea's state-led industrialization program. Under Park Chung Hee's regime in the 1960s and 1970s, the domination of the economy by *chaebols* was seen as necessary, and the challenge for the state was to try to tame them to achieve rapid and efficient late industrialization.

Industrial Policy in Taiwan

Though Taiwan previously relied chiefly on exports of labor-intensive goods as the main source for its growth, as in South Korea, the government of Taiwan has also been concerned with upgrading its industrial structure. It has not simply let free market forces determine the course of the economy. Rather, it has made active use of industrial policy to steer and sustain the long term growth of the economy. The Third Plan (1961-64) noted that:

> while priority should be given to light industries, . . . heavy industries that serve to consolidate and broaden the foundation of the developing economy . . . shall not be neglected despite heavy investment and slow returns [for] it holds the key to industrialization as it produces capital goods. We must develop heavy industries to support the long-term steady growth of the economy.

The government has long realized that cheap labor is not an adequate basis to sustain industrialization. Rather, the key to late industrialization is believed to lie in developing a well integrated economy, including basic and heavy industries (such as chemicals, wood pulp, petrochemical intermediaries and large scale integrated steel production), besides the development of products with high income elasticities (e.g., electrical appliances and electronic products), as recognized in the Fourth Plan (1965-8):

> For further development, stress must be laid on basic heavy industries, instead of end product manufacturing or processing. Industrial development in the long run must be centered on export products that have high income elasticity and low transportation cost. And around these products, there should be development of both forward and backward indus-

> tries . . . [by moving in this direction], we shall then be able to meet the changing situation in the world market brought about by the rapid industrial progress of the emerging nations and the growing sophistication of the industries of the developed countries.

Unlike South Korea, which depends on the *chaebol* as the main agent for industrialization, in many sectors in Taiwan, public enterprises have been the chosen instruments for state-led industrialization. Typically, public enterprises are among the largest, if not the only firms in their sectors. In 1980, for example, the six biggest industrial public enterprises had sales equal to the fifty biggest private industrial concerns. About half the total assets of Taiwan's corporations—worth NT$380 billion in 1980—is controlled directly or indirectly by the government and the ruling Guomindang (KMT). The government's creation of a large state sector was justified by invoking KMT founder Sun Yat Sen's People's Livelihood principles, which foresaw the state owning monopolized sectors (i.e., natural monopolies) and setting up needed industries too large or too risky for private capital (i.e., to compensate for market failure).

Public enterprises have not only been used to promote particular industries. They are concentrated in upstream sectors, where they can create incentives and pressures for growth in downstream sectors dominated by private firms. They have also tended to be strong in industries that would otherwise be dominated by foreign multi-national companies. This was especially true in the early years for fuel, petrochemicals, mining, metals, fertilizers and food processing. In sectors where public enterprises do not dominate, such as textiles and plastics, the state aggressively led private investments in the 1950s. During the late 1950s and the 1960s, public enterprises accounted for a large part of total investment in synthetic fibers, metals, shipbuilding and other industries (Wade, 1990).

Though public enterprises are often used to create and promote key industries, private firms have not been left alone. Incentives and pressures have been brought to bear on them through a mixture of controls and incentives. The control instruments include quantitative import restrictions and export licensing, incoming and outgoing foreign investment screening, approval for capital goods imports for new plants (until 1980), restrictions on non-governmental borrowing of foreign funds, and restrictions on entry to certain sectors. The incentives included tariff rebates, tax incentives and concessional credit. The state also lowered the costs of production for export with subsidies, duty drawbacks, etc. Fiscal investment incentives and concessional credit were also used to lower production costs, and to thus channel investments, first into heavy and chemical industries, and more recently, into electronics and machinery. Industrial reorganization policies have also been used, but not as frequently as in South Korea.

It is then clear that in both South Korea and Taiwan, the role of government has been much more profound and extensive than suggested by both free market and simulated market versions of neoclassical economic theory. Their main allegations—e.g., that "state intervention is largely absent and what the state provided is simply a suitable environment for the entrepreneurs to perform their functions" (Chen, 1979), and that "the basic causation of success of the NICs on the policy front, can be traced to the lessening of government intervention in the market during the export-oriented phase" (Fei, 1983)—are quite false and not based on empirical evidence.

The simulated market argument has been that "the active interventionist attitude of the state has been aimed at applying moderate incentives which are very close to the relative prices of products and factors that would prevail in a situation of free trade . . . as though the government were simulating a free market" (Berger, 1979). These claims are not only questionable empirically (Wade, 1990), but also on theoretical grounds. For example, it is unclear why Bhagwati's presumption—that resource allocation in an economy where neutrality is contrived by policy measures is basically the same as where there is no government intervention—is true. Instead the East Asian governments have intervened and altered the pattern of resource allocation in a manner quite different from what would have been produced by a free trade regime.

Conditions for Successful Intervention

While it is evident that industrial policy was critical for the success of the East Asian NICs, the crucial question now is why the governments of Taiwan and Korea were apparently able to reap the potential benefits of industrial policy while many other governments have not been able to do so. Balassa's (1988) claim (quoted in Chang, 1994), that the role of state "apart from the promotion of shipbuilding and steel in South Korea and of a few strategic industries in Taiwan . . . has been to create a modern infrastructure, to provide a stable incentive system, and to ensure that government bureaucracy will help rather than hinder exports," while in Latin American countries, "there are pervasive controls of investment, prices, and imports, and decisions are generally made on a case by case basis, thereby creating uncertainty for business decisions" is simply not true. The policy measures used in South Korea and Taiwan are not radically different from those used in Latin America and in other developing countries. The main differences seem to rest in three areas (Wade, 1988; 1990).

1. The central economic bureaucrats of the two countries seem to have realized that mere protection has not been sufficient to generate rapid growth. They sought to couple protection with *competition,*

to ensure that the lethargy-inducing effects of protection were outweighed by the investment-inducing effects.

2. Interventions have been *selective*, and the criteria of selection have something to do with future competitiveness. This serves to differentiate Taiwanese and South Korean intervention from much of Latin American and Indian intervention, where the assumption has tended to be that trade controls, coupled with unselective support of all domestic market-oriented industrial investment, would be sufficient to promote the right kind of industrialization.
3. Despite the market-augmenting method of intervention, even more important is the willingness and ability of the state to discipline capital. Incentives have not been allocated as give-aways, but rather in exchange for meeting specific concrete performance standards (e.g., with respect to output, exports, product quality, investments in training, and more recently, R&D) (Amsden, n.d.). One powerful instrument which has enhanced state capacity to mobilize businessmen for major economic programs and to penalize them for not conforming is "policy loans."

With undeveloped capital markets involving securities (stocks and bonds) in South Korea and Taiwan firms have depended heavily on credit for financing. This has resulted in highly leveraged firms heavily dependent on government/bank credit. The governments have dominated the financial sectors in both economies: in Taiwan, virtually the entire banking system is government-owned, and in South Korea, the same was true until the early 1980s, though the government continues to retain considerable influence. Thus, firms are vulnerable to government arm-twisting to the extent that a cut-off in credit raises the prospect of liquidation. Thus, the financial system permits the government to guide resource allocation to designated priority sectors; it also makes credit very difficult for less cooperative firms to obtain.[4]

Such a system, however, contains certain imperatives which must be met if the system is to work. These imperatives are reflected in readily identifiable features of the financial systems in both countries. And these have profound implications for the governments' overall roles in the economies. The governments must not only socialize risk—because it needs high interest rates to attract savings and low rates to induce investment—it must also provide "lender of last resort" facilities, deposit insurance, subsidies to banks imperiled by loan losses, and subsidies to firms in financial difficulties. It also has to ensure financial stability in the system because of the many highly leveraged firms in the economy very vulnerable to downswings in earnings.

The system also requires that the supplier of credit becomes intimate with company management, if necessary, restructuring a company's management to make it more competitive, and takes a long term view. The reason is that the creditor cannot simply withdraw when a company runs into difficulty by selling the company's securities in the secondary capital market as the market is poorly developed. And since market signals are blurred by administered pricing and socialized risk, the government must create a central guidance agency capable of supplementing market signals with its own indicators as to which sectors are viable or profitable (Wade, 1988).

Conclusion

Undoubtedly, the experiences of the NICs have tremendous relevance for late industrialization in developing countries. However, help is not to be found in the World Bank/IMF structural adjustment programs. Chang has correctly pointed out that development strategy is a complex set of interrelated policies, and should not be reduced to a simplistic dichotomy between "outward looking" and "inward looking" strategies. Development strategy is multidimensional; it is concerned with the "establishment of long term targets for growth, structural change" and the enhancement of productivity and competitiveness of the economy, rather than the static conception of an export-led strategy relying on exports of labor-intensive products for growth.

The success of industrial policy in Taiwan and South Korea have shown that the state can indeed play a positive and crucial role in late industrialization. However, direct emulation of these East Asian NIC experiences may not be feasible, as their development strategies were forged in particular historical, social and political circumstances. Nevertheless, what seems to be important is what has often been cited as the "missing element" in the less impressive performing Third World countries: a strong state committed to development with considerable autonomy in public policy formation from entrenched interests inimical to creating the conditions for late industrialization. This seems to be an important and a necessary precondition for any developing country wishing to be successful in late industrialization.

Notes

1. "...Singapore picked early winners, like shipbuilding and ship repairing. It happened in others, like shipbuilding, oil rig-building, printing and electronics. . . . There seemed to be no flaw in the formula: the government picked the winners and the people ran to order" (*The Economist*, Nov. 1988; quoted in Nolan, 1990).

"... [in South Korea], almost half of the country's GNP is produced by 15 *chaebols*. At first sight, they look like the massive Japanese companies. But they're not. They're really more like government departments. Admittedly, they're managed by people who call themselves capitalists and they've displayed great entrepreneurial flair. But in fact, it is the Ministry of Finance and the Economic Planning

Board which decide what South Korea is going to produce and whether it is for export or the home market. It then tells several of the giants to go ahead . . . and [after] a while the government decides who's doing best and orders the others to stop" (Prysor Jones, 1987; quoted in Nolan, 1990).

". . . [in Taiwan, with the intervention of the state], the main characteristic of private enterprise—the profit incentive—will be preserved and the weakness of private enterprise—concentration of wealth—can be avoided . . . private enterprise will be protected and assisted . . . consequently, the government must take part in all economic activities and such participation cannot be opposed on the ground of any free economic theory. . . ." (*Taiwan Fourth Year Plan* (1965); quoted in Nolan, 1990).

2. . . . For those who seek in the experiences of [the NICs economies] an endorsement of free trade in the context of a passive government, these facts present obvious difficulties. . . . These countries have highly energetic and involved governments. . . . The key question is not whether there is governmental action in the Far Eastern economies, but rather how these successful economies have managed their intervention and their strategic decision making better than the unsuccessful economies.

3. . . . [the] approach is problematic. It is the product of the rational-deductive method which is the foundation of neoclassical economics. As a result, the process of investigation and recommendation is inverted since the causal effect is presupposed prior to determining the effective cause. As a result, the diagnosis of the malaise is underdetermined, leaving out vital structural features which are likely to impede its implementation. . . . While there are problems with the structure of industry in Africa, hoping the market will solve the difficulties is no substitute for developing an industrial policy . . . while H-O-S would have us believe there is a natural basis for comparative advantage that the market will indicate, others might argue that opportunities are created, not inherited.

4. A firm that does not respond as expected to particular incentives may find that its tax returns are subject to careful examination, or that its application for bank credit is studiously ignored, or that its outstanding bank loans are not renewed. If incentive procedures do not work, government agencies show no hesitation in resorting to command backed by compulsion. In general, it does not take a South Korean firm long to learn that it will "get along" best by going along (Mason; quoted in Nolan, 1990).

References

Amsden, A. *Asia's Next Giant: South Korea and Late Industrialization.* New York: Oxford University Press. 1989.

Amsden, A. "A Theory of Government Intervention in Late Industrialization." Working Paper No. 27, Economics Department. New York: New School for Social Research. n.d.

Berger, F. "Korea's Experience with Export-led Industrial Development." In *Export Promotion Policies,* edited by B. de Vries. Staff Working Paper No. 313. Washington, DC: World Bank. 1979.

Balassa, B. "The Lessons of East Asian Development: An Overview." *Economic Development and Cultural Change* (Supplement) 36, No. 3. 1988.

____. "The process of industrial development and alternative development strategies." In *The Newly Industrializing Countries in the World Economy*. New York: Pergamon. 1981.

Bello, W., and S. Rosenfeld. Dragons in Distress. San Francisco: Food First Books. 1990.

Bhagwati, J. "Export-Promoting Trade Strategy: Issues and Evidences." *World Bank Research Observer* 3, No. 1. 1988a.

____. *Protectionism.* Cambridge, MA: M.I.T. Press. 1988b.

Chang Ha-Joon. *The Political Economy of Industrial Policy in Korea.* London: MacMillan. 1994.

Chen, E. *Hyper-Growth in Asian Economies: A Comparative Study of Hong Kong, Japan, Korea, Singapore and Taiwan.* London: Macmillan. 1979.

Edwards, C. *The Fragmented World: Competing Perspectives on Trade, Money and Crises.* London: Methuen. 1985.

Evans, D. and P. Alizadeh. "Trade, Industrialization and the Visible Hand." *The Journal of Development Studies* 21, No. 1. 1984.

Fei, J., G. Ranis, and S. Kuo. *Growth with Equity: The Taiwan Case.* New York: Oxford University Press. 1979.

Hamilton, C. "The Irrelevance of Economic Liberalization in the Third World." *World Development* 17, No. 10. 1989.

Johnson, C. "The Industrial Policy Debate Reexamined." *California Management Review* 27, No. 1. 1984.

____. *MITI and the Japanese Miracle: The Growth of Industrial Policy, 1925-1975.* Stanford: Stanford University Press. 1982.

Krueger, A. "Government Failures." *Journal of Economic Perspectives* 4, No. 3. 1990.

____. "Trade Policy as an Input to Development." *American Economic Review* 70, No. 10. 1980.

Lal, D. *The Poverty of Development Economics.* Hobart Paperback 16. London: Institute of Economic Affairs. 1983.

Nolan, P. "Assessing Economic Growth in the Asian NICs." *Journal of Contemporary Asia* 20, No. 1. 1990.

Steedman, I., ed. *Fundamental Issues in Trade Theory.* London: Macmillan. 1979.

Stein, H. "Deindustrialisation, Adjustment, the World Bank and the IMF in Africa." *World Development* 20, No. 1. 1992.

Stewart, F. "The Fragile Foundation of the Neo-classical Approach to Development." *Journal of Development Studies* 21, No. 2. 1985.

Tobin, J. "One or Two Cheers for the Invisible Hand." In *Pacific Basin Capital Market Research,* edited by S. Rhee, and R. P. Chang. North Holland: Elsevier. 1990.

Toye, J. *Dilemmas of Development.* New York: Basil Blackwell. 1987.

Wade, R. "East Asia's Economic Success: Conflicting Perspectives, Partial Insights, Shaky Evidence." *World Politics* 44, No. 2. 1992.

____. *Governing the Market: Economic Theory and the Role of Government in East Asian Industrialization.* Princeton: Princeton University Press. 1990.

____. "The Role of Government in Overcoming Market Failure: Taiwan, South Korea and Japan." In *Achieving Industrialization in Asia,* edited by Helen Hughes. Cambridge: Cambridge University Press. 1988.

8

China and Mexico: Comparable Development Strategies, Disparate Results

Victor D. Lippit

Starting in 1978, China embarked on major economic reforms. The reform program constituted a response to serious problems, both economic and social, that the previous "Maoist" development strategy had created or left unsolved. In the 1980s, Mexico too embarked on a major program of economic reform. Mexico, like China, acted in response to the serious economic and social problems associated with the previous development strategy. Although China claims to be following a "socialist" development strategy and Mexico is clearly pursuing a "capitalist" one, there are striking similarities in the reform programs undertaken by the two countries. Both are seeking to reduce the scope of government intervention in economic activities, to enhance the role of market forces and the private sector, and to move away from earlier policies of limited participation in the capitalist world economy by sharply increasing the role of international trade and investment.

In other respects as well, the similarity in their development strategies is unmistakable. Both are seeking ways to reform industrial structures that developed in distorted fashion through the impact of ideology. Both are retaining a key role for the state in planning or industrial policy, even while promoting the role of market forces in allocation decisions at the enterprise level. Despite these similarities, however, major differences also exist between the two countries.

In China, as the data below will show, the benefits of reform have largely accrued to the working classes, the peasants as well as the industrial workers. Although there is indeed a group of capitalist *nouveau riches* who are benefiting from the reform, the greater share of the benefits is going to the mass of the population. In Mexico, by contrast, the capitalist class has been the primary beneficiary in the early stages of reform. In effect, the unequal distribution of income and wealth at the start of the reform period has been intensified. Moreover, despite a downtrend in the overall unemployment rate setting in at the end of the 1980s, many workers in well-established firms continued to face dismissal as a result of restructuring. And when economic crisis flared up again in the mid-1990s, unemployment rose again by some one million workers and real wages again fell sharply amidst soaring inflation; once again ordinary people were forced to bear the brunt of adjustment.

If we seek to explain the reasons underlying the disparate results emanating from similar strategies, then two elements—especially in China's revolutionary heritage—must be stressed. First, the land reform in China, which distributed some 44 percent of China's arable land area between the late 1940s and 1952 (Lippit, 1974), created an equal per capita distribution of land in each village and a basically egalitarian distribution of income and wealth in the countryside. When a market system is introduced, the principal beneficiaries, at least at first, tend to be those who already have substantial income and wealth. When the initial distribution is relatively egalitarian, the beneficiaries are apt to be distributed more widely among the population.

Second, even though the people's communes proved to be incapable of significantly improving popular living standards in China's countryside (Nolan, 1988), they helped to create conditions that were extremely conducive to the success of the subsequent reform. Among the favorable effects of the commune system, we may note especially the building up of the rural infrastructure and the creation of small-scale rural industry. The communes were dissolved in 1982, but the collective enterprises they had established were preserved as township and village enterprises (TVEs), which are clearly the most dynamic element in the Chinese economy today. By 1987, they had passed agriculture in value added (Zweig, 1993: 419), and by 1992, were employing some 100 million people and affecting nearly one peasant household in two.

Thus, the egalitarian and collective heritage in China has played a central role in assuring that the benefits of economic reform are spread widely among the population. This helps to account for the fact that the consequences of economic reform have been so disparate in China and Mexico, despite the striking parallels in the reform strategies adopted in the two countries. In Mexico, the high concentration of property ownership compared to China contributed to a much more inegalitarian outcome. While Mexico's GDP per capita declined by 9 percent between 1980 and 1989, average real wages fell 24 percent and real minimum wages by 47 percent. Between 1980 and 1988, total wage payments relative to income from the ownership of capital fell from 0.64 to 0.40 (Sheahan, 1991:2).

TABLE 8.1. China and Mexico: Economic and Social Comparisons in the Era of Reform

	China	Mexico
1990 GNP per capita (US$)	370.0	2,490.0
1980-9 inflation rate (%)	5.8	72.7
1989 life expectancy at birth (years)	70.0	69.0
1985 adult illiteracy (%)	31.0	10.0
1980-89 GDP growth (%; annual average)	9.7	0.7
1980-89 agric. growth (%; annual average)	6.3	0.8
1980-89 industrial growth (%; annual average)	12.6	0.4
1987-89 index of food production per capita (1978-81=100)	128.0	98.0
1980-88 growth rate of earnings per employee in manufacturing (%)	4.2	-5.2
1980-89 private consumption growth (%)	7.5	0.7
1989 infant mortality (per 1,000 births)	30.0	40.0
1980-89 rural population below the poverty line (%)	10.0	43.0

Sources: Sheahan, 1991, ch. 2: p. 3; World Bank, 1991: 204-259; World Bank, 1992: 218-219; United Nations, 1991: 152.

Given the similarity in many of the "initial" conditions, the conditions that preceded the initiation of the Chinese reforms under Deng Xiaoping in 1978 and the Mexican reforms that began in the early 1980s and went into high gear under Salinas at the end of the decade, it is perhaps not so surprising that the two nations have adopted parallel strategies. Among the most important of the common initial conditions is the severe problem of surplus labor in agriculture. Between 1988 and 2000, for example, as many as 180 million jobs would have to be created for displaced workers in Chinese agriculture to eliminate underemployment there fully.

In Mexico too, unemployment and underemployment are severe; the difficulties in finding work at home are reflected in the massive migrations that have taken place to Mexico City and abroad to the U.S. Mexico City, possibly the world's largest city in 1995 with some 25 percent of Mexico's 92 million population or 23 million people, has reached critical pollution levels as a consequence, and still cannot begin to provide the jobs that are needed (World Bank, 1994: 162-163, 222-223; *The Economist*, 10/28/95, Mexico Survey: 4). Any reform strategy in Mexico, as in China, must address the question of employment, and in Mexico, the dispersal of employment must also be addressed—an area in which China has already achieved substantial progress.

Surplus Labor

The existence of surplus labor often reflects a pattern of distorted or blocked industrial development. In the case of China, pursuit of the Soviet-style policy of heavy industrial development created relatively few jobs, even though enterprises were forced to accept more workers than they needed. The result of this unbalanced development strategy is an intensified problem with surplus labor even while the nation's heavy industrial base requires a high level of expenditures for renovation, replacement and technological upgrading. The resources required for this would divert funding from the light industrial enterprises that could potentially absorb the excess labor in agriculture.

A number of factors contributed to the extreme emphasis on large-scale heavy industry that marked Chinese development policy in the pre-reform era, starting with a development strategy that consciously stressed capital formation as the central element in growth. Material incentives for efficiency, effort and innovation could be dispensed with, it was thought, and thus light industry and the wage goods it could produce were marginalized. Instead of balanced industrial development then, heavy industry received lopsided emphasis at the expense of light industry (and also of agriculture, which provides many of the raw materials for light industry).

In Mexico, a comparable surplus labor problem stemmed from different sources. There, the import-substitution (IS) strategy of industrialization contributed to a focus on the production of consumer durables, and the greatly unequal distribution of income and wealth limited the development of mass consumer markets and the light industry to serve them; Table 8.2 below compares income distribution in Mexico with that in China. At the same time, the IS strategy protected domestic firms, preventing Mexican industry from developing the competitive strength needed to participate vigorously in export markets.

Despite the emphasis on heavy industry in China, however, there were two major countervailing forces, both of which were to become significant during the reform period. First, because the heavy-industry industrialization strategy limited the availability in the countryside of needed agricultural inputs as well as a wide range of basic consumer goods, the strategy of "walking on two legs" was implemented in the countryside with the establishment of local industries at the commune and brigade levels of the people's communes; these later became the township and village enterprises (TVEs). Second, because at least some property rights (including rights to receive tax revenues, to appoint managers, etc.) are vested at the level of government that initiates an enterprise, competition among officials to promote the development of their own regions sometimes contributed to a proliferation of enterprises—a proliferation that the center could not always control.

TABLE 8.2. Income Distribution, China and Mexico*

Percentage share of income:	China	Mexico
Lowest 20%	6.4	4.1
Second quintile	11.0	7.8
Third quintile	16.4	12.3
Fourth quintile	24.4	19.9
Highest 20%	41.8	55.9
Highest 10%	24.6	39.5

* The Chinese data are for 1990, the Mexican data for 1984.
Source: The World Bank, 1994: 220-221.

As a consequence of these countervailing factors, China at the start of its reform period had a relatively diversified productive base, especially if comparisons are drawn with other Communist countries, such as the Soviet Union. The official focus in both China and the Soviet Union remained on the large, state-owned enterprises, but in China smaller enterprises were scattered like germinating weeds all around the officially-emphasized state sector. And when the economic reform program provided them with nutrients, they sprouted and even flowered.

Other Initial Conditions

The differences between Mexico and China are, of course, evident. The distribution of income and wealth are much more unequal in Mexico (see Table 8.2 above and the discussion concerning the Mexican billionaires below); the foreign debt (and debt service) is much higher in relation to gross national product (GNP) in Mexico—in 1992 external debt as a percentage of GNP was 12.8 percent in China and 34.1 percent in Mexico, while debt service amounted to 10.3 percent of exports in China and 44.4 percent of exports in Mexico (World Bank, 1994: 206-207); economic activity and population are more dispersed in China; Mexico's per capita GNP (US$3,470 in 1992) is much higher than China's (US$470 in 1992; World Bank, 1994: 162-163); agricultural dualism is present in Mexico—a large *ejido* population living at subsistence alongside a smaller group of prosperous commercial farmers—but not in China; and the class structures and patterns of surplus appropriation are quite different in the two countries. To understand the basis for the similarity in development strategy, however, we must focus on the common elements in their initial conditions. These are more extensive and of greater importance than might appear to be the case at first glance.

In addition to the existence of an enormous supply of surplus labor in both countries, the key role played by inefficient, state-owned enterprises is among the most important of the common factors. These enterprises contributed far less to the public purse than they might have or actually drained funds away from it. In China, for example, about one-third of the state-owned enterprises lost money in 1991. In both countries, moreover, the problems associated with these "statist" enterprises were not amenable to mild reform. On the one hand, those with privileged access to them would not readily give up the benefits they derived, and on the other, the enterprises provided employment and welfare services that could not readily be replaced and yet which built in a considerable measure of economic inefficiency.

In both China and Mexico, the industrialization strategies pursued prior to reform created great inefficiency in the industrial sector. In both countries, the parastatal (statist) corporations were shielded from competition, required to fulfill social welfare functions for their employees and permitted to provide "rents" (returns higher than were necessary to attract workers or managers) for those with privileged access to them. Thus, Pemex employed about five times as many workers per dollar of revenue as did Royal Dutch/Shell in 1986 (*Wall Street Journal*, 9/27/88: 20). Efficiency in China also suffered from an absence of market prices. Low energy prices, for example, discouraged conservation, with the resulting energy shortages preventing a substantial share of the nation's productive capacity from being utilized at any given time.

In addition to the efficiency problems with state-owned enterprises, the existence of surplus labor in agriculture (and thus, the urgent need to provide non-agricultural employment), the distorted industrial structure and the weakness of the middle market for mass-produced goods, a number of other initial conditions were comparable in the two countries. Both are near economic superpowers, creating favorable possibilities for trade and investment. Both have ample energy resources, a blessing tempered by serious environmental problems tied in large part to energy use. The two have young populations and high dependency ratios, but education is valued and the labor force relatively educated—especially the younger workers (between 1970 and 1991, the proportion of secondary school-age children attending school rose from 24 percent to 51 percent in China, and from 22 percent to 55 percent in Mexico; World Bank, 1994: 216-217). Both countries experienced productivity problems in agriculture associated with (very different kinds of) collectivization. And both suffered from an overlap of the ruling party and the state, attempting in their reforms the ticklish task of limiting corruption and of separating the two somewhat while enabling the party leadership to maintain sufficient control to implement its vision of modernization. The success in separating party and state has, of course, been limited in both countries.

The Strategies of Development

At the core of the similar development strategies being pursued by China and Mexico is the effort to incorporate their economies more firmly in the capitalist world economy and a related effort to increase the role of competition and market forces in domestic resource allocation. China carried out a process of decollectivization in 1982 in an attempt to raise agricultural productivity and Mexico began in 1993 to follow a parallel path with "de-ejidoization." Both countries are pursuing strategies of balanced growth, seeking simultaneously growth in light industry, heavy industry and agriculture. The development of industrial exports plays an especially important role in both cases—to provide jobs and earn foreign exchange—but foreign exchange is also being sought through widening doors to foreign investment, promoting tourism, and so forth.

In comparing the reformist development strategies of both Mexico and China, we have multiple objectives. In addition to the viability of the strategies being pursued, we are especially concerned with their human development implications. Both countries began by recognizing serious deficiencies in their previous strategies, strategies that involved promoting the state ownership of enterprises and limiting foreign investment and trade. The previous strategies had been justified on the grounds that they would improve popular welfare, but the failure of mass living standards to improve significantly during the Maoist period in China (mid-1950s to mid-1970s) and the serious decline experienced in the 1980s in Mexico (see Table 8.1 above) made reform imperative.

Mexico justifies its reform on the grounds that an oligopolistic but internationally competitive capitalism will provide jobs and improve popular living standards. China, following a comparable strategy, justifies its reform on the grounds that pursuing "socialism with Chinese characteristics" will have the same consequences. Despite their pursuing comparable development strategies, however, and adopting reforms that at a structural level appear to be quite similar, the class impact of the reforms in the two countries has been strikingly different, as Table 8.1 above makes clear. Moreover, the disparate welfare effects have persisted into the mid-1990s. Between 1980 and 1994, for example, per capita consumption more than doubled in China, increasing from an index of 100 to 206.5, whereas in Mexico between 1980 and 1995 real per capita income fell (State Statistical Bureau, 1995: 258; *The Economist*, 10/28/95, Mexico Survey: 4).

The greater strength of collective and egalitarian institutions in China has played a central role in creating conditions for mass benefit from economic reform. In Mexico, by contrast, the capitalist/statist social formation that is the object of reform assured that its prime beneficiaries would not be the working classes. Thus, both the streamlining of some state-owned firms and the privatization of others have typically resulted in large numbers of employees losing their jobs. In the case of Mexico's largest industrial enterprise, the state-owned Pemex, the April 1992 employment level of about 150,000 reflected the dismissal of almost one-third of its labor force during the reform program (*Los Angeles Times*, 4/26/92: D7); job loss in restructuring firms in the private sector was often even more severe. In the long run, a dynamic economy will presumably create more jobs, but as Keynes observed, in the long run, we are all dead.

The Reform Strategy in China

Favorable conditions for the overall reform strategy in China were created by the successful reform in agriculture. A brief review of collectivization and its consequences may help to clarify the reasons for this success. China began carrying out land reform during the revolutionary war and completed the process over the entire country during the 1950-52 period. As we have noted, about 44 percent of the arable land area was redistributed, resulting in roughly equal per capita holdings in each village (Lippit, 1974). Mutual-aid teams and cooperatives were organized in the ensuing years, and in 1958, "people's communes" were organized, incorporating nearly all peasant households. After a period of experimentation and adjustment, the commune structure was stabilized in the early 1960s.

The communes made a positive contribution to development in a number of respects. They made it possible to mobilize the rural population for work on water conservancy and other capital construction projects during the off-season and facilitated the spread of new technology and, at least in principle, rational land-use planning. At the same time, while assuring the subsistence needs of their members (after an initial tumultuous period during the Great Leap Forward, 1958-60), they made it possible for the state to systematically extract the surplus generated in the farm economy to carry out industrialization. Although the communes proved effective in raising land productivity (output per acre), however, they were unable to raise labor productivity. Since a rise in living standards depends ultimately on the latter, this shortcoming was quite serious.

Probably the main problem with the commune structure was a curtailment of individual incentives. This was compounded by central planning directives (such as insistence on self-sufficiency in grain) that prevented localities from specializing in crops for which they enjoyed a natural advantage, and by centrally-set terms of trade between industry and agriculture that greatly undervalued agricultural produce. Attempts to reform the incentive structure by allowing peasant households to dispose of their own surpluses—output in excess of taxes and required quota sales (at low prices)—had been attempted in various localities from the late 1950s. Each time, however, ideological arguments were used to crack down on the process, arguments to the effect that the reforms constituted a rebirth of capitalism or would lead to it. Only in December 1978 did this reform receive official Party sanction.

The agricultural reform basically re-established household farming, with the peasants free to consume or sell on the market any output in excess of the taxes and quota sales. Procurement prices were raised sharply. Specialized household production (e.g., chicken and egg production) was encouraged. Peasants could also set up individual or small-group enterprises, offering tractor services, transport, and so forth. Some of these subsequently became fairly large in scale. The commune enterprises, primarily at the brigade and commune level, became township and village enterprises (TVEs) collectively owned by the village and (former) commune members. Where the commune enterprises had been well developed, especially near major urban centers and in prosperous regions, these collective enterprises grew dramatically. In poorer regions, private enterprises did likewise. The growth of intermediate-size towns (from about 20,000 to about 200,000) was encouraged.

The dramatic expansion of rural industry, especially collective industry, became a hallmark of the economic reform in China. From 1980 to 1994, the industrial output value of rural enterprises increased at an average annual rate of 26.7 percent in real terms (State Statistical Bureau, 1995: 233, 265), and by the late 1980s the value added in rural industry surpassed that of agriculture. Employment in the township and village enterprises grew from 30.0 million in 1980 to 120.2 million in 1994 (State Statistical Bureau, 1995: 84-85).

The expansion of rural industry provided jobs for a large share of the surplus labor in Chinese agriculture (although, as we have noted, much more remains to be done). The 120.2 million workers employed by rural enterprises in 1994 amounted to 26.9 percent of the 446.5 million person rural labor force in that year (State Statistical Bureau, 1995: 85). Rural industrialization also helped rural incomes to rise sharply since the wages provided by rural enterprises were considerably higher than average peasant incomes. Throughout the 1980s, a housing boom took place in rural China, where per capita housing space rose from 8.1 square meters in 1979 to 17.2 square meters in 1989 (State Statistical Bureau, 1990: 310). Real per capita consumption rose by 94.4 percent in China as a whole over these years, with the gain for the agricultural population amounting to 101.2 percent and that for the non-agricultural population amounting to 67.8 percent (State Statistical Bureau, 1990: 274). This helped diminish inequality in China since average peasant consumption levels are much lower than those for urban residents. From 1990 to 1994, however, while rural living standards continued to improve, the relative gains for the agricultural population vis-à-vis the non-agricultural population were reversed. During these years, per capita consumption for the agricultural population rose by 29.6 percent, compared to a gain of 54.5 percent for the non-agricultural population (State Statistical Bureau, 1995: 258).

The agricultural reform included allowing peasants to grow what they pleased and to respond to market incentives. Entrepreneurial instincts remained strong in the countryside, and the response was a surge in agricultural production. Since, even in the 1980s, more than half of urban household expenditure was for food, the great increase in the quantity and quality of food supplies made a major contribution to improved urban well-being. By the early 1990s, urban nutritional standards in China were comparable to those in Japan in the 1950s or those in South Korea in the 1970s (*The Economist*, 6/1/91: 16). The rapid gains in urban consumption during the 1990s suggest that these improvements have been sustained, although as the data below indicate, a much larger share of urban income gains has been going into consumer durables.

Reforming the statist industrial enterprises is proving to be a much bigger challenge in China than reforming agriculture. The difficulty in reforming these enterprises mirrors that encountered in the Soviet Union, where the inability to raise the productivity of the state-owned enterprises was a major factor in the collapse of the state. In both China and the Soviet Union, early growth was predicated on sustaining massive investment levels. With the returns on these investments decreasing over time, economic growth slowed markedly in the Soviet Union, and in the 1980s, ground to a halt. While China did not experience as sharp a slowdown, its state-owned enterprises too had sharply decreasing returns over time. China, however, reacted to its problems in more timely fashion than did the Soviet Union.

Improving the performance of China's statist enterprises is no less daunting a task than improving the Soviet Union's was. It has been observed that managing such an enterprise in either country is/was more like being the mayor of a small city than like managing a Western corporation. The enterprises typically provide housing, retirement benefits, welfare services, and so forth. Further, they are often expected to add workers or maintain employment even when grossly overstaffed. Enterprises may also be unprofitable because a large part of their purchases and sales takes place at planned prices over which they have no control. Moreover, because of the various responsibilities the enterprises are expected to fulfill, it is difficult for the state to carry out full-scale price reform rapidly.

In China, for example, there has been virtually no market for housing. Apartments are supplied by one's employer, with nominal charges for rent and utilities. This system, combined with severe restrictions on rural-urban migration, assured relative equality in the housing market and the absence of a homelessness problem. It also assured an aging, deteriorating housing stock with cramped quarters and lack of privacy. Between 1952 and 1978, per capita housing space in China's cities fell by as much as 25 percent. Since it is not possible to move suddenly to market-level rents without unacceptable social dislocation, the state-owned enterprises must continue to subsidize the housing costs of their employees and retired workers. Saddled with these and other expenses, many of them lose money, with the state required to provide ongoing subsidies. This, in turn, puts considerable pressure on the state budget, limiting funds for other purposes while allowing inefficient firms (some, but not all of the subsidized ones) to remain in operation.

In view of these difficulties, China has been trying to move gradually toward market pricing in the urban/industrial sector. Thus, the state-owned firms still receive output plans and input allocations, both at planned prices, but once they have met their planning obligations, they are free to acquire inputs and sell their output according to market conditions. Reforms in the early to mid-1990s promise to raise sharply the role of market allocation and envision ultimately phasing out the central planning system altogether (*Beijing Review*, 11/9/92: 7). Under conditions of limited reform, the statist enterprises have been growing, but their growth is much more sluggish than that of the smaller rural enterprises. Thus, for example, between 1979 and 1989 inclusive, state-owned industry grew at an average 8.1 percent annually, while collectively-owned industry (primarily rural) grew at 19.0 percent annually (State Statistical Bureau, 1990: 395). As we have noted, rural industry alone grew at an average rate of 26.7 percent from 1980 to 1994.

One of the central elements in China's economic reform program has involved integrating its economy with the world market. Initially, four special economic zones (SEZs) and fourteen economic and technical development zones (ETDZs) were established, numbers which have since increased to five and sixteen respectively. Subsequently, a broad coastal area was also granted special rights and privileges to promote international trade and investment, and free trade zones have been established in Shanghai (at Pudong) and Tienjin.

The SEZs are separate cities with their own governments, while the ETDZs are specified areas within existing cities. The special rights include tax breaks for foreign investment, low-interest loans to provide infrastructure, exemption from or reduction of import duties and export restraints, rights to retain or obtain foreign exchange, and so forth. The SEZs have been situated in localities that would facilitate investment by overseas Chinese. The largest, for example, Shenzhen, is close to Hong Kong.

China's foreign trade has increased sharply in response to these initiatives, and the area around Hong Kong (which reverts to China in 1997) is among the most dynamically growing regions in the world. By 1995, Hong Kong firms employed some 400,000 industrial workers in Hong Kong itself, and some four million inside China, mainly in the adjacent Guangdong province (which includes Shenzhen). For China as a whole, the sharp rise in exports, imports, and foreign investment reflects the success of its internationalization strategy.

Between 1978 and 1994, exports rose from US$9.8 billion to US$121.0 billion, while imports increased from US$10.9 billion to US$115.7 billion (State Statistical Bureau, 1995: 537). Table 8.3 below indicates the annual changes.

TABLE 8.3. China's Foreign Trade, 1978-94 (US$bn)

Year	Export value	Import value
1978	9.7	10.9
1979	13.7	15.7
1980	18.1	20.0
1981	22.0	22.0
1982	22.3	19.3
1983	22.2	21.4
1984	26.1	27.4
1985	27.4	42.3
1986	30.9	42.9
1987	39.4	43.2
1988	47.5	55.3
1989	59.1	52.5
1990	62.1	53.4
1991	71.9	63.8
1992	84.9	80.6
1993	91.7	104.0
1994	121.0	115.7

Sources: Lardy, 1992: 694; State Statistical Bureau, 1995: 537.
Note: The 1978-79 figures are not strictly comparable since they include only the value added from the export processing of imported components or raw materials; this reduces the value of both exports and imports. Processing activity, however, was relatively limited in those two years, only becoming significant later in the reform.

A major force fueling the sharp rise in imports and exports has been the influx of foreign investment into China. This investment was primarily in the form of foreign loans through the 1980s, but direct foreign investment became larger from 1992, and a surge in such investment made it a far more important category by the mid-1990s as the domestic market was increasingly opened to foreign enterprises locating production facilities within China, adding to the incentives created by the booming export market. Table 8.4 below indicates the inflow of foreign capital into China between 1979 and 1994.

In economic terms, China's reform strategy has been a stunning success. This is true despite the overheating of the economy in the late 1980s, which was accompanied by a serious problem with inflation and a need for retrenchment. From 1980 to 1989, Gross Domestic Product (GDP) grew at an average rate of 9.7 percent per year (see Table 8.1). This was the same as the growth rate of South Korea and ahead of Hong Kong's 7.1 percent and Singapore's 6.1 percent. During this period, China's indus-

TABLE 8.4. Foreign Capital Used in China, 1979-1994 (US$bn)

Year	Foreign loans	Direct foreign investments	Other foreign investments	Total
1979-83	11.8	1.8	0.9	14.4
1984	1.3	1.3	0.2	2.7
1985	2.7	1.7	0.3	4.7
1986	5.0	1.9	0.4	7.3
1987	5.8	2.3	0.3	8.5
1988	6.5	3.2	0.5	10.2
1989	6.3	3.4	0.4	10.1
1990	6.5	3.5	0.3	10.3
1991	6.9	4.4	0.3	11.6
1992	7.9	11.0	0.3	19.2
1993	11.2	27.5	0.3	39.0
1994	9.3	33.8	0.2	43.2

Source: State Statistical Bureau, 1995: 554.

trial growth rate averaged 12.6 percent while its agricultural growth rate averaged 6.3 percent.

At the end of the 1980s, high inflation forced the government to adopt measures to cool the economy, and real GDP growth fell to 4.1 percent in 1989 and 3.8 percent in 1990. When the policy brakes were eased, however, China's exceptional growth potential under reform reasserted itself, and the growth rate of GDP again rose sharply, reaching 9.3 percent in 1991, 14.2 percent in 1992, 13.5 percent in 1993, and 11.8 percent in 1994 (State Statistical Bureau, 1995: 32). For the period from 1989 to 1994, real GDP growth averaged 10.5 percent. The great inflow of foreign capital, shown above in Table 8.4, helped to sustain the high rates of growth experienced during the early to mid-1990s.

The reappearance of rapid growth, however, brought with it renewed inflationary pressures. Although the tighter monetary and fiscal policies that had been adopted to reduce such pressures at the end of the 1980s brought the year-over-year increase in the consumer price index down from 18.0 percent in 1989 to 3.1 percent in 1990, it rose sharply again in the ensuing years, reaching 24.1 percent in 1994 (State Statistical Bureau, 1995: 233). While the course of China's expansion has not been smooth, the average rate overall has been extremely high, a sharp improvement in living standards in both urban and rural areas has accompanied the high levels of capital formation, and the foundation has been laid for continued rapid development.

The Reform Process in Mexico

Between 1980 and 1989, real GDP per capita fell by about 1 percent per year in Mexico. The severe economic slump was closely tied to the debt crisis, which revealed the limits of the import-substitution (IS) industrialization strategy that previously fueled Mexico's growth. The IS strategy had focused on the use of protection to foster domestic industry. The result was that domestic industry, freed from the spur of competition, emerged as a relatively high-cost producer, incapable of competing on world markets. Thus, Mexico remained heavily dependent on its oil exports, which in 1985 constituted 66.6 percent of the total (Cardoso & Helwage, 1992: 15). The sharp fall in oil prices during the 1980s put severe pressure on both the trade balance and the federal budget, with budget deficits contributing to severe inflation that reached 159 percent in 1987 (*The Economist*, 10/28/95, Mexico Survey: 4).

The burden of the 1980s' crisis was borne disproportionately by the working classes and the poor. As we have noted, average real wages fell by 24 percent in the 1980-89 period, during which time real minimum wages fell by 47 percent. In 1986, some 43 percent of rural families and 23 percent of urban ones were living below the poverty line (Sheahan, 1991, ch. 2: 3). The challenge that public policy faced in Mexico was to reorient development strategy in the midst of a severe crisis while mitigating the problems of poverty and unemployment. The reorientation was both necessary and successful in the sense of laying the foundation for sharply improved economic performance in the future (the crisis of 1994-95 notwithstanding), but in laying the burden of adjustment on the backs of the poor, Mexico stands in sharp contrast to the general prosperity associated with economic reform in China.

The broad characteristics of the reform process in Mexico included the privatization of most state-owned enterprises, with the number falling from nearly 1,200 in 1982 to about 200 in 1995 (*The Economist*, 10/28/95, Mexico Survey: 8)—Pemex, the state-owned oil company, was the most notable exception—a sharp reduction in tariffs, reduction in the national debt (the main use for privatization revenues), the elimination of the budget deficit, reducing sharply the rate of inflation—from a peak of 159 percent in 1987 to 7 percent in 1994 (*The Economist*, 10/28/95, Mexico Survey: 4)—negotiating a reduction in the debt burden with foreign creditors, creating a hospitable environment for foreign investors and the return of Mexican flight capital, and creating the basis for a rapid growth in manufactured exports.

As the World Bank data in Table 8.5 below indicate, the exports of manufactured products rose rapidly in the 1980s, albeit from a very low initial level. The leading sector was automobiles and auto parts. By 1991, auto production topped one million vehicles, with exports standing at 358,000. Output by the end of the century is expected to reach some three million vehicles, with a disproportionate increase in exports now that the North Ameri-

TABLE 8.5. Mexico: Exports of Manufactured Products (US$bn)

Year	Export value	Year	Export value
1980	2.2	1986	7.1
1981	2.7	1987	9.8
1982	1.8	1988	11.6
1983	3.3	1989	11.6
1984	4.2		
1985	4.6	1992	14.1

Sources: Sheahan, 1991, ch. 2: 3; The World Bank, 1994: 187, 191.

can Free Trade Agreement (NAFTA) has been approved (*Business Week*, 3/16/92: 98). The export competitiveness of other industries is rising as well. Mexico enjoys an advantage in wage costs, with hourly compensation in manufacturing averaging US$2.03 in 1992 compared to a US$4.10 average in the four Asian "tigers" and US$15.33 in the United States (*Business Week*, 5/4/92: 22); the peso crisis brought the rate below $1.80 in 1995, further increasing Mexico's labor cost advantage. As Mexico's former President Salinas has observed, however, if low labor costs were the sole factor determining industrial location, Haiti would be the manufacturing leader of the Western hemisphere. By opening up the economy and reducing debt and inflation, and by putting into effect a longer-term program oriented to improving education and the nation's physical infrastructure, the government succeeded in creating a favorable climate for private entrepreneurship; an influx of foreign capital and returning domestic capital helped to sustain its program until the new crisis (discussed below) emerged at the end of 1994.

While real GNP declined by 3.6 percent in 1986, it grew by an average 3.3 percent per year by 1990-92 (Comision Nacional de Valores, Banco de Mexico). The unemployment rate fell from 17.1 percent in 1986 to an estimated 8.0 percent in 1992, while the Treasury Bill interest rate, tracking the decline in inflation, fell from 98.6 percent to 17.0 percent (Comision Nacional de Valores, Banco de Mexico). These macroeconomic improvements took place despite sluggishness in the world economy, including Mexico's most important trading partner, the United States.

The North American Free Trade Agreement (NAFTA), which went into effect on January 1, 1994, appeared to provide the climax to the economic reform program. Responding to the reform and anticipating NAFTA, some $91 billion in foreign investment poured into Mexico from 1990 to 1993 inclusive (*The Economist*, 10/28/95, Mexico Survey: 5). Some two-thirds of that money, however, went into easy-to-withdraw financial investments in stocks and bonds. At the same time, domestic savings fell from 22 percent of national income in 1988 to 16 percent in 1994. Mexico thus made itself vulnerable to a decline in the confidence of foreign investors, paving the way to the financial crisis that began at the end of 1994 and the severe recession of 1995. As the discussion below indicates, however, Mexico's response to the crisis was a deepening of its reforms, and by the end of 1995, recovery was in sight.

Problems Generated by the Reform Process

The core argument presented here focuses on the disparate burdens borne by different classes in China and Mexico, and the disparate benefits received. During the 1990s, as the reform process matured in both countries, this differential pattern was sustained. At the same time, however, the reform process generated different social and macroeconomic problems in the two countries, and a comparison between the two must take these into account.

In the case of Mexico, the burden of the mid-1990s crisis has once again fallen disproportionately on the poor. In the case of China, high rates of real growth and rising living standards have been maintained, but the government has been unable to restrain inflation, while the intensification of such social problems as crime, corruption, and the exploitation of labor has begun to call into question the very character of the transformation China is experiencing. More explicitly, as the reform moved into its second decade in China, it brought with it social and economic changes that appear more likely to lead to the emergence of a welfare-state capitalism than to the officially-endorsed market socialism.

In the case of Mexico, the unequal impact of reform is expressed most vividly in the increase in the number of billionaires from two in 1991 to thirteen in 1993 and twenty-four in 1994, when the number of Mexican billionaires (expressed in U.S. dollars) was fourth in the world, trailing only the U.S., Japan, and Germany (*Forbes*, 7/17/95: 122). Following the collapse of the Mexican peso and stock market in December 1994 and early 1995, the number of Mexican billionaires fell to ten (*Forbes*, 7/17/95: 122), but for the most part the super-rich can be expected to regain their status with an economic recovery already in sight by late 1995 and a stock market recovery already begun.

The financial crisis, however, which brought an inflationary spike and sent short-term interest rates soaring as high as 90 percent, devastated small- and medium-sized companies and encouraged the restructuring of larger ones, leading to a rise in unemployment of one million and a sharp decline in real wages, which fell by 25 percent in 1995 (*The Economist*, 3/18/95: 73; *Business Week*, 11/13/95: 106). Once again the burden of adjustment fell disproportionately on those least able to bear it.

The causes of the financial crisis in Mexico lie, in large measure, outside the reform strategy itself. The uprising in Chiapas in southern Mexico at the start of 1994, combined with two major political assassinations during the year, undermined the confidence of foreign investors. At the same time, the ruling PRI party, facing a national election, was unwilling to slow the economy to keep economic activity in line with the diminished resources available. The economic problems were exacerbated by the low national savings rate in Mexico—some 16 percent of GDP compared to an average of about 20 percent in the industrialized countries and over 25 percent in developing economies (*The Economist*, 6/24/95: 72); China's national savings rate, by contrast, was well over 30 percent of GDP in 1994, when investment in fixed assets reached 36.4 percent of GDP (*Beijing Review*, 4/12/95: I).

The low savings rate in Mexico meant that much of national investment had to be financed by foreign savings, including heavy foreign portfolio investment in Mexican stocks and bonds. When foreign investors lost confidence, the portfolio investment turned from an inflow to an outflow, leading to a collapse of the peso. The Mexican government was then forced to slash budgetary expenditures and support extremely high interest rates to regain the confidence of foreign investors, resulting in a deep recession and rising unemployment.

Although political factors precipitated the crisis, the underlying structural problem of the low national savings rate provided its basis. Mexico is taking steps to raise national savings, including the introduction of a Chilean-style social security system (in which employers and employees are both required to pay into portable pension plans), but these measures can be expected to bear fruit only gradually and over time. Otherwise, the underlying reform strategy remains unchanged, and in fact an acceleration and deepening of the privatization program has been one of the means chosen to address the crisis. In the long run, the reform process can still be expected to bring employment and prosperity to a growing proportion of the Mexican population, but the 1994-95 crisis again makes clear that the burden of reform and adjustment falls disproportionately on those least able to bear it when the initial distribution of income and wealth is highly skewed.

In China, by contrast, the vast majority of the population has continued to benefit from the reforms, despite strong inflationary pressures and growing inequality. Between 1990 and 1995, the proportion of the population able to afford consumer durables has risen, as has the power and income of the small elite with substantial wealth generated from a mix of political connections and entrepreneurial skills. That is to say, the reform in China has moved into a new stage in which, although most ordinary citizens continue to benefit strongly, increasing class differentiation has become noticeable. Combined with the evidence of social decay and the growing exploitation of labor, these changes impart an increasingly capitalist cast to the character of Chinese development.

As we have noted, the growth rate of China's real GDP averaged 10.5 percent from 1989 to 1994, with direct foreign investment rising from $4.4 billion in 1991 to $27.5 billion in 1993 and $33.8 billion in 1994 (see Table

8.4). Since this was direct investment in real (as opposed to financial) assets, China was not subject to the same risk of sudden withdrawal of foreign funds that devastated Mexico.

By the end of 1994, China had 207,000 foreign-funded companies, including joint ventures with Chinese enterprises and wholly foreign-owned units. These enterprises had some $484.6 billion in assets and employed more than 23 million people (*Wall Street Journal,* 1/11/95: A10). The foreign investment was closely tied to an increase in foreign trade, with exports rising 31.9 percent in 1994 to US$121 billion and imports rising 11.2 percent to US$115.7 billion (*Beijing Review,* 4/12/95: II). Although the ongoing boom has been accompanied by strong inflationary pressures, with retail prices rising by 24.7 percent in 1994 (*Beijing Review,* 1/23/95: 18), national living standards continued to improve markedly.

In 1992-94, for example, the average height of urban and rural children at the age of six had increased by 4.6 and 4.0 cm respectively compared to a decade earlier, with average weight increases of 2.4 and 1.2 kg (*Beijing Review,* 1/30/95: 31). The number of rural poor, which had fallen from 250 million in 1978 (31.0 percent of the rural population) to 125 million in 1985 (14.8 percent), declined further to 80 million in 1993 (9.3 percent), in line with a state target to eliminate poverty by the end of the century (*Beijing Review,* 2/27/95: 20). The reduction in poverty is reflected in the rising per capita grain consumption in poverty-stricken counties, which increased from 315 kg in 1985 to 354 kg in 1992 (*Beijing Review,* 2/27/95: 20). With more than 80 percent of China's 1.2 billion people having access to television and some 30 percent of its urban population firmly ensconced in or beginning to enter the middle class, and with residential construction adding 200 million square meters of housing for the urban population and 580 million square meters for the rural population in 1994 alone (*Beijing Review,* 4/12/95: II), the evidence of continuing broad participation in China's growing national prosperity is unmistakable.

Nevertheless, the growth in corruption, crime, and other social problems mirrors a national obsession with gaining money, undermining—probably fatally—the official goal of creating a market socialist system. The children of party leaders have established elaborate networks of privilege, prospering in commercial ventures, which generally require the approval and support of party and state officials. With sharp increases in prostitution, illegal money-changing carried out openly in the lobbies of major hotels, and older women using their grandchildren to beg, China's social patterns increasingly reflect the characteristic features of capitalist development. In 1994, cases of major corruption and white collar crime each jumped 70 percent from the previous year (*Wall Street Journal,* 5/2/95: A10), and accounts of violent street crime began to break into the national press.

Perhaps representing the sharpest break with China's past, however, is the nation's dismal record of worker safety. In November 1993, for example, eighty-four young women were killed in a toy factory fire in Shenzhen (*China Daily*, 11/22/93: 3). Three of the four exits to the factory were locked and the windows barred to prevent theft. A month later sixty workers, mostly young women, were killed in a similar fire in Fuzhou. In 1993, in Guangdong province alone, 45,000 industrial accidents were responsible for about 8,700 deaths. According to a *Wall Street Journal* (6/27/94: A10) report:

> Despite authorities' vows to enforce safety rules following a rash of factory disasters in southern China, the government is moving gingerly because of reluctance to scare off Hong Kong investors. Warning against harsh policies, a Labor Ministry official told Hong Kong's *South China Morning Post*, "We cannot block (these investments) just for safety's sake."

The underlying logic of a system of market socialism reflects an effort to combine the efficiency and incentive effects of the market system with the social justice concerns of socialism. When such a system is implemented in a less developed country such as China, however, it tends to unleash a national obsession with gaining wealth by any means. When, as in the case of China, the power of the state remains critical in assuring commercial success (by providing approvals, licensing, financing, and so forth), the leading cadres with privileged access to the power of the state are placed in a position to enrich themselves, their family members, and their friends. And the traditional system of reciprocal personal obligations leads to the creation of mutually supportive networks of such individuals, undermining the principles of equality—even of opportunity—that once characterized revolutionary China.

Conclusion

China and Mexico have carried out reform programs that are strikingly similar. Both have linked their economies with the capitalist world economy and benefited from an upsurge in international trade and investment. Both have maintained a central role for government in carrying out industrial policy and setting the macroeconomic parameters for their economies, even while withdrawing from microeconomic decision-making at the enterprise level; both have sharply increased the role of market forces in resource allocation. Yet, the primary beneficiaries of the reform policies have been quite different. In China,

> Between 1978 and 1991, grain consumption of the average Chinese went up by 20%; seafood consumption two-fold; pork consumption 2-1/2 times; egg consumption more than three-fold; edible oil and poultry consumption four-fold. In 1981 each 100 urban households in China averaged less than one colour television among them; ten years later it was 70. In 1981

> there were six washing machines for each 100 city households. In 1991 more than 80; in 1981, 0.2 refrigerators, ten years later almost 50. (*The Economist*, 11/28/92, China Survey: 4)

In Mexico, by contrast, the first decade of reform was marked by increasing polarization of income and wealth. On the one hand, the stock market boomed, increasing from an inflation-adjusted index of 342.1 in 1986 to 1,572 in 1992 (Comision Nacional de Valores, Banco de Mexico), when Mexican billionaires began to appear on *Forbes'* annual survey of the world's richest people. On the other hand, real wages fell by 24 percent between 1981 and 1989, and the levels of poverty remained high. While ordinary people were major beneficiaries of the reform program in China, the reform program was built on the backs of such people in Mexico.

If we try to find the reasons underlying this striking difference, it is difficult to find anything in the programs themselves that can account for it. Ultimately, the significantly greater equality in the distribution of income and wealth that prevailed in China at the start of the reform period and the vibrant rural small enterprise sector in China appear to be the major factors responsible for the difference, with both acting to ensure the wide distribution of reform benefits. Thus, ironically, the Maoist development strategy China pursued from the mid-1950s to the mid-1970s, despite all its shortcomings, paved the way for a generalized prosperity when a radically different strategy of market-led growth was adopted.

In comparing the second decade of reform in China and Mexico, the strong differences in the popular welfare impact of the reform process continue to stand out. At the same time, however, new problems have appeared to differentiate the consequences of reform in the two countries. In Mexico, the problems have been largely macroeconomic in nature, with an outflow of portfolio investment leading to a collapse of the peso and severe inflation, forcing the government to raise interest rates sharply to restore investor confidence in Mexico's currency and its government's commitment to reform.

The sharp increase in inflation and interest rates gave rise to a severe recession in 1995, with the most disadvantaged members of the population suffering most from the accompanying unemployment and decline in real income. The long run outlook for the reform program remains favorable, but once again the primary burden of the reform has fallen disproportionately on those classes least able to bear it.

China too has experienced macroeconomic problems, especially with inflation, but in the case of China the systemic consequences of reform have been more pronounced. Even as prosperity there spreads, crime, corruption, and social stratification have increased disproportionately, subjecting the very fabric of Chinese society to extraordinary stress. These changes, combined with the ongoing difficulties of the state-owned enterprises, make it increasingly likely that the development path on which China has embarked will lead to the establishment of a system of capitalism—albeit one with welfare state characteristics—rather than the market socialism sought by the leaders of the reform.

If we consider the reform process as a whole, as it has proceeded from its inception in both countries, the disparate distribution of burdens and benefits remains its most striking feature. While the beneficiaries of economic reform have included the vast majority of the Chinese population from the very start of the reform period (1978), reform in Mexico has benefited disproportionately a very small proportion of the population. Indeed, large numbers of the most disadvantaged in Mexico have experienced absolute declines in real income and wealth during the reform period (starting in 1982). The difference in popular experience, moreover, can readily be traced to the much more unequal distribution of income and wealth that existed at the start of the reform period in Mexico. A comparison of the experience of the two countries provides powerful evidence that the initial impact of market reforms intensifies pre-existing inequalities when these inequalities are substantial to start with.

References

Beijing Review (dates indicated).

Business Week (dates indicated).

Cardoso, Eliana, and Ann Helwege. *Latin America's Economy*. Cambridge: M.I.T. Press. 1992.

Comision Nacional de Valores, Banco de Mexico (data reports).

The Economist (dates indicated).

Forbes (dates indicated).

Lardy, Nicholas. "Chinese Foreign Trade." *The China Quarterly* No. 131. September 1992.

Lippit, Victor D. *The Economic Development of China*. Armonk, NY: M. E. Sharpe. 1987.

Lippit, Victor D. *Land Reform and Economic Development in China*. Armonk, NY: M. E. Sharpe. 1974.

Los Angeles Times (dates indicated).

Nolan, Peter. *The Political Economy of Collective Farms*. Boulder, CO: Westview Press. 1988.

Sheahan, John. *Conflict and Change in Mexican Economic Strategy*. Strategy Monograph Series, 34. University of California, San Diego: Center for U.S.-Mexican Studies. 1991.

State Statistical Bureau, People's Republic of China. *China Statistical Yearbook 1990*. Beijing: China Statistical Information and Consultancy Service. 1990.

State Statistical Bureau, People's Republic of China. *China Statistical Yearbook 1995*. Beijing: China Statistical Publishing House. 1995.

United Nations Development Programme. *Human Development Report 1991*. New York: UNDP. 1991.

United Nations Development Programme. *Human Development Report 1995*. New York: UNDP. 1995.

The Wall Street Journal (dates indicated).

World Bank. *World Development Report 1991*. New York: Oxford University Press. 1991.

World Bank. *World Development Report 1992*. New York: Oxford University Press. 1992.

World Bank. *World Development Report 1994*. New York: Oxford University Press. 1994.

Zweig, David. "Rural Industry: Constraining the Leading Growth Sector in China's Economy." In *China's Economic Dilemmas in the 1990s*, edited by U.S. Congress, Joint Economic Committee. Armonk, NY: M. E. Sharpe. 1993.

9

State Intervention, Rents and Malaysian Industrialization

Rajah Rasiah

Industrialization occupies central importance in the development agenda of most economies. Economists have long grappled with the fundamental question of how to govern economic growth. Neoclassical economists point to the invisible hand of the market as the best allocating force to bring about systematic growth. The most developed of such international economic models, the Heckscher-Ohlin-Samuelson theorem views laissez fairism as the ideal means of stimulating growth. Since the allocative role is given to markets, the state is only accorded a subservient role. Even recent attempts to introduce increasing returns to scale in neoclassical analytical tools have not resulted in governments enjoying bigger roles (e.g., Krugman & Helpman, 1989).

Neoclassical economists often cite fast growing market economies to suggest causation between liberalization and economic growth. The fast growing Asian newly industrialized countries (NICs) are often claimed to be fairly liberal economies (Ranis & Fei, 1975; Balassa, 1982; Bhagwati, 1985), while less developed economies, such as India and Turkey, are often cited as highly distorted economies (Little, 1982). Being a fast growing economy (see Table 9.1), Malaysia is usually classified as liberal, with its export-oriented industries considered to be governed by markets (Sheperd, 1980; World Bank, 1993). Central to their arguments about Malaysia's success in achieving fast growth is the international competitiveness of the export-oriented sub-sector (Sheperd, 1980; World Bank, 1993), suggesting that export-orientation is market-orientation. Indeed, Sheperd (1980: 186–7) argued that the rapid growth of export-oriented industries has been achieved through competitiveness not subsidies.

TABLE 9.1. International Annual Growth Rates, 1965–89

	Gross Domestic Product			Industrial Output			Manufactured Exports		
Year	1965–73	1973–80	1980–89	1965–73	1973–80	1980–89	1965–73	1973–80	1980–88
Malaysia	9.7	6.4	5.3	12.4	10.3	6.5	0.9	12.6	11.6
LDCs	6.6	4.8	4.0	8.8	4.9	5.3	11.6	12.8	10.4
OECD	4.5	2.6	2.9	3.7	2.0	2.2	10.6	5.2	4.2
East Asia	7.9	10.0	8.0	12.7	9.2	10.3	17.5	15.5	14.5
World	4.9	3.4	3.1	4.8	2.8	2.5	10.7	6.1	5.2

Source: Compiled and computed from World Bank, *World Development Report,* 1990: 159–65; Malaysia, *Economic Statistics: Time Series,* 1986; Malaysia, *Economic Report, 1990/1991,* 1990; United Nations, *National Accounts Statistics,* various years.

The evidence on the interventionist nature of governments in South Korea, Taiwan and Singapore is now clear (Amsden, 1989; Wade, 1991; Luedde-Neurath, 1986; Evans, 1987).[1] It will be argued here that Malaysia's industrial policies—for both the import-substitution (IS) and the export-oriented (EO) manufacturing sectors—have been distortionary, i.e., relative prices were distorted. Both the IS and EO sectors were distorted, with the former protected and the latter subsidized. While growth in the IS sector was sluggish, this was due to misguided intervention rather than just protection. As for the EO sector, distortions created by the government have enabled transnationals producing for global markets to benefit from host-economy incentives.

This chapter is divided into three main parts: the next part presents foreign ownership trends in the manufacturing sector, while the following part critically examines the main industrial strategies pursued by the government since independence. These arguments are summarized in the concluding section along with recommendations for ironing out flaws in existing industrial strategies.

Foreign Ownership

Since foreign capital contributes a significant proportion of fixed assets, employment and output to the manufacturing sector (see Table 9.2), ownership trends are examined before tackling Malaysia's industrial strategies. Except for leather, wood and basic metals, foreign capital owned more than half the fixed assets in the remaining manufacturing branches in 1968 (see Table 9.3).[2] This gives a rough indication of foreign ownership in Malaysia's manufacturing sector before the 1970s. The modern manufacturing sector which emerged under colonialism began to expand after independence in 1957, with foreign firms setting up assembly, packaging and other finishing operations to benefit from the high tariffs in-

TABLE 9.2. Malaysia: Foreign Share of Manufacturing, 1968–91 (%)

	1968	1970	1972	1974	1979	1985	1987	1991
Establishment	6.0	N.A.	14.9	11.3	9.2	7.6	9.3	16.3
Fixed Asset	52.7	51.0	N.A.	46.6	34.0	18.7	22.3	40.0
Output	48.2	N.A.	52.0	49.8	42.1	34.7	40.0	47.1
Employment	N.A.	N.A.	33.0	33.5	32.7	28.8	33.8	44.2

Note: Foreign share comprises of fully owned, and majority foreign equity in joint ventures of limited companies.

N.A. — not available.

Source: Compiled and computed from Malaysia, *Industrial Surveys* (various years); Lall (1980:69); Anuwar & Wong (1993)

troduced following the Pioneer Industries Ordinance of 1958. This demand-pull effect on foreign capital began to fall gradually as the local market became saturated.

The next wave of foreign relocation came after the Free Trade Zone Act of 1971. This Act mainly attracted export-oriented labor-intensive industries. The electric/electronic, textile/garment and rubber industries were the main beneficiaries of this thrust, with a rise in foreign ownership from 1971. Rapidly growing domestic demand in the early 1970s, especially in the agricultural and transport sectors, also led to the expansion of foreign participation in chemicals, machinery and transport equipment. During 1975–79, foreign ownership declined relatively in almost all manufacturing branches, while foreign manufacturing fixed assets grew slower in this period. Wood was the only manufacturing branch with a clear increase of foreign ownership, but remained relatively insignificant. The exodus of labor-intensive firms from developed economies slowed down in this period,[3] while the state offered few additions to existing incentives.

Relative foreign ownership fell gradually in the 1970s, except for 1971–74, when it was stable. The foreign share in manufacturing fell further until the mid-1980s with some growth in foreign investment in the 1980s,[4] mainly due to the dramatic rise of state-sponsored heavy industry. In the second half of the 1980s, the relative share of foreign capital, especially from Japan and the Asian NICs, rose again following the appreciation of their currencies, growing labor shortages and increasing trade restrictions imposed on their exports by governments from the major markets of the West. Privileges under the generalized system of preferences (GSP) were withdrawn from the East Asian NICs in 1988. Malaysia was an important beneficiary of such investments, explaining the trend rise in foreign ownership of fixed capital in most manufacturing industries.

Import-substitution

As with most newly independent economies, Malaysia adopted an IS strategy with the Pioneer Industries Ordinance of 1958 to promote industrialization. Unlike the experience of more nationalistic regimes such as South Korea and Taiwan, local capital was not given a paramount role as industrial policy during the IS phase did not discriminate against foreign capital. Both foreign and local firms enjoyed similar incentives in the industries promoted. With IS being the main industrialization strategy in the 1958–68 period, foreign firms relocated operations in many industries to benefit from the high tariffs. Indeed, foreign firms dominated ownership of most industries as late as 1968 (see Table 9.3). Both the modern textile and electronics industries emerged during this phase; a textile factory was first established in 1957, while an electronics joint-venture plant was started in 1967. Unions were also discouraged in new industries following the Pioneer Industries Ordinance of 1958 and the Trade Unions Act of 1959.

IS was prescribed by structural economists, such as Lewis (1955) and Myrdal (1957), to spawn and develop local infant industries for eventual international competition upon maturity. However, the Malaysian government also used IS incentives to attract foreign firms but did not see IS as a means towards eventual export promotion.[5] Foreign firms from Singapore and Britain, in particular, relocated "screw-driver" assembly operations to benefit from the high tariffs imposed on finished goods (see Edwards, 1975; Saham, 1980). As raw materials and intermediate goods generally faced low tariffs, IS firms were highly protected in the 1958–68 period. Most foreign firms which expanded operations during this phase also had production operations elsewhere that generally discouraged exports from Malaysia. Besides, pioneer status incentives were only offered to IS firms during this decade. Thus, when the small domestic market became saturated by the mid-1960s, there was little demand-pull to stimulate further expansion. Manufacturing's contribution to the gross domestic product (GDP) therefore stagnated at 9 percent between 1960 and 1965 (World Bank, 1980).

Although the high protection reduced competition in the IS phase, misguided IS, rather than merely the lack of competition, mainly accounted for the eventual stagnation in manufacturing growth during the IS phase. If the state in South Korea offered IS rents to local capital in return for meeting stringent performance standards (Amsden, 1989; Chang, 1991), the Malaysian state offered monopoly rents to foreign firms without imposing performance conditions, i.e., the carrots were given without the stick.[6] The state simulated competition to press for technical change and efficiency improvements in South Korea as new firms could hardly be expected to compete with foreign transnationals on their own. Hence, the South Korean government succeeded in creating dynamic comparative advantage by initially encouraging IS as a step toward export-orientation.

TABLE 9.3. Malaysia: Foreign Share of Fixed Assets in Manufacturing Branches, 1968-90 (%)

Branch/Year	68	69	70	71	72	73	74	75	76	77	78	79	80	81	82	83	84	85	86	87	88	89	90
Food	74	73	71	72	69	62	56	55	56	48	45	39	32	31	29	28	27	25	26	26	28	30	30
Beverage/tobacco	93	91	89	86	82	81	81	79	78	77	77	76	76	66	66	67	67	67	70	69	70	69	62
Textile/garment	52	41	39	48	53	66	65	63	62	60	58	56	54	54	52	49	48	48	53	54	53	59	61
Leather[a]	17	56	56	54	54	53	51	48	46	45	44	45	48	54	56	57	56	54	48	45	51	58	59
Wood	15	8	11	12	13	11	9	8	10	12	13	14	13	14	14	12	10	9	8	9	15	15	19
Furniture/fixture	50	73	71	69	66	65	63	61	56	48	42	38	31	19	28	22	19	19	16	14	25	36	45
Paper, printing & publishing	N.A.	N.A.	N.A.	N.A.	24	21	18	16	15	13	12	10	10	9	11	10	19	20	19	20	21	10	14
Chemical	53	59	61	66	66	69	65	63	61	59	54	56	53	51	48	44	42	16	21	19	21	23	24
Rubber	14	9	14	16	28	36	44	42	46	46	45	44	46	34	36	65	38	42	41	45	56	56	55
Petroleum/coal	78	75	77	77	79	78	81	79	79	78	79	80	78	66	65	36	43	37	37	40	41	44	44
Plastic	N.A.	N.A.	N.A.	N.A.	N.A.	N.A.	N.A.	N.A.	N.A.	N.A.	N.A.	N.A.	12	12	12	14	12	13	15	15	18	27	27
Non -metal mineral	57	59	60	63	61	56	58	52	46	42	36	24	19	36	37	36	29	32	31	33	33	34	33
Basic metal	49	45	45	46	44	43	43	42	41	42	39	36	35	29	28	32	31	32	33	34	34	23	17
Fabricated metal	66	76	69	69	72	71	69	59	45	42	39	36	26	30	27	27	24	23	23	25	26	28	30
Machinery	74	66	58	57	59	61	54	51	51	51	48	45	42	49	45	36	34	35	39	43	48	50	53
Electric and electronics	70	69	67	74	82	83	83	84	85	82	82	81	80	79	76	74	77	73	77	77	81	86	89
Transport equipment	N.A.	N.A.	58	57	62	61	56	51	49	49	48	42	32	27	22	11	18	15	21	22	22	25	25
Other	60	25	67	72	75	72	71	69	66	62	58	56	57	64	63	60	55	53	58	62	63	62	69
Total	61	61	59	57	57	57	56	52	50	47	46	50	39	36	38	36	37	33	34	36	39	40	42

Note: 1971-79 figures have been estimated from projects approved by MIDA.
[a] - excludes rubber footwear.
N.A. - not available.
Source: Computed from unpublished MIDA data.

The Malaysian state did not similarly use IS, progressively which could have been due to a weak sense of economic nationalism due to the state's ethno-populist priorities.[7]

Following the shift to export-orientation after 1968, import-substitution gradually lost significance in terms of output and employment generation, although it continued to co-exist with the former. IS also declined in significance as several tariffs gradually fell, thereby reducing the distortionary rents enjoyed by these industries. For example, between 1969 and 1987, the effective rate of protection (ERP) fell from 160 percent to 16 percent for basic industrial chemicals, from 125 percent to –26 percent for tobacco, from 300 percent to 8 percent for fertilizers and insecticides, and from 35 to one percent for structural metal products, according to unpublished data from C. B. Edwards. While EO firms continued to enjoy generous incentives, tariff protection for most IS firms gradually declined. Some IS industries, earmarked for strategic promotion by the government, experienced increases in their ERP; e.g., the ERP for basic iron and steel rose from 28 percent in 1969 to 131 percent in 1987.

From 1981, the government intervened strongly to promote heavy industries, through the Heavy Industries Corporation of Malaysia (HICOM). This was not merely second-order import-substitution as one key feature of the strategy involved direct government participation in developing heavy industry. The earlier IS concentrated merely on attracting import-substituting investment irrespective of control, structural content and scale, while the early 1980s saw the introduction of state sponsored and controlled investment in heavy industry. These heavy industries enjoyed top priority from the government and were not integrated with either the earlier IS sector or the EO sector. Hence, there was no programmatic sequencing typical of other second rounds of import-substitution.

In addition to protection, the government also offered subsidized capital, imposed stringent controls on competitors in the domestic market and introduced other promotional tools to spawn the manufacture of cement (Kedah Cement and Perak Hanjoong), steel (Perwaja Steel) and motorcars (Proton). The government's objectives, *inter alia,* included the development of a strong capital goods sector and linkages with the domestic economy, especially *Bumiputera* [8] enterprises. These industries remain strongly subsidized and protected. Indeed, by controlling Proton's purchases, the government has been gradually requiring domestication of supply and *Bumiputera* participation involving an "umbrella" approach to vendor development. Despite collaboration with Japanese capital, ownership in these industries has been dominated by the government. In this way, by 1993, Proton had achieved domestic sourcing of 80 percent of car components, and had forced firms supplying Proton to raise *Bumiputera* equity participation. Despite its IS origins, the automobile industry has been increasingly geared towards gradual export-orientation. For the time being at least, the monopoly rents enjoyed in the domestic market due to high tariffs are supposedly meant to subsidize exports. The state also revamped the management of Perwaja Steel and Proton following losses in the early years, suggesting the deployment of some elements of discipline. While elements of IS for EO are apparent in these heavy industries, it is unclear if such rents will be gradually withdrawn with rising sales volumes and competitiveness.

Except for beverages and tobacco, "inward looking" industries have gradually become increasingly locally owned (see Tables 9.3 and 9.4). It also appears that EO industries generally involve higher levels of investment, employment and output growth than inward-oriented industries (see Table 9.5). This is also reflected in the EO industries' rising contribution to overall manufacturing. However, the government-dominated heavy industries may have experienced great productivity improvements in the 1985–90 period. Output/capital and output/labor ratios of non-metal mineral products, iron and steel, and transport equipment—which are dominated by government ventures—improved in this period; however, data on these aggregated industries include privately owned enterprises and hence should be treated accordingly. Also, their improved financial performance may have been partly due to the government writing off debts on fixed assets as well as accelerated depreciation allowances, as reflected by the decline in capital-intensities in iron and steel, as well as transport equipment (see Table 9.6). Rapidly expanding demand—with the expansion of EO industries and government-sponsored heavy industries—is likely to have improved the performance of "inward looking" industries. Demand generated by input requirements, employee incomes and service utilization is likely to have strengthened "inward looking" firms.

Although nominal tariffs on several IS industries were gradually reduced in the 1980s, locally dominated industries were generally still inward looking. Of the 12 industries shown in Table 9.4, more than half the output of seven was for the domestic economy. Only five were outward-oriented, of which electric/electronics and textiles/garments were the most export-oriented. IS industries showed productivity improvements in the 1980s, especially in the 1985–90 period. Falling levels of protection appear not to have negatively affected the performance of IS industries, which could be a consequence of growing domestic demand stimulated by the manufacturing sector and the economy generally. Given the natural protection offered by proximity, resource-based industries do not usually require considerable protection to secure competitiveness. As Malaysia is rich in timber, rubber, palm oil, petroleum and tin ore, it is generally economic to support downstream activities when demand reaches sufficient levels. Minimum efficiency scales are also significantly smaller in light and primary heavy industries, which are different from second-order heavy industries. Transport equipment as well as iron and steel require significantly larger minimum efficiency scales and greater technological capacity. Of the three industries with heavy government involvement, cement has required less protection as a consequence of rapidly rising construction demand. The replacement of Proton's and Perwaja Steel's original managements in the late 1980s were the most dramatic examples of the stick being applied to force efficiency improvements in government-supported industries.

Export Orientation

The limited success of import substitution forced the switch to export-orientation, beginning symbolically with the Investment Incentives Act in 1968. The promotional efforts of the World Bank, United Nations Industrial Development Organization (UNIDO) and other international agencies, and the success of other East Asian export processing zones were important external factors influencing the switch. Meanwhile, local capital began to grow, especially in IS industries, gradually reducing foreign ownership proportionately. The government has opened free trade zones (FTZs)[9] and licensed manufacturing warehouses (LMWs)[10] since 1972 to ensure better security, coordination and control for export processing activities. Initially, these export platforms mainly attracted electronics and textile firms. Tax incentives shifted from IS to EO firms. Lucrative incentives—such as pioneer status and investment tax credit for periods of between 5 to 10 years—became the main carrots for attracting EO firms. Whenever pioneer status expired, firms were easily given investment tax credits for additional periods of five years. Other firms enjoyed accelerated depreciation allowances. When these expired, some firms opened new plants to enjoy a new round of incentives (see Rasiah, 1993b). In addition, many foreign firms have been allowed to retain total ownership. Hence, though IS industries continued to enjoy high tariffs, financial incentives shifted to EO firms.

As the aggregate data in Table 9.4 show, EO industries have enjoyed various other government subsidies. Although export incentives that offer double deduction benefits on corporate income tax are given to all exporting firms, given the scale of their exports, the prime beneficiaries have been EO industries. Furthermore, EO firms also tend to most utilize the double deduction benefits given for training, as well as for research and development (R&D). This is primarily because of rapid changes in product and process technologies in international markets, and the minimum efficiency scale needed to engage in state of the art training, as well as process and design research and development. Apart from resource-based industries (e.g., wood and rubber) and government controlled car, steel and cement production, foreign firms were the other major beneficiaries of training and R&D incentives. Hence, apart from a few IS industries (especially the government-dominated heavy industries, i.e., steel, cars and cement), EO firms have gradually become more subsidized than IS firms.

TABLE 9.4. Malaysia: Manufacturing Protection and Subsidies

			Incentives (1991)[e]				
	ERP (1987)[d] %	X_i/Y_i (1990) %	Projects Approved with Special Export Incentives	Training	R&D	PS/ITA	Government ownership
Food		21.7	57.5	W	W	M	N
Beverage & tobacco	13[a]	5.1	31.3	W	W	W	N
Textiles & garments	10	85.7	74.2	M	W	S	N
Wood	233	25.4	71.1	M	M	M	N
Chemicals	57	19.6	45.4	M	M	M	N
Rubber	20	9.4	95.5	M	M	S	N
Non-metal mineral	86	24.6	46.6	M	M	M	Y
Iron & steel	131[b]	15.0	N.A	S	M	W	Y
Metal	22[c]	60.4	54.9	W	M	M	N
Machinery	18	81.9	59.6	M	M	M	N
Electric/electronics	–5	94.0	88.5	S	M	S	N
Transport equipment	230	41.9	22.9	S	M	W	Y

[a] - includes food, beverage and tobacco; [b] - of basic industries only (ERP of primary iron and steel was 447%); [c] - of wire and wire products; [d] - from Edwards data bank; [e] - based on interviews with MIDA officials; X_i - export of industry i; Y_i - gross output of industry i; W - weak, M - moderate, S - strong, N - no, Y - yes; PS - pioneer status, ITA - investment tax allowance; N.A. - not available.

Source: Compiled from MIDA (unpublished data); C. B. Edwards, personal communication, 1991; Malaysia, *Industrial Survey*, various years; Malaysia, *External Trade Statistics*, various years.

It is little wonder then that EO industries have expanded rapidly since the early 1970s. The electric/electronics sub-sector has become the most important manufacturing industry in terms of fixed assets, employment, output and exports (see Table 9.5). However, the average capital-intensities of the electric/electronics and textile/garment industries have fallen since 1985 and 1973 respectively, probably due to East Asian investments in consumer electronics since the yen appreciation as well as relatively little new investment from the mid-1970s until the 1980s in textile firms and stronger expansion in the more labor-intensive garment industry after 1985 (see Rasiah, 1993b). The electric/electronics industry experienced a decline in average capital-intensity after 1985 following strong expansion in more labor-intensive consumer and industrial electronics (see Rasiah, 1993). Initial expansion in EO industries tended to undermine output-capital ratios, which fell sharply in the 1968–73 period despite falls in capital-labor ratios, a general tendency in that period (see Table 9.6). Falling capital-intensities were largely due to the growth of export-oriented labor-intensive foreign firms from the early 1970s. It was only from 1979, and especially after 1985, that labor productivity and capital productivity began to improve. However, long-term productivities generally declined in EO industries. Both output-capital and output-labor ratios in EO industries fell over the longer 1968–90 period, the fall being very significant in the foreign-dominated electric/electronics industry. As industry-level growth rates aggregate both old and new firms, the falling average productivities recorded do not necessarily imply declining productivities for all firms.

Two plausible reasons can, however, be offered here.[11] The first, which is likely to have been the most important, is the many lumpy fixed investments by both existing and new firms. Hence, aggregate data tends to exaggerate factor inputs (the denominator) in productivity computations. Productivity measures—being spread over longer periods regardless of the lumpiness of investments in fixed assets—tended to show falling output-labor and output-capital ratios. Secondly, as tax holidays encourage transnationals to inflate exports and underestimate imports, as means to transfer profits to low tax and no-tax zones, such practices may raise productivity, especially during the early years of operation of EO industries. This—along with subsidies offered in the form of tax exemptions and accelerated depreciation allowances—distorted prices sufficiently to attract investment, i.e., discount rates significantly exceeded interest rates to attract lumpy investments. This supports Schumpeter's (1987) assertion that monopoly rents or "entrepreneurial profits" are essential to attract investments into risky, lumpy and innovation-related investments. Using neoclassical analytical tools, Lucas (1988), Romer (1986) and Krugman & Helpman (1989) acknowledge this insight in the context of increasing returns, where discount rates exceed interest rates.[12]

Similarly, the operations of foreign transnationals producing for the external market stimulated export expansion. EO industries easily dominated exports, with the electric/electronic and textile/garment industries together contributing more than 63 percent of total manufactured exports (see Table 9.7). EO industries also greatly improved their trade balances. However, with the exception of resource-based industries, EO industries had higher import penetration with little trend declines, reflecting fairly weak backward pecuniary linkages.[13] With incentives more tied to EO industries, the entire manufacturing sector gradually experienced greater export-orientation.

Since the introduction of the Industrial Master Plan, 1986–1995 (IMP), and especially from 1988, efforts to deepen domestic participation and localization have taken new dimensions. As shown in Table 9.4, incentives for exports, training, as well as research and development have been offered (see also Malaysia, 1992). Pioneer status and investment tax allowances are generously offered to "strategic firms," and since 1991, this has included firms with at least 30 percent domestic sourcing of inputs. While the government merely offered incentives to EO investments to firms meeting employment, investment and locational targets until the mid-1980s, it

TABLE 9.5. Malaysia: Growth and Composition of Manufacturing Industries, 1968–90

	Average Annual Growth (percentages)					Composition (percentages) #				
Years	68–73	73–79	79–85	85–90	68–90	1968	1973	1979	1985	1990
Output										
Food	5.45	5.41	5.45	6.62	5.70	18.91	16.61	27.68	26.17	16.71
Beverage & tobacco	8.70	8.15	–0.26	2.41	4.51	7.66	5.11	3.67	3.72	1.97
Textile & garment	20.46	10.95	4.73	12.79	11.70	2.76	8.53	6.11	4.20	5.46
Wood	14.70	3.66	–4.53	13.11	5.79	6.78	10.50	7.93	4.68	5.51
Chemical	3.20	8.86	2.81	7.89	5.67	5.69	5.23	4.72	9.59	6.94
Rubber	0.42	1.35	4.22	24.99	6.88	18.41	14.63	9.58	6.01	5.51
Non-metal mineral	4.43	8.18	3.60	7.40	5.88	3.20	3.11	2.96	3.95	3.27
Iron & steel	19.82	5.14	6.86	9.05	9.69	1.04	3.14	2.02	3.38	4.14
Metals	14.27	1.58	9.78	4.68	7.30	25.29	19.71	10.78	5.51	3.08
Machinery	14.92	1.98	8.97	6.56	7.77	1.71	2.62	2.44	1.58	4.66
Electric/ electronics	7.99	15.83	7.99	16.37	14.08	1.56	5.24	12.59	12.92	25.37
Transport equipment	10.95	10.20	9.04	14.99	11.12	2.23	2.61	2.71	3.15	4.80
Employment										
Food	27.66	5.49	3.01	4.11	9.12	11.11	14.66	13.61	14.28	10.42
Beverage & tobacco	12.13	–0.14	–2.12	–0.92	1.78	6.67	4.60	3.07	2.37	1.35
Textile & garment	44.42	8.19	1.50	11.97	14.43	5.35	13.08	14.14	13.58	14.26
Wood	16.35	3.83	1.22	10.75	7.38	19.09	15.84	13.37	12.63	12.56
Chemical	19.38	6.05	2.71	6.56	8.11	4.04	3.81	3.65	3.77	3.09
Rubber	5.24	3.56	–1.20	16.13	5.32	19.09	9.59	7.97	6.51	8.21
Non-metal mineral	12.81	6.33	5.67	–6.45	4.50	14.04	9.98	9.72	11.88	5.08
Iron & steel	16.41	4.34	4.80	5.38	7.34	2.93	2.44	2.12	2.47	1.91
Metals	20.44	1.31	2.43	10.66	7.83	7.37	7.27	5.30	5.37	5.32
Machinery	25.34	0.62	–0.61	15.28	8.72	4.34	5.23	3.65	3.09	3.76
Electric/ electronics	65.99	19.31	1.96	21.64	23.76	2.02	9.90	19.25	19.00	30.19
Transport equipment	19.70	9.71	4.20	5.89	9.46	3.54	3.38	3.97	4.47	3.55
Fixed Assets										
Food	19.52	12.46	11.35	2.40	11.32	14.27	18.74	20.71	13.00	9.90
Beverage & tobacco	1.53	12.32	13.84	–4.09	6.29	6.80	3.95	4.33	3.11	1.70

(continues)

TABLE 9.5 *(continued)*

	Average Annual Growth (percentages)					Composition (percentages) #				
Years	68–73	73–79	79–85	85–90	68–90	1968	1973	1979	1985	1990
Textile & garment	38.79	13.61	−1.35	12.55	14.17	3.60	9.98	11.73	3.56	4.35
Wood	28.16	6.18	8.58	8.00	11.93	6.43	11.97	9.37	5.06	5.03
Chemical	3.13	5.14	50.32	−1.42	13.72	12.14	7.63	5.63	21.39	13.46
Rubber	58.65	10.87	11.17	19.72	22.49	1.16	6.28	6.38	3.97	6.60
Non-metal mineral	7.60	11.03	25.71	4.87	12.57	10.51	8.16	8.36	10.86	9.32
Iron & steel	61.05	−2.05	50.40	0.73	24.06	0.89	5.20	2.51	9.57	6.71
Metals	−1.40	7.90	18.26	12.68	9.46	9.71	4.87	4.21	3.79	4.65
Machinery	27.64	1.80	13.76	28.40	16.45	1.87	3.41	2.07	1.48	3.49
Electric/ electronics	33.31	21.83	19.97	24.58	24.46	2.52	4.71	8.42	8.27	16.77
Transport equipment	3.52	24.97	20.47	−2.46	12.05	4.69	2.48	5.16	5.19	3.10

Note: Includes primary processing; excludes leather, furniture & fixtures, paper, printing, publishing, plastics, petroleum & coal products and other manufactures; #—composition figures are for all manufacturing; growth rates for capital and output computed using 1978 price data.

Source: Computed from Malaysia, *Industrial Surveys*, various years.

has assumed a more pro-active stance since the second half of the 1980s. Incentives have been increasingly tied to technological deepening and to exports, and since 1991, also for increasing domestic sourcing of inputs. This strategy has, *inter alia,* encouraged EO transnationals, especially Japanese firms, to relocate their suppliers, including their own subsidiaries, in Malaysia (see Rasiah, 1993). The policy shift also strengthens backward linkages within the economy. The 1990s have also seen a shift in the provision of financial incentives. For example, the government has reduced tax benefits for export-oriented firms other than strategic industries from 100 percent to 70 percent.

Especially after 1986, locally-dominated inward-looking industries also appear to have experienced faster growth, due to a combination of government promotion and growing domestic demand. Even government dominated industries have shown strong growth since the late 1980s. Despite continuing to be primarily inward looking, some IS industries have gradually become outward-oriented. IS industries not set up by the government are gradually losing tariff protection. Such protection is expected to fall further with the development of the Association of Southeast Asian Nations (ASEAN) Free Trade Area (AFTA) from 1993; tariffs for fast track products are expected to fall to 0–5 percent by 2000–2003. Since AFTA aims to liberalize the ASEAN economies to encourage intra-ASEAN trade, several

TABLE 9.6. Malaysia: Capital-intensity and Productivities in Manufacturing, 1968–90

	Average Annual Growth Rates (percentages)				
	68–73	73–79	79–85	85–90	68–90
Ki/Li					
Food	–6.4	6.6	8.1	–1.6	2.0
Beverage & tobacco	–9.5	12.5	16.3	–3.2	4.4
Textile & garment	–3.9	5.0	–2.8	0.5	–0.2
Wood	10.2	2.3	7.3	–2.5	4.2
Chemical	–13.6	–0.9	46.4	–7.5	5.2
Rubber	50.8	7.1	12.5	3.1	16.3
Non-metal mineral	–4.6	4.4	19.0	12.1	7.7
Iron & steel	38.4	6.1	43.5	–4.4	15.6
Metals	–18.1	6.5	15.5	1.8	1.5
Machinery	1.8	1.2	14.5	11.4	7.1
Electric/electronics	–19.7	2.1	17.7	2.4	0.6
Transport equipment	–13.5	13.9	15.6	–7.9	2.4
Manufacturing	–6.0	3.2	18.2	3.1	3.9
Oi/Ki					
Food	–11.7	–6.3	–5.3	4.1	–5.1
Beverage & tobacco	7.1	–4.4	–12.1	6.8	–1.7
Textile & garment	–13.2	–2.3	6.2	0.2	–2.2
Wood	–10.5	–2.4	–12.1	4.7	–5.5
Chemical	0.1	3.5	–31.6	9.5	–7.1
Rubber	–36.7	–8.6	–6.3	4.4	–12.7
Non-metal mineral	–3.0	–2.6	–17.6	2.4	–5.9
Iron & steel	–25.6	7.3	–29.0	8.3	–11.6
Metals	15.9	–5.9	–7.2	–7.1	–2.0
Machinery	–10.0	0.2	–4.2	–17.0	–7.5
Electric/electronics	–19.0	–4.9	–10.0	1.4	–8.3
Transport equipment	7.2	–11.8	–9.5	17.9	–0.8
Manufacturing	–6.7	–3.5	–13.5	6.6	–4.7
Oi/Li					
Food	–17.4	–0.1	2.4	2.4	–3.1
Beverage & tobacco	–3.0	7.5	2.3	3.4	2.7
Textile & garment	–16.6	2.6	3.2	0.7	–2.4
Wood	–1.4	–0.2	–5.7	2.1	–1.5
Chemical	–13.6	2.7	0.1	1.3	–2.3
Rubber	–4.6	–2.1	5.5	7.6	1.5
Non-metal mineral	–7.4	1.7	–2.0	14.8	1.3
Iron & steel	2.9	0.8	–2.0	3.5	2.2
Metals	5.1	0.3	7.2	–5.4	–0.5
Machinery	–8.3	1.4	9.6	–7.6	–0.9
Electric/electronics	–34.9	–2.9	5.9	3.9	–7.8
Transport equipment	–7.3	0.4	4.6	8.6	1.5
Manufacturing	–10.6	–0.6	2.8	8.4	–0.9

Note: Growth rates for capital and output computed using 1978 prices data; Ki—fixed assets of industry i; Li—employment of industry i; Oi—output of industry i.

Source: Computed from Malaysia, *Industrial Surveys*, various years.

TABLE 9.7. Malaysia: Manufacturing Trade Indicators, 1968–90

	1968	1973	1979	1985	1990	1968	1973	1979	1985	1990
	(Xi–Mi) / (Xi+Mi)					Mi / (Yi+Mi–Xi)				
Food	–0.562	–0.358	–0.274	–0.308	–0.163	0.623	0.510	0.227	0.234	0.277
Beverage & tobacco	–0.752	–0.106	0.150	–0.800	–0.509	0.221	0.188	0.170	0.120	0.141
Textile & garment	–0.897	–0.482	–0.058	0.106	0.159	0.789	0.416	0.410	0.635	0.813
Wood	0.778	0.935	0.913	0.874	0.932	0.025	0.011	0.010	0.014	0.012
Chemical	–0.736	–0.628	–0.710	–0.721	–0.675	0.030	0.023	0.017	0.006	0.009
Rubber	–0.149	0.230	0.470	0.113	0.342	0.429	0.225	0.491	0.586	0.457
Non-metal mineral	–0.665	–0.507	–0.335	–0.518	–0.038	0.129	0.094	0.068	0.052	0.093
Iron & steel	–0.910	–0.780	–0.759	–0.826	–0.736	0.616	0.259	0.306	0.251	0.198
Metals	0.707	0.627	0.570	0.252	–0.307	0.569	0.357	0.802	0.669	0.890
Machinery	–0.824	–0.778	–0.706	–0.746	–0.573	0.820	0.640	0.685	0.948	0.806
Electric/ electronics	–0.877	–0.723	–0.031	–0.037	0.100	0.873	0.647	0.669	0.987	0.902
Transport equipment	–0.808	–0.813	–0.652	–0.624	–0.595	0.869	0.822	0.810	0.839	0.834
	Xi / Yi									
Food	0.316	0.329	0.143	0.139	0.216					
Beverage & tobacco	0.039	0.157	0.217	0.015	0.051					
Textile & garment	0.170	0.199	0.382	0.683	0.857					
Wood	0.170	0.257	0.176	0.170	0.254					
Chemical	0.179	0.275	0.235	0.098	0.196					
Rubber	0.017	0.032	0.055	0.041	0.094					
Non-metal mineral	0.088	0.096	0.114	0.084	0.246					
Iron & steel	0.167	0.167	0.240	0.084	0.150					
Metals	0.889	0.612	0.919	0.730	0.604					
Machinery	0.506	0.408	0.488	0.917	0.819					
Electric/ electronics	0.160	0.110	0.728	0.990	0.940					
Transport equipment	0.393	0.287	0.398	0.394	0.419					
	Xi / SXi					Mi / SMi				
Food	0.175	0.196	0.123	0.127	0.081	0.308	0.225	0.152	0.134	0.076
Beverage & tobacco	0.009	0.029	0.025	0.002	0.002	0.030	0.019	0.013	0.010	0.005
Textile & garment	0.014	0.061	0.072	0.100	0.105	0.124	0.095	0.057	0.045	0.052

(continued)

TABLE 9.7. *(continued)*

	1968	1973	1979	1985	1990	1968	1973	1979	1985	1990
			Xi / SXi					Mi / SMi		
Wood	0.034	0.097	0.043	0.028	0.031	0.002	0.002	0.001	0.001	0.001
Chemical	0.030	0.052	0.034	0.033	0.031	0.097	0.122	0.143	0.113	0.106
Rubber	0.009	0.017	0.016	0.009	0.012	0.006	0.006	0.004	0.004	0.004
Non-metal mineral	0.008	0.011	0.010	0.011	0.018	0.020	0.018	0.015	0.020	0.013
Iron & steel	0.005	0.019	0.015	0.010	0.014	0.054	0.083	0.078	0.058	0.062
Metals	0.658	0.433	0.307	0.140	0.042	0.056	0.054	0.059	0.047	0.053
Machinery	0.025	0.038	0.037	0.051	0.086	0.130	0.166	0.152	0.194	0.213
Electric/ electronics	0.007	0.021	0.284	0.446	0.534	0.055	0.070	0.214	0.269	0.296
Transport equipment	0.026	0.027	0.033	0.043	0.045	0.119	0.141	0.112	0.105	0.120

Note: Manufacturing trade includes simple processing; Xi - exports of industry i; Mi - imports of industry i; Yi - output of industry i.

Source: Computed from Malaysia, *Industrial Surveys*, various years; Malaysia, *External Trade Statistics*, various years.

quantitative and non-quantitative restrictions may also go by the year 2008, which may undermine Malaysia's relatively non-competitive industries and enhance the position of her competitive industries vis-à-vis her ASEAN neighbors (see Rasiah, 1994).

Concluding Remarks

Growth in Malaysia's manufacturing sector has been guided by two major trade strategies, namely import-substitution and export-orientation. The former has been constrained by the small domestic market, while the latter has enjoyed access to global markets. Exports expanded easily as foreign transnationals already enjoyed considerable global market shares prior to their relocation in Malaysia. Electric/electronics and textiles/garments, the two most export-oriented industries in Malaysia, are also dominated by foreign ownership.

IS and EO industries have both faced distorted relative prices due to protection and subsidies respectively. IS rents attracted investments, especially from abroad, until the near saturation of the domestic market by the mid-1960s. Later, government-sponsored heavy industries expanded quickly from the late 1980s. Although it is difficult to establish the efficiency of government-owned heavy industries (as large debts incurred by them were written off), they did expand considerably to dominate the domestic market. EO rents largely attracted foreign transnationals engaged in the processing of imported inputs for re-export. The sheer size of global markets facilitated rapid expansion so that EO industries gradually became leading generators of employment, output and exports in the manufacturing sector. A combination of rents—in the form of financial (especially tax) incentives, low wages, good infrastructure, political stability and government collaboration—has attracted risky, lumpy investments in export processing, and even in some design activities, since the 1980s.

Like import substitution, export orientation has also involved distorting relative prices. Initially driven primarily by employment generation considerations, IS and EO involved relatively little pro-active participation by the government until the 1980s. Given the government's relatively weak bargaining power vis-à-vis foreign capital and limited strategic economic vision from the late 1950s until the early 1980s, the government hardly supported the expansion of domestic productive capacity. Apart from schooling and infrastructure, the government invested little in the development of industry skills, research and development as well as support for local manufacturing firms.

From the mid-1980s, with the introduction of the IMP, the government assumed a more progressively interventionist stance in some regards, while withdrawing from other areas in line with its commitment to economic liberalization, giving the overall impression of incoherent industrial policy. On the positive side, rents were increasingly tied to the development of domestic production capacity,[14] rather than simply to investment and employment generation, as was the situation before the mid-1980s. Human capital, research and development, linkages, exports and technologically strategic manufactures have all become privileged, e.g., enjoying tax incentives. The period since the mid-1980s has also involved new distortions on the part of the government to use its improved bargaining position vis-à-vis foreign capital to encourage technological deepening.

Despite the government's pro-active role, existing industrial strategy in Malaysia also has some flaws. In at least three areas, changes will be necessary to further strengthen the manufacturing sector. First, weak links between IS and EO industries need serious attention. Enforcement of the 30 percent domestic sourcing condition does not sufficiently address this problem. Large numbers of foreign suppliers have flocked to Malaysia, especially since 1986, securing supply contracts which local firms may have otherwise have hoped for (see Rasiah, 1993). While foreign parts suppliers that use technologies well beyond existing local technological capacities (e.g., fabricated wafers and lead frames) are both desirable and unavoidable, studies show that several foreign firms are actually penetrating markets previously supplied by local firms (see Rasiah, 1990; 1993). This issue may have become more serious with the implementation of the common effective preferential tariff (CEPT) scheme from 1993, which aims to reduce trade barriers among ASEAN economies. To prevent further undermining of promising ASEAN enterprises, efforts should be taken to shelter them against unfair competition, especially in the initial phase.

Second, there needs to be a rigorous assessment of the incentives offered to IS and EO firms to eliminate unnecessary carrots offered to firms so that only efficiency-enhancing, linkage-spawning and technologically-strategic firms are supported. Even for these firms, rents should be gradually withdrawn to force them to become competitive internationally. To achieve productive efficiency, rents that do not generate improvements in competitiveness should be terminated. In this regard, there needs to be greater dissemination of performance data on the state-controlled heavy industries so that assessments can be made on their trend performances. While the stick should be applied to non-performing firms, the choice of products and industries for promotion should not only be limited to profitable ones as complementary effects may require non-profitable industries and products essential for the continued growth of the profitable ones. Hence, the issue of complementary influences in industrial structural change is crucial.

Finally, there needs to be greater emphasis on process and product research and development. Rents should be tied to such aspects of technological deepening. Indeed, the manufacturing sector has reached a level where further expansion strongly depends on moving on to higher technological niches greatly dependent on higher investments in research and development. Only with more emphasis on innovation can manufacturing firms move on from being mere assemblers and subcontractors to becoming original equipment manufacturers. Although initiatives are being taken to increase innovative research, there is no clear strategy to implement them. To minimize costs and maximize gains, an extended version of transaction cost considerations should govern the development of institutional networks to support technology development and dissemination in industries (Rasiah, 1995). From the original transaction cost argument expounded by Coase (1937) and later expanded by Williamson (1985), where markets generally influence the establishment of large firms and institutions, the extended version also emphasizes cooperation as an additional coordination mechanism. To strengthen participation and long-term efficiency gains, collaborative networks between firms and these institutions should be encouraged (see Wilkinson & You, 1992; Rasiah, 1993).

While visible governance appears to have been important for Malaysia's industrial growth, this should not be interpreted to imply a total rejection of the market. The market has performed the useful role of generating resources and signaling current pecuniary influences. Moreover, like the market, government intervention also involves costs. Hence, a combination of visible and invisible governance should guide future industrial policy in Malaysia.

Notes

1. See Rasiah (1995) for a theoretical critique of neoclassical arguments on growth.

2. Ownership data prior to 1968 are not available.

3. I do not think that the Industrial Coordination Act of 1975 was a major cause of the relative fall in foreign manufacturing investment. MIDA (1988) promotional brochures stipulated *Bumiputera* equity participation only for firms with paid-up capital beyond a certain level selling more than 20 percent in the local market.

4. Note that this figure is higher than that shown in Table 9.2. While the figures in Table 9.3 have been calculated from fully owned and controlled fixed assets (including those with less than 50 percent foreign equity) according to MIDA surveys, the figures in Table 9.2 are compiled from surveys conducted by the Statistics Department, presented in its annual *Industrial Survey.*

5. See Krugman (1980; 1989) for an analytical account using neoclassical tools to demonstrate gains from IS as a strategy for promoting exports.

6. See Amsden (1989) for an excellent account of the South Korean experience.

7. See Jomo (1986) for a class account of the political economy of the ethnic redistribution-oriented New Economic Policy (NEP) introduced in 1971.

8. *Bumiputera,* literally translated, means son of the soil, and generally refers to the indigenous peoples of Malaysia.

9. FTZs lie outside the principal customs area (PCA); thus, goods imported to and exported from FTZs are not liable for customs duty. Goods imported from and exported to the PCA are liable for customs duty unless exemptions have been granted by the Treasury (Malaysia, 1988: 55). Generally, firms producing not less than 80 percent for export can apply to locate in FTZs. Until the 1990s, FTZ firms were expected to import most of their inputs.

10. LMWs were introduced to encourage spatial dispersal of factories producing not less than 80 percent for export. LMW status is granted to firms sited in places where the location of FTZs is neither practical nor desirable (Malaysia, 1988: 56). Until the 1990s, LMW firms were also expected to import most of their inputs.

11. It might also be noted that the data compiled by the authorities concerned are confusing; e.g., there are data discrepancies in the MIDA data bank, UNIDO's *Industrial Statistics Yearbook,* the United Nations' *Yearbook of International Trade Statistics* and the Statistics Department of Malaysia. Although growth rates computed from these sources were slightly different, the trends were generally similar. We used data from the Statistics Department, which is the cited source for the two international sources.

12. As Scherer (1992) has noted, apart from presenting more elegant quantitative models, neoclassical analysis has not significantly extended past arguments.

13. An analysis of linkage coefficients to support this point was not undertaken as the latest available Malaysian input-output tables are for 1983.

14. This is in line with Kalecki's (1976) prescription for developing economies.

References

Amsden, A. *Asia's Next Giant: South Korea and Late Industrialization.* New York: Oxford University Press. 1989.

Anuwar Ali, & P. K. Wong. "Direct Foreign Investment in the Manufacturing Sector." In *Industrialising Malaysia: Policy, Performance, Prospects,* edited by Jomo K. S. London: Routledge. 1993.

Balassa, B. *Development Strategies in Semi-Industrial Economies.* Baltimore: Johns Hopkins University Press. 1982.

Bhagwati, J. "Foreign Trade Regimes." In *Dependence and Interdependence,* edited by J. Bhagwati. Oxford: Basil Blackwell. 1985.

Chang, H. J. *The Political Economy of Industrial Policy.* Basingstoke: Macmillan. 1994.

Coase, R. H. "The Nature of the Firm." *Economica* 4(16): 386–405. 1937.

Edwards, C. "Protection, Profits and Policy: Industrialisation in Malaysia." Ph.D. thesis. Norwich: University of East Anglia. 1975.

Evans, P. "Class, State and Dependence in East Asia: Lessons for Latin Americanists." In *The Political Economy of the New Asian Industrialism,* edited by F. Deyo. Ithaca: Cornell University Press. 1987.

Jomo K. S., ed. *Industrialising Malaysia: Policy, Performance, Prospects.* London: Routledge. 1993.

____. *A Question of Class.* Singapore: Oxford University Press. 1986.

Kalecki, M. *Essays on Developing Economies.* Hassocks: Harvester. 1976.

Krugman, P. "Import-Protection as Export Promotion: International Competition in the Presence of Oligopoly and Economies of Scale." In *Monopolistic Competition and International Trade,* edited by H. Kierzkowski. Oxford: Clarendon Press. 1989: 180–93.

____. "Scale Economies, Product Differentiation and the Pattern of Trade." *American Economic Review* 70, 1980: 750–9.

Krugman, P., and E. Helpman. *Trade Policy and Market Structure.* Cambridge: M.I.T. Press. 1989.

Lall, S. *The Multinational Corporation.* London: Macmillan. 1980.

Little, I. *Economic Development: Theory, Policy and International Relations.* New York: Basic Books. 1982.

Lucas, R. E. "On the Mechanics of Economic Development." *Journal of Monetary Economics* 22, 1988: 3–22.

Luedde-Neurath, R. *State Intervention and Export-oriented Development: A Reassessment of the South Korean Case.* Boulder: Westview Press. 1986.

Malaysia. *Incentives and Guidelines for Malaysian Manufacturing.* Kuala Lumpur: Malaysian Industrial Development Authority. 1992.

____. *Investment in the Manufacturing Sector: Policies, Incentives and Procedures.* Kuala Lumpur: Malaysian Industrial Development Authority. 1988.

____. *Industrial Surveys,* various years. Kuala Lumpur: Department of Statistics. 1968–90.

Ranis, G., and J. C. H. Fei. "A Model of Growth and Employment in the Open Dualistic Economy: The Cases of Korea and Taiwan." In *Employment, Income Distribution and Development,* edited by F. Stewart. London: Frank Cass. 1975.

Rasiah, R. *Foreign Capital and Industrialization in Malaysia.* London: Macmillan. 1995.

____. "AFTA and Its Implications for Industrial Restructuring: Televisions and Airconditioners in Malaysia." Report submitted to the Thailand Development Research Institute (TDRI), Bangkok. 1994.

____. "Transnational Corporations and Backward Sourcing in the Electronics Industry: A Study of Subcontracting Links with Local Suppliers in Malaysia." Bangkok: United Nations Economic and Social Commission for Asia and Pacific. 1993a.

____. "Free Trade Zones and Industrial Development in Malaysia." In *Industrialising Malaysia: Policy, Performance, Prospects,* edited by Jomo K. S. London: Routledge. 1993b.

____. "Competition and Work in the Textile and Garment Industries in Malaysia." *Journal of Contemporary Asia* 23(1). 1993c.

____. "Foreign Manufacturing Investment in Malaysia." *Economic Bulletin for Asia and Pacific* 63(1): 63–77. 1992.

Romer, P. "Increasing Returns and Long-run Growth." *Journal of Political Economy* 94, 1986: 1002–37.

Saham, J. *British Industrial Investment in Malaysia, 1963–71.* Kuala Lumpur: Oxford University Press. 1980.

Scherer, F. *International High Technology Competition.* Cambridge: Harvard University Press. 1992.

Schumpeter, J. *Capitalism, Socialism and Democracy.* London: Unwin. 1987.

____. *The Theory of Economic Development.* Cambridge: M.I.T. Press. 1934.

Sheperd, G. "Policies to Promote Industrial Development." In *Malaysia: Growth and Equity in a Multiracial Society,* edited by K. Young, W. C. F. Bussink, and P. Hasan. Baltimore: Johns Hopkins University Press. 1980: 182–210.

UNIDO. *Industrial Statistics Yearbook, various years.* Vienna: United Nations Industrial Development Organization. 1968–1991.

United Nations. *Yearbook of International Trade Statistics, various years.* New York: United Nations. 1968–91.

United Nations. *National Accounts Statistics, various years.* New York: United Nations. 1968–91.

Wade, R. *Governing the Market: Economy Theory and Role of Governments in East Asian Industrialization.* Princeton: Princeton University Press. 1991.

Wilkinson, F., & J. I. You, J. I. "Competition and Cooperation: Towards an Understanding of the Industrial District." Small Business Research Centre (SBRC) working paper. Cambridge: University of Cambridge. 1992.

Williamson, O. *The Economic Institutions of Capitalism: Firms, Markets and Relational Contracting.* New York: Free Press. 1985.

World Bank. *The East Asian Miracle: Economic Growth and Public Policy.* New York: Oxford University Press. 1993.

____. *World Development Report.* New York: Oxford University Press. 1990.

____. *World Development Report.* New York: Oxford University Press. 1980.

Young, K., W. C. F. Bussink, and P. Hasan, eds. *Malaysia: Growth and Equity in a Multiracial Society.* Baltimore: Johns Hopkins University Press. 1980.

10

Japanese Investments and Technology Transfer to Malaysia[1]

Lynne E. Guyton

One significant trend in several developing countries in East and Southeast Asia has been the growing importance of, and emphasis on, the role of industrial technology in the process of economic and industrial development. It is increasingly recognized in these countries that an essential prerequisite to industrialization is the rapid development of technological capability in the use, absorption and adaptation of foreign technology in the growth of indigenous techniques and processes.

Despite this, in most developing countries, only during the last two decades have specific policies been adopted that directly affect the application and development of technology, particularly at the level of production. Previously, technological development was mainly promoted by institutional programs for technical education and training, on the one hand, and by the establishment and operation of government-owned or supported research institutions in selected fields, on the other. It was generally considered that capabilities for the application, use, and development of technologies in various industrial sectors would emerge as an integral part of the process of industrialization, and that policies formulated to accelerate this process, would, at the same time, ensure technological development. Thus, policies and programs designed to establish production capacity in various sectors were also expected to result in the necessary flow of production technology and management techniques. Only in recent years has technological development—including issues of foreign technology transfer and its absorption and adaptation, and development of indigenous technological capability—become an important feature of current policies and programs in developing countries. These aspects are, in turn, closely linked with policies toward FDI and the role of activities of MNCs in these countries (Marton, 1986: 3–4).

This chapter then, will examine the impact of Japanese FDI in the form of technology transfers upon Malaysia's industrialization. In view of the fact that Japan has been the major player in the industrial development of the country—from the import-substitution phase beginning in the late 1950s through to the current export-oriented phase—there have been many expectations of its role in technology transfer to domestic industries. Since Malaysia needs to upgrade its industrial base and technological capabilities, the extent of technology absorption and assimilation is indeed critical.

FDI has been sought in Malaysia with the expectation that it will expand employment opportunities in the manufacturing sector and enhance the country's technological capability. Throughout, technology transfer from parent MNCs in Japan to their subsidiaries and to smaller Japanese firms acting as suppliers in Malaysia will be distinguished from technology transfer by Japanese subsidiaries to Malaysian subcontractors. The following brief discussion of different types of technology transfer will be followed by an analysis of the costs associated with procuring foreign technology in general, and Japanese technology in particular. Evidence and examples will be drawn from the fieldwork conducted within the Malaysian consumer electronics industry. The final section will offer some policy recommendations to Malaysia and other developing countries on how to benefit more fully in the future from Japanese technology transfers.

Types of Technology Transfer

Technology transfers (TTs) to developing countries generally involve the transfer of written information, human-embodied skills, know-how and the adaptation of production processes by technology suppliers. Such transfers involve a variety of different channels, the main ones being the purchase of technology through licensing agreements, imports of machinery and equipment, technical assistance contracts and turn-key arrangements. Options may vary from industry to industry and firm to firm, but choices are usually influenced by the technological capabilities of the users as well as the desire of the supplier to extract maximum rent from the provision of its technology.

Technology transfer is generally referred to being either "packaged" or "unpackaged." The former refers to an arrangement whereby technology is purchased as an important component of an investment package to be complemented by management, marketing services and equity participation. The main disadvantage of this approach is that it tends to perpetuate technology dependency upon industrial countries and to create bottlenecks which can hamper the pace of industrial growth in a developing economy. Depending on the extent of their technological capabilities, many developing countries try to "unbundle" technology packages to facilitate separate treatment of the different components offered, such as management, production methods, marketing strategies and control systems.

"Unpackaged" technology refers to technology acquisition by licensing, involving "pure technical collaboration agreements" which exclude foreign equity participation. Japan's early industrial development can be partly explained by its capabilities in acquiring and adapting technologies from more industrialized countries in this manner. However, the effectiveness of this approach depends upon both the industrial infrastructure and technological capabilities in the national economy. Within Malaysia, a number of manufacturing firms have used such methods to acquire technologies from advanced countries such as Japan. But given the country's narrow industrial base and dominance of FDI in key industries, technology acquisition and assimilation has been all the more difficult. A number of other factors have to be considered when a domestic industry acquires technology, including the willingness of foreign investors—mainly MNCs—to transfer their technologies, the appropriate price of such technologies, as well as domestic absorptive capacity (Anuwar Ali, 1994).[2]

One of the most important modes of transferring technology is through subcontracting relationships between MNCs and local suppliers. Wong identifies the following four ways technology can be transferred.

Direct Transfer of Know-How

Here, the MNC buyer may make conscious efforts and commits resources to transfer certain technology that it commands to its suppliers. This involves the MNC giving advice to the local subcontractor on plant layout, training for a quality management system and other "good manufacturing practices" (GMPs), on-site audit of plant operation and troubleshooting of specific productivity problems, loan of equipment and machinery, either temporarily or permanently, and training the subcontractor's staff through formal courses or informal consultations/visits.[3]

Learning Facilitation

Even if the MNC buyer does not effect any direct transfer of technical know-how, MNC insistence on local subcontractors meeting very high and stringent quality standards for the products they supply will, of itself, greatly facilitate technological learning by local subcontractors. Such learning facilitation is specifically aided by the provision of testing and feedback on quality and other dimensions of performance of suppliers' products, sourcing of technical experts to solve specific technical problems encountered by suppliers and advance indications on requirements and targets of quality, performance and features of products to be supplied by suppliers.[4]

Indirect Technology Transfer or Spillover Transfer

The very process of carrying out transactions between the MNC and the local subcontractors will, of itself, involve some transfer of technical knowledge and information from the buyer to the seller. Such transfer is often effected through (i) the buyer providing its requirements on product design specification and performance to the seller, (ii) the early involvement of the supplier in the stage of prototype development and value engineering, (iii) providing technical and market information on competitor's products (iv) informal sharing of technical information and ideas among the technical staff of both buyer and seller, and (v) exposure to the MNC system of managing and organizing manufacturing activities and observation of MNC corporate culture (organization and management technology). It must be stressed that the transfer of technical knowledge as carried out here is unintended, unlike the conscious, deliberate effort under direct transfer.

Inducement

Finally, the very existence of the subcontracting relationship may induce the supplier to commit itself to making certain technological investments which it would otherwise not make in the absence of such a relationship. This is because the presence of the subcontracting relationship reduces the perceived risk of the investment decision by, for example, the tacit agreement and commitment on the part of the MNC to procure the new product or to increase procurement of an improved product if the investment turns out to be successful and to offer technical assistance if needed (Wong, 1991).

The technology transfer process begins with adoption, that is, the recipient, aware of the availability of the technology, works to adopt it. In the sample, all firms concluding technology transfer agreements (TTAs) were considered as having adopted technology. The second stage of the transfer process can be termed as rooting. This refers to the extent to which the adopted technology takes hold in the domestically-based firm. It consists of three steps and as each step is accomplished the rooting may be considered to be deeper. Rooting begins with operational skills, progresses to duplicative abilities (including repair and maintenance capabilities) and continues to the third stage of innovation, enabling the recipient to undertake, unaided, technological design and innovation. The final stage of diffusion completes the process of technology transfer, and refers to the spread of technological expertise throughout the host economy.

Evidence of adoption of technology was found in all the companies surveyed. Rooting of technology appeared to be in its infancy, although within the components sector of the electronics industry evidence of the second tier of rooting was found. On the diffusion of technology, it was found that Japanese-owned firms in Malaysia have not diffused technology unless they had developed strong secondary linkages with the domestic economy through local ancillary firms.

The channels through which Japanese technology is transferred in Malaysia will now be examined. The discussion will consider TT through agreements, training, and manufacturing practices as some of the more common practices used by Japanese firms.

Technology Transfer Agreements (TTAs)

Initial research on TTAs in Malaysia found that the electronics industry had the highest number of TTAs within the manufacturing sector. As a percentage of the total number of agreements in the manufacturing sector, the share of the electronics industry rose from 17 percent during 1976-1985 to 24 percent between 1986 and November 1992 (Malaysia, 1993). The higher proportion of the electronics TTAs suggests that this industry made relatively more use of TTAs as a means to obtain foreign—almost exclusively Japanese—technology.[5] From this, it can be deduced that the higher proportion of TTAs in this industry was related to the dominance of foreign-owned or controlled firms. It was also found that firms producing components within the consumer electronics industry had a particularly high number of TTAs. This can be explained by the fact that the subsector has had the longest history in Malaysia, and being export-oriented and technology-driven, it faced the greatest pressure from the international market to constantly upgrade its technology.

All seventeen MNC subsidiaries surveyed said that technology transfers did occur between the parent company and the subsidiary. Of the seventeen MNCs, sixteen responded that transfers were in the form of a written agreement with the parent company. Examining the type of agreements in operation, technical assistance agreements (TAAs) and know-how agreements (KHAs) were common in twelve firms.[6] Eleven companies had licensing patent agreements with the parent company, while sixteen had turnkey agreements. The reason for the relatively large number of turnkey operations is due to the fact that they are a common mode relied upon in the initial operational phase of a firm, so as to obtain foreign expertise in the construction of the plant, installation of machinery etc. The fact that many of the sample firms had only been established for three years explains the high proportion of such agreements. Turnkey operations as a mode of TT should decline with the aging/maturing of the firms.

Training

TTAs are not the only means of technology transfer in the electronics industry. Most important are the knowledge and skills necessary not only to operate and maintain, but also to repair, modify and improve on the machinery and technology. All the firms surveyed believed that regular train-

FIGURE 10.1. Type of Agreements in Operation

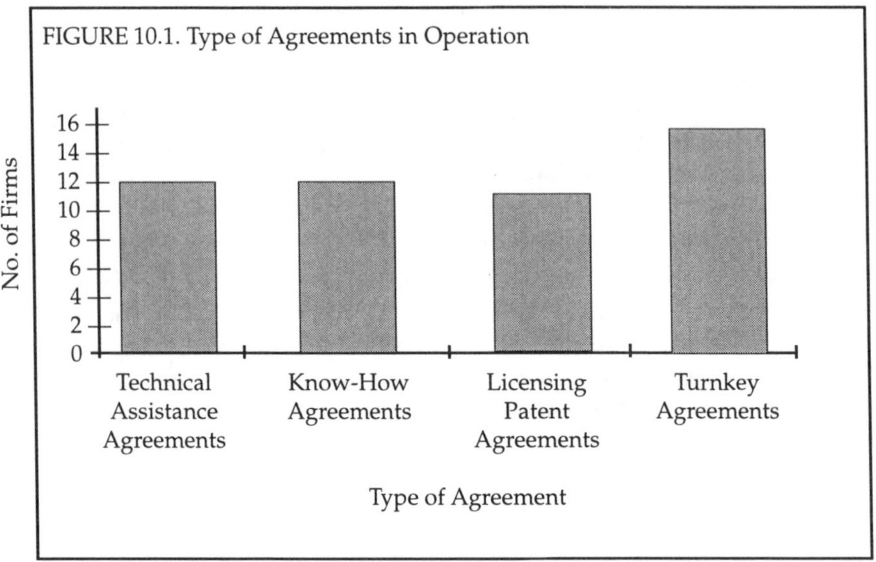

ing for employees was an essential part of company policy which not only led to a more skilled workforce, but also created an important attachment between the worker and the company. All the companies extended on-the-job-training (OJT) to both managerial and line staff. In general, OJT tends to be carried out by Japanese expatriates, although senior local staff also contribute towards OJT.

In-house training. In-house training or OJT involves various aspects. In general, the multinational subsidiaries surveyed tended to provide training to improve performance in the current job specifications and also to increase the worker's ability to perform other jobs as well. Such multi-skilling has several obvious benefits. First, it removes the need to increase the number of workers employed as the number of job specifications increase. Second, and more importantly, it increases the flexibility of the workforce, enabling them to be redeployed as and when the management deems it desirable or necessary. Third, it reduces the problem of a skilled labor shortage. Finally, it provides some security against absenteeism.

The second level of training is geared towards upgrading the workforce. Again, on the whole, it was the multinationals, rather than the smaller firms, which tended to have the vision (and the resources) to carry out such programs. Workers at every level have a fixed training timetable by which they gradually move up the job scale. However, the length of this process tends to be between three to five years, revealing that the Japanese MNCs are keen for their employees to demonstrate their loyalty to the company before they are rewarded with higher level training and promotion.

Training abroad. Without exception, all the companies surveyed sent a number of their employees on regular training visits to the parent company in Japan. The type of employees chosen to go were overwhelmingly technicians and engineers, although supervisors and managers were often asked to go as well. Most of the companies dispatched between one to seven persons annually for training overseas. The length of the training visit varied from two weeks to six months, depending largely on the type of skill to be mastered. The average time span appeared to be about six weeks. All companies viewed such overseas training trips as an important measure to overcome skilled manpower shortages.

The effect of an inadequately skilled workforce on the transfer of technology. All the firms sampled reported that the prevailing level of skills in their workforces prevented them from being able to absorb sophisticated technology. Such views were normally expressed by the Japanese managers interviewed. Malaysian managers, however, felt that because high-level TT was not necessarily forthcoming, workers were not necessarily given the opportunity to upgrade their skills. Most companies sampled were involved in the manufacture and assembly of CTVs and VCRs—relatively old technology. In light of the research findings, it appears that the comparative advantage for more sophisticated electronic products (such as camcorders and high definition TVs) is likely to remain in Japan for some time to come, in part because of the inability of overseas workers to absorb such technology, but primarily due to the fact that such technology is often slowly and reluctantly transferred by the parent companies.

The Purchase/Loan of Machinery and Other Capital Goods

This has been a commonly used method by Japanese subsidiaries to import technology from their parent companies. The subsidiary often has little discretionary power in choosing where to source machinery and capital goods (this was often from the parent company in Japan). As a consequence, the majority of subsidiaries interviewed revealed that their parent companies had frequently already planned where certain machinery would be procured from. In the long term, the high cost of purchasing from Japan will not only have an adverse effect upon Malaysia's balance of payments deficit (in terms of capital goods imports and freight charges), but also upon the development of Malaysia's SMIs. The continuous reliance upon Japanese suppliers for machinery and equipment (either in Japan or in the host country) will have a detrimental impact on Malaysia's own machinery-producing firms.

Manufacturing Practices

Malaysia can now be considered to be in the technology phase of industrialization, where it has acquired operational and process adaptation knowledge and experience in the production process, to the extent of running a fairly sophisticated assembly of a wide range of products. There is now a relatively much higher degree of automation, especially in the bigger companies.

However, the level of automation in Japanese subsidiaries in Malaysia is generally much lower than in similar operations in Japan. Many of the manufacturers surveyed use the conventional conveyor-belt type of operations that mainly involve handwork processes. Some of the firms had introduced computer numerically controlled (CNC) machines and adopted automatic control in operations such as printed circuit board (PCB) insertion and in-circuit testing. Furthermore, there was some use of robots in technology intensive production.

As seen from Figure 10.2, a number of the firms practice just-in-time (JIT) or the principle of *kanban,* but due to the reliance on imported parts, the Japanese subsidiaries tended to carry a higher volume of inventory compared to their parent companies. Generally, manufacturers have also adopted quality assurance systems, with a high percentage using quality circles and total quality control (TQC). All the firms indicated that the nature of the manufacturing practices within the subsidiaries had been determined by the respective parent companies.

In the area of product design for manufacture, it was found that there has been little deepening as most product design still originates from the parent company. Consequently, the majority of the sampled firms were only engaged in assembly, inspection and testing activities. Where product design did occur, it tended to involve either customization or standardization rather than total design activities. What this demonstrates is that the type of Japanese manufacturing practices which Malaysia has been so keen to attract (such as R&D and design), are not necessarily being readily transferred to either subsidiary companies, let alone to Malaysian vendor companies.

Technology Transfers in the Context of Industrial Upgrading

A deepening of industrial development requires the promotion of high-tech industries such as electronics and automobiles. Consequently, it is crucial that human resource development be focused not only on the development of skills needed by those industries, but also on the enhancement of the workforce's capacity to innovate. However, existing human resource development in Malaysia does not really emphasize the capacity to innovate. The lack of domestic funds for R&D is a constraint, but equally important is the fact that FDI preferences and existing investment incentives generally encourage the importation and adoption of highly capital-intensive equipment and technology packages from the industrial countries. This not only discourages the adoption of more appropriate and indig-

FIGURE 10.2. Manufacturing Practices

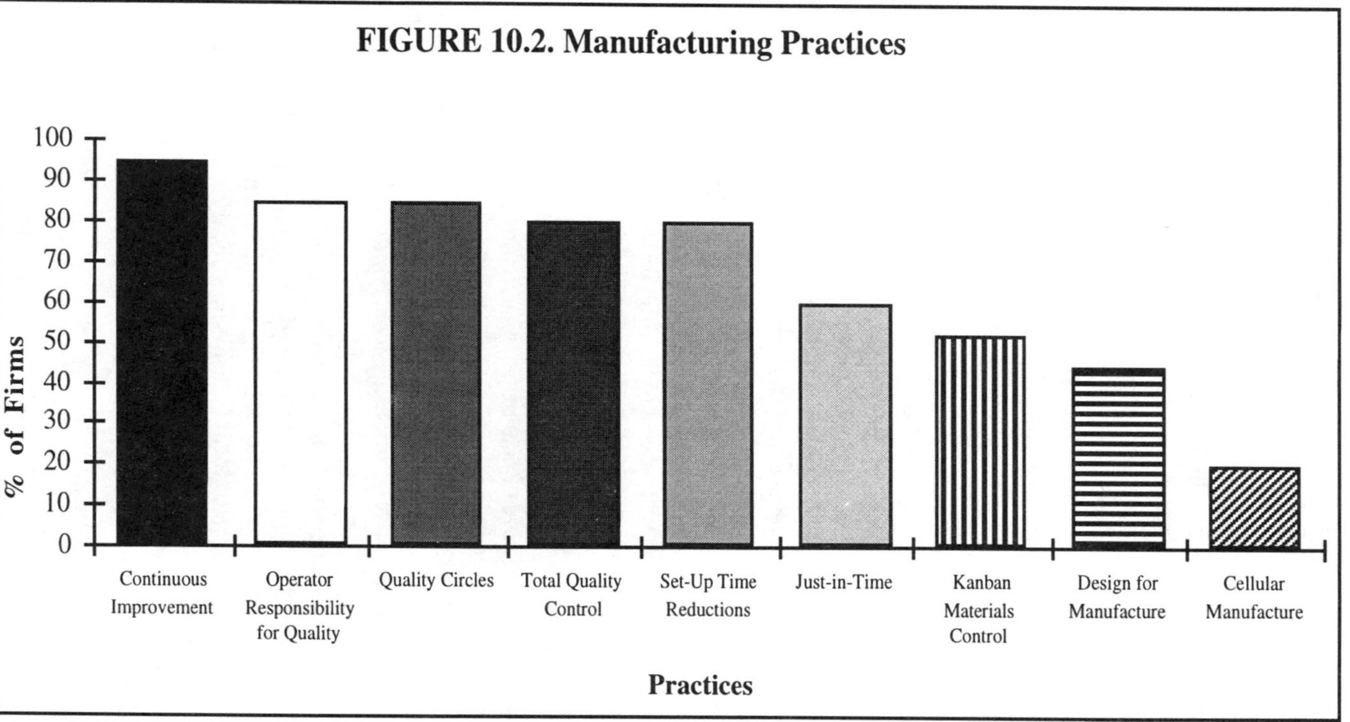

enously-developed technologies, but also undermines the capacity to innovate as the dependence on imported technologies is perpetuated (Anuwar Ali, 1994).

Qualified and experienced technicians and engineers are an important determinant of R&D facilities. In Malaysia, such personnel are lacking and, as a consequence, management from Japanese MNCs tend to fill top positions, stifling the development of domestic entrepreneurship. Such a situation creates an industrial structure which leaves domestic entrepreneurship utilizing only low-level technologies which contribute little towards a more independent industrialization process. Anuwar Ali notes that this tendency is reinforced by other structural features characteristic of skewed, open economies like Malaysia, where high demand for luxury consumer goods tends to ensure that the most profitable areas of economic activity, to which domestic entrepreneurs are attracted, are commercial activities related to consumption (Anuwar Ali, 1994).

At the same time, the recent influx of FDI, including small- and medium-scale enterprises, puts considerable pressure on domestic capital, crowding out enterprises, especially the weaker ones (Lim, 1990: 39–46). While in theory, technology transfer involves the purchase of technology from another country based on the mutuality of interests, for the importing country there is a price to be paid for the technology import; hence, domestic industries need to assess whether the technology transferred is suitable in relation to their own technological capability.

The Costs of Procuring Technology Through FDI

While FDI can have positive effects upon the economic development of a host country, the costs incurred by countries attracting FDI are often overlooked by its proponents. Foreign firms have been frequently criticized for their failure to develop technologies and products appropriate to factor price conditions, income levels, and other local conditions of the countries in which they operate.[7]

FDI can be an efficient means of transferring a package of capital, skills, technology, brand names and access to established international networks. It can also provide beneficial spillovers to local skill creation and, by demonstration and competition, to local firms. Where local skills and capabilities are inadequate, FDI can sometimes be the only means to upgrade technologies and enter high-tech activities. The very fact, however, that FDI is such an efficient transmitter of packaged technology based on innovative activity in advanced countries has serious implications. With few exceptions, the subsidiary in a developing country receives the results of innovation, not the innovative process itself: it is not efficient for the enterprise concerned to invest in skill and linkage creation in a new location. Consequently, the subsidiary develops efficient capabilities up to a certain level, but not beyond. Such a truncation can not only diminish the subsidiary's own technological development, but also its linkages with the host country's technological and production infrastructure, thus limiting beneficial externalities. Moreover, a strong foreign presence with advanced technology can prevent local competitors from investing in deepening their own capabilities (as opposed to becoming dependent on imported technology or, where the technology is not available at reasonable prices, withdrawing from the activity altogether). For these reasons, countries with technological potential may find it beneficial to restrict FDI and import technology in "unpackaged" forms, including foreign minority-owned joint ventures (Lall, 1992: 179). And in certain technologies, monopolistic or oligopolistic market situations can even increase the bargaining position of technology owners and the price of the technology in question.

While the bulk of Japanese technology in Malaysia is transferred from parent company to subsidiary, the technological needs of the subsidiary are limited, however, only to the production know-how for the specific task it performs, rather than for the entire product or for its design. Often, this narrow production task of the foreign subsidiary continues indefinitely—unless the subsidiary diversifies its production to other areas—since export-oriented foreign subsidiaries are generally not subject to progressive increases in local content requirements. Hence, if Japanese technology transferred to its own subsidiaries are limited, the chances for meaningful technology transfer to host country firms remain low.

Export-oriented manufacture, whether undertaken by domestically-owned companies or by MNC subsidiaries, has relied heavily on foreign technology, more so than production for the domestic market. In developing countries, it is often expected that MNC subsidiaries must play a major role in increasing non-traditional exports of manufactured goods. This has required some reorientation of policies toward FDI. Although in most developing countries, the trend has been toward exercising greater regulatory control over the activities of foreign companies, an important and overriding exception has been made in the case of MNCs whose local production is largely designed for exports. Export-oriented operations have often been exempted from such regulations that are applicable to foreign investments and are usually evaluated mainly in terms of their contributions to a country's foreign exchange revenues. Foreign subsidiaries engaged in export-oriented production have often been exempted from regulations relating to permissible operations and have been allowed to retain 100 percent foreign holdings or foreign majority holdings, as in Malaysia. Besides relaxation of regulatory provisions for the entry of foreign investments, ownership structure, local content, and other such aspects, export oriented companies have also been eligible for a comprehensive package of incentives available to foreign subsidiaries, whether operating in or outside FTZs.

Technology transfer by Japanese companies to their subsidiaries located in free trade zones (FTZs) has been directly related to the type of operation. Such production has been characterized by high import propensities and the specialization of the subsidiaries in narrowly defined production processes, such as the manufacture of specific parts and components, or assembly activity. Since production in these zones is for export rather than for domestic sale, the technological skills imparted to the labor force are seldom relevant to the needs of local industry. In the majority of FTZs, over 70 percent of the labor force is female, and most of their tasks can be learnt in one day to two weeks. Such skills are mainly for a specific phase of production of a component or product.[8] Transferred know-how is partial and related to a specific production stage. The type of technology to be utilized in FTZs must be geared to competitive factors in external markets. The need to use the latest technologies for export-oriented production has increased dependence on foreign technology. At the same time, technology owners seldom license their latest technology to unaffiliated companies; this is usually transferred on an intra-firm basis, tending to increase the potential role of MNCs in export-oriented sectors (Marton, 1986: 45). Because of the enclave characteristics of export-oriented Japanese subsidiaries in Malaysia (and also in other Southeast Asian countries) technological linkages with local industry have been weak and often absent. Instead, what is usually transferred is production know-how rather than the capability to design and innovate.

In small- and medium-sized industries (SMIs) in developing countries, limited access to the latest foreign technologies required for competing in global markets has been a major constraint. The latest technologies are generally difficult to obtain through licensing without equity participation. Host-country firms have also had inadequate information on available foreign technological alternatives and development, often acquiring technology that is considerably behind recent technological developments. Rather slow absorptive abilities have further constrained companies in fields such as electronics, where rapid technological changes have been occurring.

Evidence of Japanese Technology Transfer from the Firm Sample

While Japanese FDI inflows have contributed to more rapid growth of Malaysia's manufacturing sector, such inflows also provide substantial opportunities for Japanese industries to increase their exports of intermediate and capital goods to Malaysia. At the same time, they also encourage greater investments by related Japanese industries, particularly by supporting small- and medium-scale enterprises. The close links between these industries and their major industries in Japan via sub-assembly and subcontracting systems have encouraged them to expand their activities to overseas locations to more effectively supply and support their parent or core companies' requests. Hence, in Malaysia, subsidiaries and small firms worked in tandem, held together by the dictates of the parent company and *keiretsu* group as a whole.

While the Malaysian government is currently promoting small- and medium-sized industries, Aoki, in his study of Japanese investment in Malaysia, comments that "the enterprises that have contributed to this most effectively are affiliates/subsidiaries of Japanese firms that have shifted their production facilities and established factories in Malaysia" (Aoki, 1992: 73–110). This has important implications for long-term industrial expansion, as such a phenomenon will inevitably stifle domestic entrepreneurship and enterprises and the potential for inter-firm linkages involving Malaysian industries (Anuwar Ali, 1994).

Despite the rapid pace of technological progress and global commercialization of technologies since the early 1970s, the actual choices open to locally-owned enterprises as far as applied technologies are concerned are still limited. Technology transfer transactions which take place under very imperfect market conditions, generally favor the technology suppliers of the industrial countries. This is particularly evident in the transactions between the MNC technology supplier and its subsidiary in Malaysia. Japanese FDI in the Malaysian consumer electronics industry appears to discourage meaningful technology transfer and development of domestic innovative capacity. Furthermore, of the forty firms interviewed, over half did not view technology transfer as a priority in choosing to locate their manufacturing facilities in Malaysia, since their main rationale for establishing such facilities there was to export to third countries and to avoid the higher costs in Japan due to yen appreciation. It was found that if there is any transfer at all, it is normally between the parent company and its subsidiary or between subsidiaries and small Japanese firms. Under such an arrangement the technology transfer is internalized within the confines of the MNC's—or the *keiretsu* group's—global production system.[9] Fieldwork in Malaysia also revealed that 77.5 percent of firms interviewed were reluctant to allocate R&D funds to their overseas subsidiaries, let alone their affiliates or host country firms, since most of these activities are controlled by their head offices in Japan where R&D facilities have already been established in close consultation.

An important consideration in weighing the effectiveness of TTAs as a mode of technology transfer is the nature of restrictions imposed by Japanese licensers. The most common types of restrictions, as identified by the responding firms, pertain to the region to which the licensees can export their products, and the price that can be charged for the products. Together the frequency counts of these two restrictions accounted for one half of the total frequency counts found in the survey. Another significant restriction relates to sourcing. Eleven of the twelve firms which said they had formal written TTAs with the parent companies revealed that there were strict conditions tied to the agreements to ensure they would source raw materials and capital equipment from firms designated by the parent company. Furthermore, there were also restrictions on the export of products. Turnkey arrangements only appeared to contain restrictions on sourcing. This is not surprising since this type of agreement deals with the setting up and initial operations of the plant, where capital equipment and raw materials are important inputs for successful operations.

Consequently, Malaysian-owned or managed firms may be substantially disadvantaged if restrictive conditions are imposed by their Japanese technology suppliers. Restrictions on export outlets, the level of technology transferred, and domestic R&D activities are often observed. In view of the negative impact of such restrictions, Malaysia's MITI is trying to minimize them to allow domestic manufacturers greater flexibility to expand their operations and become less dependent on their technology suppliers in the long run. There have been many cases in which the technology licensers insist on fixing the prices of the licensed products, while others insist that the local licensees purchase all material inputs and components from them at prices fixed by them, which has significant implications for efforts to broaden the country's industrial base.[10] Such tie-in purchases undoubtedly strengthen the position of the technology suppliers, enabling them to maximize their gains by selling over-priced components, intermediate inputs, capital equipment and spare parts, thus creating opportunities for transfer pricing. Additionally, the obligation to purchase key inputs from the technology licenser enables the latter to monitor the activities of the local licensee, by constantly checking the production volume of the licensee, mainly for the purpose of determining royalty or technical fees (Anuwar Ali, 1994).

The supplier-buyer relationship in Japanese technology purchases could be viewed as a "bilateral monopoly," where the price is largely determined through a series of negotiations between the two parties assumed to be of equal strength. But if this is true, then the final negotiated price for technology should be reflective of prices in competitive markets. However, if one party is in a weaker bargaining position, as is frequently the case for Malaysian firms, the final negotiated price would favor the stronger party. Thus, where a licensee has less than sufficient mastery of and knowledge about the technology, the licenser is usually able to extract larger economic rents from the technology transaction. In Malaysia, the largest proportion of technology transfer payments made by firms involves payments for new machinery and equipment. Such purchases are normally made through parent companies of Japanese-controlled firms.

The constraints faced by local firms are reinforced by other factors such as the Japanese firms' inherent strengths and their considerable negotiating and bargaining skills built up through extensive experience in selling technology. Hence, the bargaining position of Japanese companies tends to be greater at the beginning of a relationship, when the need for their resources and expertise is most critical. Once the manufacturing facilities are established, the recipient enterprise becomes more adept, while the services of the Japanese counterpart then becomes less indispensable. In such a situation, there could be a shift in the relationship in favor of the local enterprise. Even then, when Japanese interests maintain equity and management control, the relationship may not be so straightforward, as Japanese companies generally tend to have a higher proportion of Japanese personnel working in Malaysia compared to most other foreign companies.

Malaysian firms' bargaining positions vis-à-vis Japanese technology suppliers with respect to technology transfer have tended to weaken in recent years due to intensifying competition among developing countries for FDI in general and "high-tech" investments in particular. In addition, high tech industries characterized by rapid technological changes are unable to catch up, and as such, are much more vulnerable and dependent upon the Japanese MNCs to provide the latest improvements.

One major observation which came to light during the survey was the fact that 76 percent of the companies surveyed felt that technology was transferred too slowly to them. This was expressed by subsidiaries of MNCs as well as by smaller independent Japanese companies. A number of the Malaysian managers interviewed in the firms had previously worked for other American/European electronic companies. They maintained that U.S./European firms transferred far more technology at a much faster pace than their Japanese counterparts. Furthermore, they indicated that non-Japanese firms were better at providing technical manuals to local personnel. This can perhaps be attributed to greater language difficulties (compared to Americans and Europeans) and some cultural aspects of Japanese training. The Japanese technical training relationship is based to a great degree on personal contact rather than documentation. Furthermore, one Malaysian personnel manager commented that Japanese training of a person takes a number of years (the common practice in Japan is to remain in a company for life), while widespread job-hopping in Malaysia discourages Japanese from imparting full knowledge and skills. In contrast, U.S. and European firms are used to shorter employment records, and hence do not perceive a high turnover rate as an impediment to training and TT.

Linkages between the Japanese electrical and electronic firms and supporting/ancillary firms have the potential not only for spurring the growth of the latter, but also for facilitating their technological upgrading.[11] The stringent quality, delivery and reliability requirements of the Japanese companies can force their suppliers to improve their own capabilities. However, the survey revealed that local (majority Malaysian-owned) suppliers were rarely used. While these *secondary* effects of technology transfer are undoubtedly important, Southeast Asian industries still need more and fairer transfer deals to develop to a stage when they can innovate technology. Because the Japanese production network is closed and tightly controlled by the firms that operate within it, it is difficult for local firms to receive the type of TT needed to develop and expand.[12]

While the need to automate per se may have simply led to increases in the imports of machinery, the parallel need to modify and adapt machinery has provided the crucial push to look for expanded machine tool facilities that are reliable and easily accessible. Three options have been open to Japanese firms: to expand in-house machinery workshops, to convince Japan-based subcontractors to relocate locally, or to seek out local (Malaysian) subcontractors with the potential to meet their needs. Of these three, the study found that the second option was the most popular with Japanese firms. Hence, while some local (Malaysian) firms are undoubtedly now being used as subcontractors, the closed nature of the *keiretsu* and *shitauke* system of subcontracting makes it exceedingly difficult for "outsiders" to penetrate this system on a large scale.

Although Malaysia's Ministry of International Trade and Industry (MITI) has laid down a number of guidelines for the purchase of components or intermediate inputs, it is difficult to ensure effective technology transfer given the Ministry's lack of experience and capacity to assess the "technology content" imparted to domestic licensees or local personnel. As in most developing countries, technology transfer regulations in Malaysia have not been utilized to screen for more "appropriate technologies," partly because the technology transfer agreements are monitored and processed by administrators lacking the necessary technology background. It is therefore critical that Malaysia's technology assessment capability be upgraded to minimize the negative effects of technology transfer arrangements (Malaysia, 1991: 193).

Enhancing Domestic Technological Capability: Lessons For Developing Countries

The above observations suggest that technology transfers through Japanese FDI allow Japanese parent firms to control production methods, leaving local subsidiaries or Malaysian-owned subcontractors very limited control over technology. Most Japanese subsidiaries are technologically dependent on their parent companies for their requirements such as machinery, equipment and components. The subsidiaries are simply given product specifications and technology as decided by the parent company.

While it is important for Malaysia to try to reduce problems of technology absorption with appropriate strategies, it is equally important that advanced industrial countries like Japan appreciate aspirations for technological enhancement. Although the amount of FDI may be important in inducing economic growth in the short term, the quality, type or nature of foreign investments will be crucial from a long term perspective. This implies that investments made by Japanese firms must be viewed in terms of their impact on Malaysian technology acquisition and enhancement as well as inter-industry linkages within the domestic economy.

This would mean that FDI must be selectively encouraged so that it will not stifle domestic investments or enterprises. The experiences of Japan and South Korea, for example, suggest that FDI was discouraged in favor of licensing arrangements for the purpose of domestic technological enhancement, as domination by foreign capital would have been detrimental for the development of domestic industrial enterprise.

Lessons for Developing Countries

There appears to be a growing need for Malaysia—and other developing countries—to have a flexible approach to industrial development, for as industrial technologies evolve rapidly and constantly, their skill, infrastructure and informational needs are changing in concert. All these changes raise the need for existing industries in the developing world to improve their productivity and competitiveness to world standards, which in turn, calls for flexibility in government policies, institutions, factor markets and technological efforts within firms (Lall, 1994: 1). Issues arise about the form that industrial adaptability may take, as well as on national and firm-level factors that influence adaptability, and the role of the government and institutions in promoting adaptability.

Lall argues that if developing countries want to continue to attract and absorb FDI, domestic firms must be able to do two closely related things. First, since many developing country enterprises tend to operate below international levels of "best practice" technical efficiency, they must improve the efficiency with which they use given technologies by investing in organizational and technological capability improvement. Second, they must upgrade and add to their range of technologies. At the industrial level, greater adaptability to technical progress and growing international competition calls for a restructuring of existing activities and for entry into new, generally more complex activities. Restructuring involves the closure of inefficient firms, the selection or creation of facilities of a size and capability to compete in world markets, and the promotion of inter-firm co-operation, and linkages that are conducive to effective transfer of technology and information (Lall, 1994: 3). What Lall tends to overlook is the fact that while this is sound advice, entry into new markets and inter-firm co-operation often hinges on the receptiveness and generosity of foreign firms from developed countries (with developed techniques and technologies). Where the general "goodwill" is lacking, so too is the capacity for host country firms to upgrade themselves.

Manufacturing enterprises do not develop capabilities in isolation. They operate, in most industries, in a dense network of formal and informal relationships with suppliers, customers, competitors, consultants and technology, research and educational institutions. These networks take the form of complex, long-lasting contractual and non-contractual relations. These linkages help individual firms to deal with each other, to gain access to expensive information and facilities, and to create information, skills and standards that all firms need but no individual firm will generate on its own. As the complexity of activities grows with economic development, so does the need for firms to take account of linkages. This process is an essential part of the increasing specialization between firms that is essential to industrial development. As economies progress and mature, it involves "deepening" in any or all four forms—technological upgrading of products and processes within industries, entry into more complex and demanding new activities, increasing local content, and mastering more complex technological tasks within industries.

As noted earlier, internalized modes of transfer (like FDI, where the seller of technology retains ownership and control over its utilization) tend to centralize the innovation process in developed economies and to transfer the results of research to a firm's own subsidiaries and affiliates. In externalized modes (licensing, equipment purchase, copying, etc.) the recipient may not get technology as rapidly, and generally has to do much more "homework" to absorb and build upon it. But it may, if given the right incentives and skills, be able to develop its innovative capabilities far more than if it never had to develop the skills that it imports.

Due to the risk of market failure in capability deepening due to learning costs, it may be necessary to selectively restrict technology imports to ensure they can be absorbed and utilized. Since the skills and information needs of various industrial activities differ, interventions in these factor markets have to be integrated with interventions to promote activities or technological deepening. If the government targets the electronics industry, for example, it has to ensure that electronics skills are provided by universities, technical information and support facilities on electronics by infrastructure and so on. Market-friendly interventions are therefore necessarily selective once skills and information become specific rather than generic, and since protection reduces the incentive to invest in capability development, industrial policy must provide offsetting incentives in the form of performance requirements.

Lessons for Malaysia

During the course of this study, many comments and suggestions of measures which could improve the investment climate from the point of view of both Japanese investors and Malaysian firms were made. Below is a

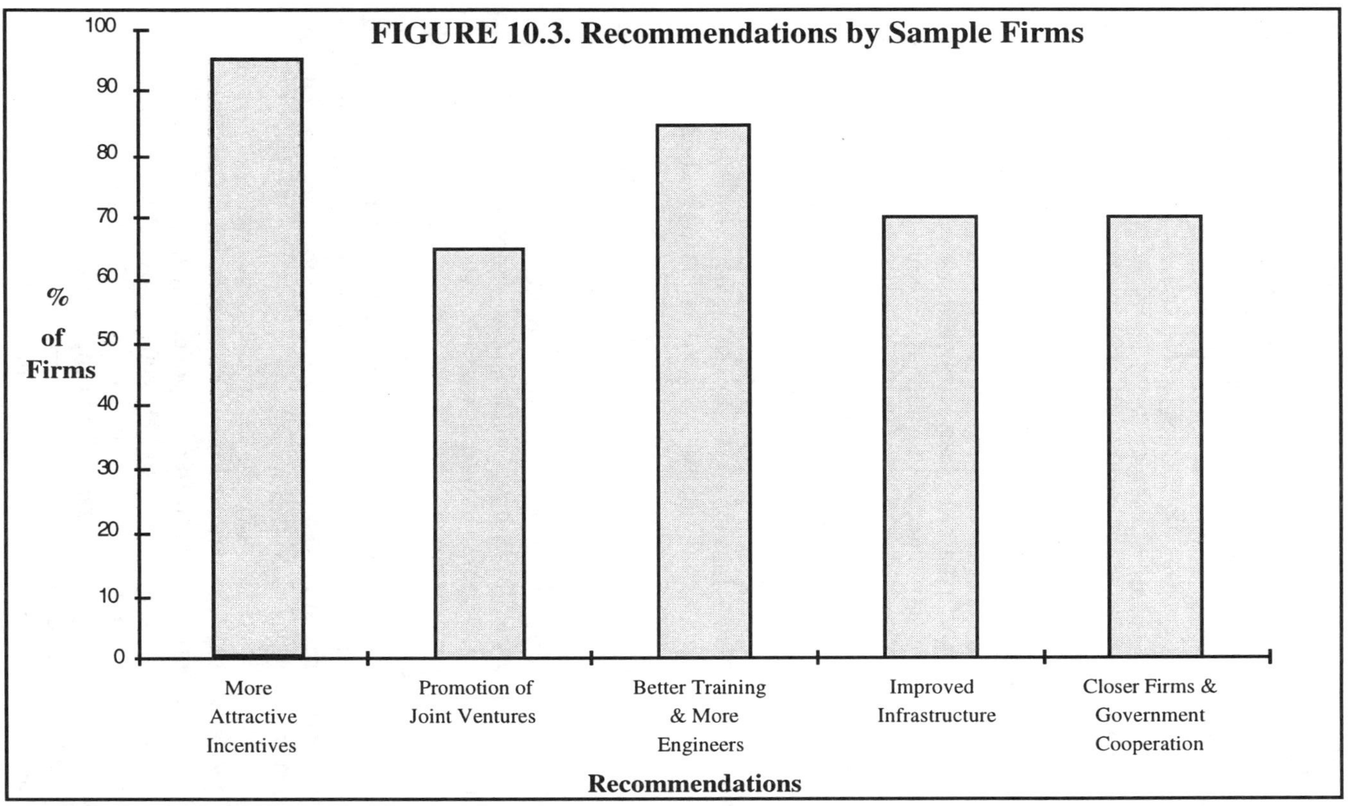
FIGURE 10.3. Recommendations by Sample Firms
100
90
80
70
60
50
40
30
20
10
0
% of Firms
More Attractive Incentives
Promotion of Joint Ventures
Better Training & More Engineers
Improved Infrastructure
Closer Firms & Government Cooperation
Recommendations

summary of the most frequent comments made by the Japanese and Malaysian managers interviewed.

While many of the firms surveyed generally felt that the incentives offered to encourage investments into the country have been good, they believed that more incentives were needed if they were to transfer more technology or to shift R&D operations to Malaysia, as was often requested of them.

Present government incentives such as the DDI (double deduction incentive) which is designed to encourage TT through investments in training and R&D had not been taken up by any of the firms interviewed. Many had not heard of the initiative, while those who had, felt that the procedures were too rigid, involved too much red-tape and unnecessary queries by the relevant government agencies. Furthermore, the notion of spending money on TT and claiming back through the scheme at a later date also deterred firms as the expenditure incurred may later be determined as non-deductible for income-tax purposes. Firms expressed their approval for a "direct grant" system similar to that which operates in Singapore, where the government provides the cash in advance and thus eliminates any element of risk.[13]

A further problem highlighted by this study has been the lack of linkages between Japanese and Malaysian firms. Despite the finding that backward sourcing of Japanese MNCs from Malaysian subcontractors is occurring, the survey found that apart from supplying service-based sectoral contributions, metal and plastic engineering and packaging appear to be the main inputs sourced from local firms. Consequently, a significant proportion of backward purchases of parts and components by Japanese subsidiaries are procured from small Malaysia-based Japanese firms.[14] While it may be difficult to completely eradicate the presence of intra-MNC and intra-*keiretsu* purchases, much can be done to increase local sourcing. Malaysia may have policies to attract foreign investment, but specific policies to influence the rate and direction of technology transfer and subsequent rooting (or absorption) are sorely lacking. Not surprisingly, a large percentage of the firms surveyed felt there was a need for much stronger government-firm cooperation.

One such link is the subcontract exchange scheme (SCX) set up by Malaysia's MITI in 1986. This is a computerized clearing house designed to link Malaysian firms producing components with those MNCs which need them. The SCX provides a link between the buyers' requirements and the vendors' capabilities and capacity to supply. Based on data from the SCX, 2,289 firms were registered for subcontracting work. To date, the actual linkages established through subcontracting have been minimal, and only eighteen firms have made inquiries through the SCX scheme. In light of this observation, better coordination and publicity for the scheme could make its attractions more noticeable to foreign companies.[15] However, it must be said that although some firms expressed an interest in learning about the attractions of Malaysian vendors, the majority of firms were not particularly enamored by the potential advantages of the SCX scheme.

Issues Facing Malaysia

The most important issues facing the electronics industry in this context are those of raising local content, maintaining the high rates of growth of exports through diversification and product upgrading, and developing the skill and institutional base to support these objectives. The industry remains at the lower end of the technological scale in comparison to those in industrialized countries.

A further appreciation of the yen in 1993 has prompted the beginning of another wave of Japanese investment into Southeast Asia.[16] The ability of Malaysia to attract and absorb these investments will be critical to the structural upgrading of Malaysia's consumer electronics industry. However, Japanese FDI in Malaysia in general, and in the consumer electronics industry in particular, will not reach the high levels of the late-1980s for four reasons. Hence, Malaysia's heavy dependence on Japanese MNCs to drive electronics production and exports may not serve the country well in the future. First, labor and land costs in Malaysia are rising, making it less attractive for Japanese investors. For many firms, the primary reason for relocating in Malaysia was due to such factors; now they are disappearing, there would seem to be less reason to invest there. Second, there is a technology absorption problem in Malaysia, largely due to the shortage of skilled labor. This is a problem which is of great concern to a number of the firms interviewed, and many of them expressed their frustration at the low level of education of the Malaysian workforce. Unless the government invests more into education and training, the skills shortage in Malaysia is likely to continue. Third, the potential of China and Vietnam as alternative investment sites is becoming increasingly attractive. Not only are labor and land cheap and in abundance in these areas, but the sheer size of the domestic market holds enormous opportunities (and potential profits) for Japanese companies. Some electronics companies in Malaysia have already chosen to close down their operations in Malaysia to relocate in China, the most prominent case being Thomson, a French electronics company. Finally, Malaysia's GSP (Generalized System of Preferences) privileges were another major factor which influenced Japanese companies to initially invest, as a way of gaining access to North American (and EC) markets. With these privileges likely to disappear very soon, many companies may think twice about setting up new or additional production operations in Malaysia, and opt for China or Vietnam instead.

In light of the unstable future of Japanese investment in Malaysia, Malaysia's MITI and MIDA should look to new ways to encourage and actively promote domestic investment. Domestic investment in the electronics sector amounted to just 9.2 percent of the total investments for 1992. This can be attributed to the lack of indigenous technologies and technological capability among local operators as well as poor linkages with overseas markets. Another factor was the Government's policy of allowing export-oriented projects to be wholly foreign-owned.

While the study directs much criticism at Japanese firms for pursuing relatively closed business strategies, the current environment for policy making and implementation guidance has also been a factor. Hence, the Malaysian government must also take some of the blame for the lack of development of its consumer electronics industry. The proposed regulation to remove "export" status from sales within FTZs and between LMWs would have provided a strong inducement for increasing the participation of Malaysian companies in the operations of the MNCs (MITI Directive, July 1993). However, due to objections from JACTIM, Malaysia's MITI chose to make these measures effective only for new investments into Malaysia.[17]

The subsequent decision to limit the application of the regulation to only new investments must be viewed as a lost opportunity in piercing the prevailing closed circle of business among Japanese investors. Undoubtedly, the Government's consideration of the potential discouraging effect of such a move on existing investments has had a part in restricting the scope of the said regulation. However, although this may be a factor influencing parent companies in Japan not to relocate new or additional production operations in Malaysia, other factors already noted (the loss of GSP privileges, the low costs and potential of China) are far more likely to affect the flow of investment to Malaysia.

While initiatives such as the vendor program have been engineered, many firms feel that the lists of vendors registered with the government are biased in favor of Malay firms, who in their opinion, were often lacking in quality, skills and appropriate machinery. In the words of one manager serving on the board of directors for a large Japanese CTV producer: "there is no freedom of choice in industry due to the fact that the government favors Malay companies by suggesting them as local partners/vendors for foreign firms." It was expressed that the government's strong promotion of Bumiputra vendors in the electronics industry has been in response to the predominance of Chinese companies in this sector, and is consequently a significant factor in explaining why measures to encourage domestic investment and joint ventures have not been particularly forthcoming or effective. Such was the strength of feeling on this issue among a number of Malaysian managers that it was suggested that foreign direct investment is virtually being subsidized at the expense of domestic investment.[18]

Suggestions for Malaysia and Other Developing Countries

The challenge for Malaysia now is how to promote more R&D-intensive investments, both domestic and foreign, and how to accelerate the restructuring of local manufacturing industries towards higher value-added activities.[19] The case of Singapore illustrates this industrial restructuring strategy shift into higher value-added activities. Despite significant relocation of MNC consumer electronics assembly operations from the island republic to Malaysia and Indonesia, Singapore continued to capture part of the value chain of activities of consumer electronics by being the regional headquarters or international procurement office for many consumer electronics companies sourcing their supplies from the region, and by being the logistics hub for the warehousing and distribution of components and finished goods to and from the manufacturing plants in the region and for consumer markets.

Opinions and Suggestions on Japanese Government Assistance. A number of the firms surveyed offered suggestions on how the Japanese government can step up both the quantity and quality of its technological assistance.

1. One such suggestion is that the Japanese government should consider establishing a management training school in Malaysia. Such a school should provide training to school leavers and graduates of universities in the broad field of business management but with particular focus on quality control, production planning and engineering management.

2. Currently, assistance from the Japanese government (development aid, technical assistance, manpower training, etc.) has far too many conditions attached, and should subsequently be reduced. Instead, greater technical assistance/know-how should be provided through Japan's technical aid agencies to certain industries targeted for support and promotion by the Malaysian Government.

3. One firm suggested that funds should be made available by the Japanese government for setting-up a technical school for training workers attached to industries that have subcontracting relationships with Japanese firms operating in Malaysia. This will help overcome the problem of the lack of skilled workers currently faced by Malaysia. At the same time, such technical and vocational training will help enhance the technological capability of local firms supporting Japanese industries.

4. A number of the Malaysian managers interviewed felt the Japanese Ministry of Education should encourage some of the Japanese universities to offer twinning programs at the tertiary level in Malaysia through local educational institutions affiliated to them. The programs should have an engineering, technical and management bias.

5. Another suggestion is that the Japanese government should open up further the Japanese market for manufactured goods from Malaysia, to

stimulate the expansion of Malaysia's manufacturing sector besides enhancing the proportion of Malaysian exports to Japan made up of manufactured goods.

Ultimately, the foreign investor cannot do all the homework needed to support capability development. All it can do is to create islands of static efficiency. There is no substitute for indigenous capability development effort, and technological transformation cannot be a passive process based on an open door policy to foreign investors. In the past, some policies have been too restrictive of FDI. But simply opening the door to FDI is not a solution to the problems of technological development. A wholesale dependence on foreign investors for technological development will limit the learning process, and may channel industrialization into shallower, less dynamic paths (Lall, 1993: 743).

Suggestions for the Malaysian Government. In view of the limited Japanese technology transfers occurring within the Malaysian consumer electronics industry, there are a number of things the government can do to increase the potential of its own SMEs.

1. Identification of materials and products that can be sourced locally. The government should list all domestic producers—from basic plastic molding to electrical parts. Such a list could be sent to all foreign MNCs operating in the country. This could eventually lead to a displacing of some foreign domestic suppliers.

2. Prioritization to promote local small and medium-scale industries. As the gradual development of local productive capacity should occupy paramount importance, government policy should offer prioritization to promote local SMIs. In addition to expanding local capacity, the Government can also help reduce the incidence of transfer pricing among MNCs.[20] As demonstrated earlier, Japanese intra-firm sourcing suggests that MNCs can transfer prices in such a way as to record profits in the subsidiaries that enjoy tax holidays or reduced taxes. Rasiah suggests that one way of encouraging the promotion of backward sourcing with local SMIs is through a tariff system that discriminates positively. Where local SMIs offer similar products/services of acceptable quality, a tariff on imports or a subsidy to the local SMI can be a very strong inducement to shift from imports to local inputs.[21] Local SMIs can be better supported if the government offers incentives to MNCs for sourcing from local SMIs (Rasiah, 1993).

3. Research and development support. Local SMIs should be given subsidized means of learning and working on product technologies. An R&D division within a separate SMI unit that emphasizes innovation should be given priority. In this way, R&D support can be pooled at the industry level so that the costs of manning it will be economic.

4. Emphasis on process technologies. Local SMIs should be exposed to state-of-the-art process technologies. In a world of increasing competition, the competitive edge firms enjoy are built around both product and

process technologies. Productive efficiency of local SMIs can obviously be raised considerably with more dynamic production techniques. It is necessary for Malaysia to identify the types of technology that can potentially generate optimal growth in the consumer electronics industry and the electronics industry as a whole. Downstream activities, such as computer manufacturing, and upstream activities, such as wafer fabrication, are cases in point. Furthermore, the acquisition of basic process technologies can lead to expansion into different industries utilizing similar technologies (Rasiah, 1993).

5. Incentives for MNCs and local firms offering promoted technology to local small and medium-scale industries. The Government should take the opportunity to promote technology diffusion to local SMIs by offering MNCs incentives for transferring designated technologies to local firms. Many of the old and better established firms in Malaysia are now in their post-pioneer status period, and consequently should be encouraged to reinvest in more advanced technology. Therefore, technology-related incentives should form an important part of any reinvestment incentive package.

6. Institutional set-up to support the development of local and medium scale industries. The Technology Transfer Agreement Unit within MIDA can be expanded and entrusted with the task of formulating specific policies exclusively for TT. A panel of industry experts should be set up to assist in identifying appropriate industries for active promotion. There currently appear to be too many agencies involved in policies pertaining to investment and technology transfer; these are widely dispersed in different ministries. This reduces their effectiveness, increases duplication of effort, and poses problems for firms dealing with these agencies. An all-encompassing agency (like the LIUP program in Singapore) should be established to handle all aspects of technology acquisition and transfer (Rasiah, 1993).[22]

7. Basic manufacturing skills emphasis in schools. A widespread concern emerging from the survey involves the lack of skills among Malaysian workers. As many in the workforce leave school at 15/16 years of age, it is necessary that some basic training be given within schools. A number of the managers interviewed also felt that the establishment of technical and engineering colleges should be encouraged. Such colleges could then foster links with MNCs and local firms to improve learning capabilities.

This chapter has demonstrated that the tightly organized structure of the Japanese MNCs, their subsidiaries, and indeed their whole keiretsu network is having a negative impact upon the nature and extent of technology transfers to Malaysia. While elementary technology has become rooted in a variety of areas in the electronics industry, very few Malaysian-owned consumer electronics firms have obtained sophisticated technology whereby it could be considered to have been diffused. Because so few Japanese companies in the survey had strong secondary linkages with local ancillary firms, technology transfers in this vein were minimal. Hence, while many of the above suggestions are worthy of discussion, and perhaps implementation, unless Japanese firms are willing to change their organized business relationships and foster links with Malaysian firms, the extent of FDI and accompanying technology transfers will remain limited.

Conclusion

The actual speed or magnitude of technology absorption by a SME supplier is jointly determined by its own internal technology absorption capacity and by the scope for indirect technology transfer through subcontracting, i.e., learning facilitation, spillover, and inducement (Wong 1991: 23). The greater this absorption capacity, the greater the technical knowhow that can be absorbed. The internal technology absorption capacity of SMEs is, in turn, influenced by their business vision and the technology strategy of the entrepreneurs, as well as their managerial/technical/financial capacity (Wong, 1991: 23).

Competition, domestic and foreign, is probably the most powerful incentive for building up technological capability. However, the upgrading of industrial activities usually involves high learning costs in areas such as training, experimentation, linkage creation and R&D (Katz, 1987; Lall, 1987; Amsden, 1989). Besides, firms may be reluctant to invest in technological capability building because of difficulties in capturing the externalities from investments in technology and skills; capital markets may be reluctant to finance investments in capacity acquisition because of the riskiness of new industrial activities. Such arguments constitute a valid case for carefully designed interventions to improve the functioning of markets in developing countries. Specifically, in the context of enhancing firm-level technological capability, there is a strong case for direct government intervention in building up the stock of skills (particularly engineering, technical and vocational), as well as creating an environment more conducive for private industry funded R&D in Malaysia.

The relatively underdeveloped linkages between Japanese MNCs and host-country firms persist as a result of the operation of a vicious circle. Japanese MNCs are unwilling to build up long stable subcontracting relationships because of their perception that local firms do not have the technological capability. On the other hand, local firms are unwilling to build up such capabilities unless assured of substantial procurements by the former. Carefully designed state intervention via huge investments in human resource development, the correct incentive structure and institution building are in order and will help to overcome market failures, thereby breaking this vicious circle.

Notes

1. Forty Japanese electronics companies were studied during the period from January to April 1994. Twenty companies were located in the Kelang Valley, while the remaining twenty were in Johor. Companies were selected for being primarily involved in consumer electronics, either in the assembly of products or in the manufacture of components for consumer goods. Hence, the sample is a mixture of subsidiaries of large multinationals and of smaller independent firms acting as suppliers to the MNCs. In all companies, at least two interviews were conducted, one with the managing director (Japanese) and one with either an operations or human resources manager (Malaysian). A tour of the factory and a survey of the manufacturing process also took place.

Interviews were also conducted with officials in the Kuala Lumpur offices of the Malaysian Industrial Development Authority (MIDA), the Malaysian Ministry of International Trade and Industry (MITI), the Japan External Trade Organization (JETRO), the Japan International Co-operation Agency (JICA), the Japanese Association of Commerce, Trade and Industry of Malaysia (JACTIM), the Overseas Economic Co-operation Fund (OECF), the Federation of Malaysian Manufacturers (FMM), and the Malaysian Economic Planning Unit (EPU).

2. Payments for technology may be explicit, in the forms of royalties paid for the use of technical services and industrial property rights, or implicit, like profit earnings and various forms of internal transfer pricing.

3. This was found to be a fairly common practice between parent MNCs and subsidiaries located in Malaysia. The study also found that advice on plant layout and on trouble-shooting occurred between Japanese subsidiaries and smaller Japanese firms acting as suppliers. However, when asked whether any Malaysian suppliers were offered technical assistance and advice, only a handful of companies responded that this was the case.

4. Malaysian managers interviewed within thirteen subsidiaries of Japanese MNCs commented that although technology may be transferred too slowly from the parent company to Malaysia, the strict quality control requirements of the company has positive spillover effects for the workers, and also for local suppliers.

5. It should be noted, however, that in industrial electronics and related component sectors, technology transfers from other foreign firms—principally from U.S. firms—have an important impact upon the development of the industry. Many of the Malaysian managers interviewed (a significant number of which had previously worked for U.S. electronics firms) argued that their contribution in this sphere has been more significant than the Japanese effort.

6. It was found that TAAs which allow lump sum payments are assumed to nurture the first two stages of rooting. However, of the twelve firms indicating that they used TAAs, only two firms used lump sum payments, suggesting that these TAAs would not appear to nurture TT beyond the first phase of rooting.

7. Although this view does, perhaps, overlook the considerations of the cost of developing new technologies, and the need for an appropriate payoff—it is presumably cheaper to transplant an already known technology to a different environment to which it is not entirely appropriate, paying some extra cost in terms of inferior efficiency, than to develop a new technology more appropriate to that en-

vironment; otherwise firms would not engage in the practice and there would be no FDI (Kindleberger, 1970: 41).

8. For a detailed account of the role and treatment of women in Malaysia, see Lim (1978).

9. A number of the smaller Japanese firms surveyed indicated that they benefited from the specifications and other technical information supplied by their buyers. Six of the companies surveyed reported that their buyers (larger Japanese MNCs) were sometimes heavily involved in the requirements for a particular component. This involvement could range from discussions over how to improve quality control; suggestions for (and in three instances, financial assistance in) the upgrading or renewing of machinery to ensure better quality; assistance in the training of the workforce. The MNCs surveyed perceived it to be in their interests to transfer technology to their Japanese suppliers, who were often in the same keiretsu group.

10. For several industries, the import content of their raw material requirements reached 97 per cent for the electronics industry. This is a reflection of the fact that few inter-firm linkages have developed between FTZs and the rest of the national economy.

11. Rasiah found in his 1992 study of electronics MNCs in Malaysia, that in Penang, first tier firms (Japanese subsidiaries) have fostered the growth of second and third tier firms through subcontracting relationships. The second-tier firms (Malaysian-owned), are those that have the first links with the Japanese firms, and have chosen to specialize in certain functions, preferring to pass many of their previous tasks on to third tier Malaysian-owned firms. In this manner, Rasiah claims there has been a gradual expansion in the number of machine tool manufacturers in Penang. However, although this suggests a wide diffusion of technology, the amount of spin-offs for the second and third tier Malaysian firms is minimal, as it was found that they are frequently used to supply the most basic of materials and services for Japanese firms.

12. While eleven Japanese companies revealed that they do offer advice on quality control and give assistance with training to their Malaysian suppliers, only three firms reported that they offered financial assistance to their Malaysian suppliers.

13. The officials from the selected Malaysian government agencies interviewed agreed with the Japanese firms that the incentives offered for investments were important, but disagreed with the reasons given for the ineffectiveness of incentives to promote TT. They agreed that the procedure of "spend first, claim later" had made the DDI less attractive, compared to the Singapore example. However, they disagreed that there is excessive red-tape or delays. The officials, accordingly, contend that the real reason as to why Japanese firms are reluctant to apply for the DDI is the fear of revealing true information about the firm's finances which may be used against the firms for tax purposes (Interviews with officials from various divisions of MIDA and MITI between January and April 1994).

14. Rasiah (1993) revealed that despite attempts to find evidence of backward sourcing between Japanese electronics subsidiaries and Malaysian components firms, few examples could be found. The majority of backward sourcing arrangements with Malaysian firms appeared to amount to procuring very basic services and materials from those firms.

15. However, under this scheme, the Chinese owners of SMEs are reluctant to participate for fear that the data base will be used to force them to restructure their equity in favor of ethnic Malays. One illustration is that ethnic Chinese auto parts firms have refused to accept the Japanese-style supplier purchase agreement designed by Mitsubishi for firms supplying parts to the Malaysian national car. Their fear is that ethnic Malay employees of the national car firm will use price information from the suppliers to establish new parts firms (Frankel, 1993: 194).

16. A Ministry of Finance Report (Tokyo, November 1993) indicated that the appreciation of the yen was leading to a new wave of Japanese FDI. Furthermore, it was reported that production of consumer electronics in Japan fell by 12.7 per cent in 1993—the lowest drop for a decade. Sanyo Electric, which currently makes 40 per cent of its CTVs outside of Japan, plans to raise that to 90 per cent by 1995. Sony also has plans to boost overseas production by 15 percent to reach 50 per cent (*Business Times,* 3 March, 1994).

17. In MITI's annual on-going dialogue with the private sector JACTIM was successful in getting concessions on this issue (*Business Times,* 2 March 1993).

18. Such an approach will be enormously damaging to the future of Malaysia's consumer electronic industry. According to two members of the Federation of Malaysian Manufacturers (FMM), a small number of Chinese-Malaysian firms have relocated in China due to the favorable investment climate there. These are exactly the kind of firms Malaysia needs to contribute to the upgrading of its consumer electronics industry and the economy as a whole.

19. However, many of the Japanese managers interviewed expressed a reluctance to conduct R&D locally. First, MNCs treat R&D expenditures as costs rather than as investments, as opposed to production using available technologies which can bring about returns immediately. Second, all of the MNCs involved in the survey had a corporate strategy whereby the subsidiary firms concentrate on production using available technology and leave the R&D efforts to be undertaken by the parent companies. Third, MNCs are export oriented, and prefer to conduct the R&D closer to places of export, which are mainly Europe and the U.S.A.

20. Given the higher technological capability of Japanese SMEs, their longer relationship with the Japanese core firms and the discriminatory procurement practices of the latter in favor of Japanese SMEs, local firms fear that they may be unable to compete unless some subsidies are provided. A recent study found that 78.9 per cent of Malaysian firms surveyed felt their should be more tax incentives for them (UNDP-USM, 1994).

21. This is the experience of Taiwan. See Fransman (1985) for a detailed account.

22. The Singapore Government has actively encouraged the development of local SMEs in recent years, emphasizing a multi-government agency approach involving action plans in all fronts, including financial, marketing manpower training and technology development assistance. As part of these government programs to promote SME development, a special Local Industry Upgrading Program (LIUP) was launched by the EDB in 1986, particularly to foster closer collaborations between MNCs operating in Singapore and their local supporting industries. The program aims to upgrade, strengthen and expand the existing local supporting industries to meet the increasingly stringent sourcing requirements of MNCs on the one hand, and to tap the technical and managerial expertise of the MNCs to enhance the technological capability of local enterprises on the other.

The program is implemented through a "partnership" between the EDB and selected MNCs, whereby an experienced engineer from the MNC is identified and seconded to the EDB to assume the responsibility of the LIUP manager, whose remuneration is fully paid for by the EDB for a specified period, usually two to three years. The main task of the LIUP manager is to identify selected local SME suppliers for focused assistance in all relevant business areas. With the recommendation of the LIUP manager, the SME suppliers can gain ready access to various financial assistance packages to carry out upgrading projects (EDB: published documents, 1986, 1990; unpublished documents, 1994).

References

Amsden, A. *Asia's Next Giant: South Korea and Late Industrialization.* New York and Oxford: Oxford University Press. 1989.

Anuwar Ali. "Japanese Industrial Investments and Technology Transfer In Malaysia." In *Japan and Malaysian Development: In the Shadow of the Rising Sun,* edited by Jomo K. S. London: Routledge. 1994.

Aoki, T. "Japanese FDI and the Forming of Networks in the Asia-Pacific Region: Experience in Malaysia and Its Implications." In Japan's *Foreign Investment and Asian Economic Interdependence,* edited by S. Tokunaga. Tokyo: Tokyo University Press. 1992: 73–110.

Business Times. "Aim of Offering Perks is to Boost Investment." 3 March, 1994.

____. "More Sweeteners to Boost Investment." 2 March, 1994.

Fransman, M. *Technology and Economic Development.* Brighton: Wheatsheaf. 1986.

Kindleberger, C. P. *The International Corporation: A Symposium.* Cambridge: M.I.T. Press. 1970.

Lall, S. "Industrial Adaptation and Technological Capabilities in Developing Countries." Forthcoming. 1994

____. "Understanding Technology Development." *Development & Change* 24, 1993: 719-753.

____. "Technological Capabilities and Industrialization" *World Development* 20, No. 2, 1992: 165-186.

____. *Learning To Industrialise: The Acquisition of Technological Capability to India.* Basingstoke: Macmillan. 1987.

Lim, L. Y. C. *Women Workers in MNCs: The Case of the Electronics Industry in Malaysia and Singapore.* Michigan Occasional Paper, No. IX, Fall. Ann Arbor: University of Michigan. 1978

Lim, I. "A Domestic Investment Initiative: Justification and Strategies." *Forum 1990,* The Annual Economic and Business Journal of the Federation of Malaysian Manufacturers (FMM). Kuala Lumpur. 1990.

Malaysia. *The Sixth Malaysia Plan ,1991-1995.* Kuala Lumpur: Economic Planing Unit. 1991.

Marton, K. *Multinationals, Technology and Industrialization: Implications and Impact in Third World Countries.* Lexington: Lexington Books. 1985.

Ministry of Finance Report. Tokyo: MOF. 1993.

Rasiah, R. "Transnational Corporations and Backward Linkages. An Evaluation of the Contribution of TNCs to the Development of Backward Linkages in the Electrical and Electronics Industries: A Case Study of Malaysia." Paper presented at the Expert Group Meeting for the Economic and Social Commission for Asia and the Pacific, Bangkok. 1993.

____. Flexible Production Systems and Local Machine Tool Subcontracting: the Case of Electro*nic Components Transnationals in Malaysia.* Unpublished paper, Economics Department, Cambridge University. 1992.

Singapore Economic Development Board (EDB). Various papers. Singapore. 1986–1994.

UNDP-USM. Technological Transfer to Malaysia: The Effects on the National Technological Capability and Implications for Human Resource Development. Kuala Lumpur: UNDP. 1994.

Wong Poh Kam. Technological Development Through Subcontracting Linkages. *Singapore: Asian Productivity Organization. 1991.*

World Bank. *The East Asian Miracle: Economic Growth and Public Policy.* Policy Research Report. Washington DC: The World Bank. 1993.

11

The Economic Development of Guangdong and Its Impact on Hong Kong and Taiwan

Thomas M. H. Chan

Geographically, the South China region consists of four local economies: the British colony of Hong Kong (which will return to China on 1 July 1997), the Chinese provinces of Guangdong and Fujian, and Taiwan, which was colonized by Japan and has been under the Guomindang (KMT) government since 1949.

When China adopted its "open-door" policy of economic liberalization in the 1980s, the relationship among these four local economies changed. Hong Kong was the first to establish extensive economic relations with China, including the neighboring provinces, Guangdong and Fujian. In the previous three decades, the territory has received basic food and water supplies from China, but did not have any further economic relations with China. It oriented its economy basically towards the outside world, particularly the advanced capitalist markets of North America and Western Europe. The opening up of China since the late 1970s offered Hong Kong access to the huge demand for imports in the Chinese market, and to its cheap and abundant labor and land resources. However, as Hong Kong's manufacturing industries have long been oriented to overseas markets and foreign tastes and demands, it was not easy for it to restructure to meet the different consumption and production needs of the developing economy of China. Even in the mid-1980s, when China massively imported consumer durables, Hong Kong's local economy could only benefit as an intermediary in the trade, which saw enormous amounts of consumer electronics, passenger cars and other durables, machinery and equipment going from Japan, Taiwan, South Korea as well as from other industrialized nations to China, either directly or via Hong Kong. It was only after the mid-1980s, when the outside world was convinced of China's firm commitment to market-oriented reform and economic opening, that investors from Hong Kong began to explore and quickly learn the competitive advantages offered by the cheap labor and land resources in China for industrial investment. And it was from then that the local economies of Hong Kong and Guangdong started to transform themselves in tandem.

Guangdong and Fujian were given the same policy prerogatives by the central government of China to experiment with special economic zones (modeled after export processing zones in the developing countries in the 1970s), and an aggressive policy of economic liberalization. However, Guangdong benefited from it far more than Fujian. This was partly because of its more favorable factor endowments and its proximity to Hong Kong. The Special Economic Zones, especially that of Shenzhen, facilitated an extensive exchange in goods and personnel across the border separating Shenzhen/Guangdong/China from Hong Kong. Shenzhen served very well as a window for investors and traders from Hong Kong and elsewhere to learn about and reach China. It was also the place to which timid Hong Kong manufacturers began to shift part of their export-oriented labor-intensive industries away from the rising costs in Hong Kong from 1982. The more liberal or lax foreign trade and foreign exchange controls in Guangdong also gave local firms and governments a chance to reverse its losing edge in the competition for domestic sourcing for exports with the traditional industrial and growth centers of China, like Shanghai and the northern coastal cities. Guangdong's access to the outside world and its consequent cooperation with Hong Kong became the most important means for it to make best use of its rich human and natural resources that had been dormant under the socialist planning regime. The policy and institutional changes brought a change in the orientation of the economic development of the local economy, and has been responsible for the economic growth miracle in the province since the mid-1980s.

Despite the still impressive growth of Fujian in the 1980s, it lagged very much behind Guangdong in local industrial development and structural transformation. The province was one of the poorest in China, and has long been sustained by heavy central government subsidies. The lack of infrastructural investment in the past four decades—because of the military hostility between China and Taiwan, which lies just opposite Fujian across a strait—did not significantly improve its geographical isolation from the other provinces of China. Through almost the entire course of the 1980s, hostility between China and Taiwan remained. This discouraged direct foreign investment and investment from other provinces and cities of China. The latter have been the most important source of new capital to Guangdong's Special Economic Zones. The smaller local market and the physical distance and transport difficulties from Hong Kong also made it far less attractive to investors, traders and even tourists from Hong Kong, and those who came through or were based in Hong Kong. It was only in the second half of the 1980s, when political relations across the Taiwan Strait improved, that it began to reap economic benefits from its physical and cultural proximity to Taiwan, a newly industrialized economy with economic dynamism and strength comparable to Hong Kong. Even then, the unfavorable investment environment there and the lack of economic ties of the province with the more prosperous local and regional markets of China have also turned many Taiwanese investors away to Guangdong, and to a lesser extent, to the Shanghai region. Fujian has been unable to repeat the pattern of relocating Hong Kong's export-oriented, labor-intensive industries in Guangdong. Only a small portion of Taiwan's industry seeking relocation comes to Fujian. It remains subordinate to Guangdong, and due to the political prohibition of direct trade between China and Taiwan imposed by the KMT government, it has to rely on Guangdong and Hong Kong for most of its trade and investment links with Taiwan.

Taiwan is a latecomer to the China scene. Yet, its entry into the China market has been more dramatic and aggressive than Hong Kong's. It was only in 1987 and more importantly in 1988, when policy changes in Taiwan removed hostility towards China, that investment into China began to come from Taiwan. By 1991, in the short span of 3-4 years, Taiwan has succeeded in relocating most of its export-oriented labor-intensive industries in China, mainly in Guangdong and Fujian, and had started to move even upstream industries to China as well while Hong Kong seems to have almost completed its northward industrial relocation and has concentrated on the development of services in Guangdong and in Hong Kong. With the greater economic dynamism of Taiwan, a result of the greater comprehensiveness and higher technological and capital intensity of its industry, there is more room for economic cooperation and integration of Guangdong (and Fujian) with Taiwan through a further increase in trade and investment.

This chapter will not examine the concurrent development of all four local economies in the region. Instead, it will focus on that of Guangdong alone, and see how its outstanding development in the 1980s has been related to its links with Hong Kong and later with Taiwan. Fujian will be mentioned in Guangdong's economic relationship with Taiwan, because before the coming of Taiwan on to the scene, Fujian's economic development had not been changed much by its newly acquired direct foreign trade rights and investments from Hong Kong. It seemed to remain beyond the dynamic interaction between Guangdong and Hong Kong. The impact of Guangdong's rapid economic growth and structural transformation in the 1980s on the local economies of Hong Kong and Taiwan will form the second part of this chapter.

Guangdong's Economic Development in the 1980s

Despite its historical prosperity before 1949, local development in Guangdong was retarded by the priority given to heavy industry and especially to the defense industry, and therefore to other localities in China, by the central planning system. In the past, Guangdong excelled in tropical agriculture, consumer goods industries and trade. All these were not given adequate attention by the central and provincial authorities. The perennial preparation for war and invasion denied Guangdong like other front-line provinces, including Fujian—the necessary capital investment to upgrade its dated industry, or to transform the local industrial structure to make it compatible with the heavy industry-biased industrialization strategy of the central government.[1] The province was also denied access to its traditional outlets in the outside world. Trade between the province and Hong Kong was drastically reduced and placed under tight central administrative controls. Even after the Great Leap Forward (1958-61)—which brought three years of natural disasters and heightened the need to increase exports so as to have hard currency to pay for imports of food and later, technology and machinery from the West—the revived trade with Hong Kong was small and concentrated in agricultural and related products that did not have any significant impact on existing local industry in the province. Probably since the Cultural Revolution (1966-9), the central government has imposed a quota system on the exports of agricultural products to Hong Kong, the main exports until the 1980s. Other provinces, in particular, Hunan, had been assigned a large share of the quota. This reduced the scope for expansion of Guangdong's exports to Hong Kong, even though there was great demand and it was more cost-effective to do the sourcing in Guangdong, than, e.g., to ship live pigs from Hunan via Guangdong to Hong Kong. The redistributive and monolithic central planning system in the first three decades of the People's Republic succeeded in altering and suppressing the structure of comparative advantage of China's provinces. Guangdong was no exception, and it was assigned a predominantly agricultural production function in the national division of labor. Not even the three decentralization (or local industrialization) drives in 1958-9, 1964, and 1970-2 were able to change the predicament of Guangdong.

It was the adoption of economic reform, particularly the open-door policy, that has given Guangdong an opportunity to escape from this centrally imposed pattern of underdevelopment. In 1978, the central government agreed to an aggressive program of export expansion.[2] Although the initial aim was to bring in enough hard currency to support the ambitious import-led industrialization program proposed by the heavy industry lobby in the central leadership,[3] it allowed greater autonomy to Guangdong, which had historically been one of the major exporting provinces of the nation, and which, together with Fujian, had the biggest overseas population. The desire to drastically increase China's exports in a very short time span also led the government to look for overseas examples and to take up the concept of export processing zones. To avoid risks, which also reflected the lack of understanding and the little faith of the central government at that time, in export processing zones and export-led industrialization, three such zones were set up in Guangdong, which was regarded as relatively underdeveloped and far away from the main industrial centers of the nation. A fourth one was established in Fujian with the same caution, when it was requested by the Fujian government. In 1979, the two provinces were granted special status in the Chinese system of economic management, which mainly meant that they would be exempted from many national policies and requirements. The Special Economic Zones, the Chinese-style export processing zones, were formally established in the same year.

The economic development of Guangdong since then may be divided into two stages, the first from 1979 to 1984, and the second from 1985 to the present. The choice of 1984-5 as the transitional point between the two stages marks the institutional and performance effects of the radical market-oriented, non-rural economic reforms enforced between the second half of 1984 and early 1985.[4]

First stage: 1979-85

During 1979-85, the provincial economy of Guangdong began to realize its comparative advantage under a regime of more liberalized economic policies. By both international and national standards, its pace of growth was very impressive. In 1981-4, provincial gross domestic product (GDP) recorded an average annual growth of 10.3 percent. This contrasted with the much slower growth in the year before the reform.[5]

Growth in this period was initially propelled by rapid development of the rural sector. Agricultural production expanded at an annual rate of 14.8 percent in 1980-4.[6] Foreign direct investment began flowing in during this period, but the bulk of it was devoted to the service sector. Starting from 1982, there was investment coming from Hong Kong for export-oriented processing activities, though mainly on a small scale and by small establishments.[7] Apart from capital accumulation generated by rapid agricultural development and direct foreign investment, there were other major sources of funds for investment and consumption in the province. They were investment from the central government, mostly confined to the special economic zones for initial infrastructural development,[8] remittances from overseas Chinese originating from Guangdong, who were attracted to visit and support their local relatives because of changes in the Chinese political atmosphere, and borrowing through the state banking system from outside the province.

In 1980, Guangdong had already attained a high degree of foreign trade dependency. Total foreign trade turnover was equivalent to about 30 percent of the provincial GDP.[9] This was the result of the export promotion policy of the government, which had begun in the 1970s. Total exports increased by 57.4 percent from US$1.388 billion in 1978 to US$2.195 billion in 1980.[10] After 1980, the pace of export expansion was much slower until 1985. It increased by only 34.5 percent in the five years, 1980-5. Traditional agricultural products and consumer goods from the province seemed to have reached the limits of export growth.

The slower pace of export growth suggested that the scale of outward-oriented processing activities from Hong Kong was rather small, and thus its contribution to local capital accumulation was also insignificant. In the early 1980s, Guangdong had a very sizable trade surplus, over US$1 billion per year. Yet, before 1985, when China adopted a local retention system for foreign exchange earned from exports, Guangdong was not entitled to keep all its export earnings, nor did it have a free hand in spending them on imports.[11] Most of the earnings and the surplus went to the central government.

Before 1985, Guangdong also had a large trade deficit with the rest of China, although this narrowed from Renminbi(R)1.28 billion in 1978 to R1.06 billion in 1980 and to 0.56 billion in 1984.[12] The overall balance of trade (with foreign countries and with the rest of China) was small compared with the size of investment and the increase in consumption in the province during the period. Fixed capital investment in 1978 was only R2.72 billion. In 1981, it reached 6 billion, rising rapidly thereafter to 18.46 billion in 1985. The average annual increase in investment was an extremely high 37.4 percent in 1981-5.[13] This formed the basis for the first extensive industrialization of the provincial economy after 1949. Retail sales also grew very strongly, with an average annual increase of 18.5 percent in the same period.[14] Such a phenomenal growth of investment and retail sales formed the demand that pushed up industrial output at a similarly extraordinary growth rate. At constant prices, industrial output growth rate averaged 16.4 percent p.a. in 1981-5. The ratio of gross agricultural output (minus output from sideline activities, including rural industrial output) to the gross output of the province is a good indicator of the progress of the industrialization process during this period. The ratio was 1:2.98 in 1978 and changed to 1:3.24 in 1980, and to 1:3.88 in 1985.[15] Foreign investment totaled US$1.78 billion in 1980-4, equivalent to R4.98 billion at the central government's internal settlement rate.[16] It was a large sum, but far smaller than capital from domestic sources, the most important of which are probably loans from the state banking system.

In 1980, total bank deposits in the province were R8.88 billion, while loans were 15.64 billion, giving a deficit of R6.76 billion. In 1984, the gap widened to R14.73 billion.[17] The credit deficit represented a net inflow of surplus savings from the rest of China into Guangdong. This was used to finance ever increasing investment and consumption.[18]

This first stage marked the beginning of the economic transformation of the Guangdong economy. It was the interplay of internal factors that brought in surplus savings from the rest of China to invest in the province. Exports and direct foreign investment only played a secondary role. As such, the transformation had not yet created a significant impact on the neighboring economies.

Second stage: 1985-91

The radical economic reforms introduced in 1985 placed the Chinese economy on a "double-track" system with the market track expanding instantaneously, giving rise to a semi-market economy. This offered Guangdong a chance to exploit the more accessible domestic market north of the province. The boost to the local economy came from a combination of two factors.

The last quarter of 1984 saw unexpected credit liberalization and expansion that led to an immediate jump in investment and consumption in the Chinese economy as a whole.[19] Unfortunately, China's promotion of traditional consumer goods industry and the steady rise in urban residents' living standards in the early 1980s had already satisfied consumers' needs and demand for these traditional goods. The increased purchasing power from the sudden credit expansion found no appropriate outlet in the domestic consumer goods market. It was attracted instead to foreign-made consumer durables that were demonstrated to the Chinese by their overseas visitors and through their increased exposure to foreign advertisements and living styles. As China had not reformed its domestic price structure, which inherited a large differential between domestic and international prices in consumer durables, the upsurge in demand found the special policy and lax customs controls in Special Economic Zones, in particular Shenzhen, an institutional loophole in the import regulation policy of the state. The result was an extensive and rapid growth of illegal and officially tolerated transshipment of custom duties-exempted foreign-made consumer durables and passenger cars into and through Guangdong's Special Economic Zones and Hainan Island, then still under the jurisdiction of Guangdong. All these imported goods were directed to the domestic market that extended beyond the northern border of the province, which should more precisely be considered as entrepot trade.

In 1985, Guangdong reversed its traditional trade pattern. Imports from the rest of China increased by 44.2 percent, whilst exports rose by an impressive 114.8 percent to R8.51 billion, resulting in a first-time trade surplus of R1.98 billion.[20] The source for the exports to the rest of China was Guangdong's imports from overseas, which climbed to US$2.43 billion (R7 billion) in that year. As export figures to the rest of China only covered official commercial transactions, the actual size of sales of foreign-made goods to the interior market—including direct purchases by internal tourists and journeymen in the local markets of Special Economic Zones and other towns and cities in the Pearl River Delta—should be much larger.[21]

This had led not only to rapid capital accumulation in the area and by the firms involved, but also import substitution attracted by the excessively high profit margin in production and sales of these consumer durables that were subject to seemingly insatiable demand from Chinese consumers. Despite the subsequent clamp down on the illegal "entrepot trade" by the central government in late 1985 and 1986, Guangdong still benefited from the explosion in domestic demand for these "foreign" consumer durables. It succeeded—through massive local investment and direct foreign investment—in capturing the domestic market for these goods by import-substitution, by assembling imported components and parts, rather than manufacturing them. A large number of production lines for these consumer durables were imported and set up in the province either by local firms, including township enterprises, or by joint ventures and solely-owned foreign firms. This had, in a very short time span, built up a new consumer goods industry in Guangdong, oriented towards the domestic market within and without the province.

The most obvious success of import substitution industrialization was to be found in the production or assembly of color television sets. The provincial output of color television sets was 21,500 in 1983. It jumped to 256,900 in 1984, and quadrupled to 1,009,800 in 1985. The output fell a little in 1986 to 924,400, but leaped to 1,278,400 in 1987 and reached 2,034,400 in 1988[22] and stayed at 2,620,000 in 1990.[23] The quantum leap in production was only possible with the massive import of turn-key production lines and the inflow of components and parts required for assembly which could lead to either another round of import of turn-key production lines for their production or a long period of gestation for the provincial industry to develop the production capacity for these components and parts through technology transfer or acquisition. Guangdong seemed to be consistent in relying on importation for every round of its import-substitution industrialization, rather than in allowing time for the development of its production and process technology. The same pattern was repeated in the development of other "imported" consumer goods production in the province in the same period.

The import substitution industrialization provided Guangdong with new and popular consumer goods for export to the northern provinces. In 1985, the province supplied to the rest of China a net surplus of 395,600 television sets including black and white as well as color sets, 192,000 washing machines, and 166,400 refrigerators. A year later, the northward shipment consisted of 360,200 color television sets, 222,600 washing machines, and 52,700 refrigerators.[24] A rough estimate, at current retail prices, would mean a surplus of about R800 million. When converted into wholesale prices, the surplus should constitute close to 40 percent of the total net trade surplus of R1.877 billion in the year, or about 10 percent of the total "exports" of the province to the rest of China.

The finance for the new consumer durables industry came from three main sources.

First, the province began to borrow on a much larger scale from overseas. During 1985-8, which saw the rapid expansion of the local economy with massive investments, the foreign debt of the province amounted to US$2.65 billion (or an equivalent of about R10 billion at the official exchange rate). Of the total, over 80 percent were foreign commercial loans, with a large percentage borrowed by state firms and for the importation of production lines.[25]

Second, there was a net inflow of surplus savings from other provinces through the state banking system. For instance, a net credit deficit of R25.19 billion was recorded in 1988 alone.[26] This provided a cheap source (because of the low interest rate and the soft constraints the bank imposed on its loan) of local funds to supplement foreign borrowing for investment in new production capacity as well as to supply working capital to producer firms.

Third, profits generated from the assembly and sale of these consumer durables. For instance, the sales of color television sets made in the province in 1985 and 1986 amounted to R3-4 billion. The profit margin was over 20 percent.

The second most important economic consequence to Guangdong of the radical economic reform of 1984-5 was the sudden upsurge in exports.

Until 1984, Guangdong's export expansion had been stalled. Total exports grew by an insignificant 8.4 percent from 1980, while commodity exports were practically shrinking, with a nominal growth of 1.3 percent for a period of four years. The reforms liberalized the domestic and external trading relations of the Chinese economic system. Decentralization and the introduction of a regionally biased local retention system of foreign exchange earnings from exports favored Guangdong tremendously. It could use the 100 percent retention ratio of its Special Economic Zones and the foreign exchange swap markets there to divert tradable goods from traditional export outlets like Shanghai, which was only accorded a 25 percent retention ratio, by offering higher renminbi returns to exporters.[27] The retained foreign exchange earnings would also be used to import components and parts for assembling consumer durables in short supply, thereby turning in even higher renminbi return for exporters. By this institutional advantage, Guangdong was able to immediately increase its exports, even without much investment in its industry and agriculture to enhance their export competitiveness. Commodity exports of the province swelled by

39.8 percent in 1986, 28.1 percent in 1987, and 29.8 percent in 1988. Only when the central government began to reduce the gap between special economic zones and other provinces in the country in the retention system in 1988 and again in 1989 was the upsurge in Guangdong's exports arrested, with negative growth of 10.7 percent in 1989 and a small recovery of 17.6 percent in 1990.[28] The much more sluggish growth of Guangdong's commodity exports revealed that institutional factors—more than economic factors—were responsible for the high growth in the province's exports. The comparative advantage of the province's export-oriented industry and agriculture has been more evident in its trade with the rest of the nation, rather than with the rest of the world.

Despite the failure of the province in sustaining its strong commodity exports after the removal of its advantage in 1988, Guangdong has seen the continued rise of total exports. This was because since 1984, the aggressive economic reform undertaken by the central government had convinced Hong Kong manufacturers of the Chinese commitment to attract direct foreign investment, which led them to relocate their failing export-oriented labor-intensive industries—which were suffering from cost inflation in the territory—to neighboring Guangdong. Exports from sub-contracted processing activities constituted about 10 percent of the total exports of the province in 1984, and doubled gradually to US$0.583 billion, or 5.5 percent in 1990. The bulk of the exports from processing or assembling activities by Hong Kong manufacturers were reported under a different category, that of exports of foreign-owned firms. Records of this item first appeared in 1984, at only US$74 million. It climbed to US$222 million in 1985, US$389 million in 1986, and US$611 million in 1987. Since then, exports from this source have taken off. In 1988, it was US$1.202 billion, jumping to US$2.277 billion the next year, and to US$3.724 billion in 1990, constituting a massive 35.8 percent of the province's total exports.[29] If Guangdong's economy is to be classified as export-oriented in the conventional way—that is, geared to the overseas market, instead of the domestic market—it is this foreign sector that provides the dynamism. Since commodity exports included a high proportion of agricultural and mineral exports, while exports by foreign-owned firms were all industrial products, the increase in the share of exports in Guangdong's gross industrial output from 23.1 percent in 1989 to 27.4 percent in 1990[30] was mostly the result of the great advance in the foreign sector.

To conclude, the economic miracle of Guangdong that has been praised so much in the Chinese and foreign press has been founded on a process of import-substitution industrialization, also found in many developing countries. Import substitution of this type lies in the substitution of imported consumer goods by those assembled and later manufactured domestically. It is therefore heavily dependent on the import of components and technology in the form of turn-key machinery and equipment, and involves little technology transfer. The industrial and technological foundation for sustained economic growth may not be present under this type of industrialization. However, Guangdong has been more fortunate than the Latin American countries that carried out similar import substitution in the 1950s and 1960s, as it has a huge domestic market, which has been expanding rapidly, and a newly industrialized Hong Kong lying next to it, which has started relocating most of its export-oriented labor-intensive industries to Guangdong to take advantage of the cheaper labor and land resources there. In addition, Guangdong has access to the huge labor surplus from the vast countryside of China, a condition not present in any other country except India.

The two sectors, the predominantly import substitution local sector and the mainly export-oriented foreign sector, have not been closely linked, even though there has been technology transfer from the latter to the former. By 1991, Guangdong had benefited so much from the success of these two sectors that it had turned from a capital-deficient economy into a capital-surplus one. By December 1991, after 9 months of credit surplus in its banking system, the province had accumulated almost R20 billion in surplus savings. This offered the financial resource for the province to embark on its ambitious Eighth Five-Year Plan and 10-Year Perspective Plan for secondary import substitution, following the footsteps of Taiwan and South Korea in building up local heavy and chemical industries in the 1990s.[31]

Impact of Guangdong's Economic Development on Hong Kong

The structural transformation of Hong Kong's economy went hand in hand with the economic development and export expansion of Guangdong in the second half of the 1980s. Until 1987, the total manufacturing work force employed in Hong Kong had been very stable, staying between 850,000 to 950,000, even though the fast growth of its trade with China had gradually increased the size of the work force in the import and export sector from below 100,000 in 1978 to above 200,000 after 1986. Hong Kong had been able to keep some of its manufacturing industry and gained further economic growth from the re-export of consumer durables and intermediate goods to Guangdong.

By 1987, the impact of the relocation of Hong Kong's labor-intensive industries to Guangdong was clear. Employment in the manufacturing sector began to decline. In the four years from 1987 to 1991, it shed over 20 percent of its work force, or about 200,000 workers, while the import and export sector gained 130,000 workers, or increased its work force by more than 50 percent in 1987. This change in employment structure reflected the shifting importance of Hong Kong's exports. Re-exports were secondary before rapid economic growth started in Guangdong. They constituted only 24.1 percent of the total exports of the territory in 1978. Re-exports grew along with the increase in domestic exports, and since 1983, when China, and Guangdong in particular, began to boost domestic consumption with the import of foreign consumer goods, domestic exports, together with re-exports, have fluctuated with the ups and downs in China's (and Guangdong's) imports. This explains the drop of 15 percentage points in annual growth in 1982, negative growth of 6 percent in 1985 from a 32 percent increase in the previous year, and the slowdown in growth to below 3 percent for three years from 1989 after 11 percent growth in 1988.[32] The timing of the drop in growth coincided with tightening control over imports by the central government in China. Re-exports have shown a similar pattern of high acceleration interrupted by modest increases, but even the downs were modest increases above 15 percent except in 1982 when it was 6 percent. The latter may be accounted for by the insignificant re-exports from Hong Kong's outward-oriented processing in Guangdong.

The slowdown of domestic exports after 1988 was not a simple consequence of the reduction in China's imports. In fact, in the three years beginning with 1989, domestic exports to China continued to show a strong upward trend, with annual growth rates ranging from 10 percent to 15 percent. It was the growth of the China market that prevented her domestic exports becoming negative. If the China share is taken away, Hong Kong's domestic exports stayed flat in the period, with increases in 1989 less than 1 percent and declines in 1990 and 1991 of 1.3 percent and 1.0 percent respectively.[33] This should be seen as the effect of the relocation of local export-oriented labor-intensive industries to Guangdong, and the transfer of exports from Hong Kong to Guangdong, which either went directly to overseas markets as exports of Guangdong (but in a relatively smaller proportion, as suggested by a survey of Hong Kong firms in Guangdong),[34] or came back to Hong Kong first as imports and later left as re-exports after transshipment through the local port.

Judging by the shift in local employment and the overtaking of domestic exports by re-exports (the latter passing the 50 percent mark of total Hong Kong exports in 1988, and representing 69.8 percent by 1991), since at least 1987, Hong Kong's economy has been transformed from an industrial economy into one characterized by a fast-growing service sector that is founded upon business with China. Thanks to the restrictive quota and country of origin system of export controls imposed by Hong Kong's major overseas markets, a large proportion of the local industries has been retained in the territory and forced to go into higher value-added product ranges under the pressure of rising local production and labor costs.

The service sector expanded for three reasons. First, Hong Kong has been the main bridge linking up China and the outside world because of its excellent infrastructural facilities and its expertise and experience in dealing with China. Both foreign businessmen and Chinese economic organizations need Hong Kong as the most convenient place to meet each other or as the starting point to enter either China or the outside world. The greater opening up of China has not reduced Hong Kong's importance as an intermediary. On the contrary, it attracts new firms from new countries to come to China via Hong Kong.

Second, services industries have been created to facilitate and service the import and export trade of China with Hong Kong and through Hong Kong.

Third, the relocation of Hong Kong's industries to Guangdong has improved their export competitiveness and led to their expansion in Guangdong and into other parts of China. Such relocation has not moved the entire operations of the Hong Kong firms to Guangdong or other parts of China, but turned the remaining operations in Hong Kong mainly into those of strategic planning, financial management, design, new product development, marketing and business negotiation. This has led to a proliferation of professional services and the organizational restructuring and expansion of firms, which have their production operations in Guangdong and China growing much faster than in Hong Kong.

The development of the service sector in Hong Kong has created two unexpected consequences. The relocation of most manufacturing industries inevitably causes structural unemployment for the manufacturing work force. Many of the manufacturing workers are unable to adapt themselves to vacancies found in the service sector. Meanwhile, the rapid expansion of the service sector has come as a surprise to the government and the economy; no manpower planning has been made to forecast the growth of labor demand in this sector. The result is a disequilibrium in the labor market for this sector, which has pushed up wages. The strain in the supply of services to cope with sudden demand arising from the relocation and the rapid expansion of trade and business with China has also pushed up prices of services. The combined consequence is strong inflationary pressure being built up in the local economy.

On the other hand, the repatriation of the huge profits gained in the export-oriented processing activities (wage savings for at least 1.5 million manufacturing workers employed in Guangdong would amount to US$500 per month per worker, making total savings of US$9 billion per year for Hong Kong) would find no manufacturing investment outlet. The political risk involved because of the return of Hong Kong to Chinese sovereignty in 1997 and the smaller size of individual capital funds discourage investment in capital- and technology-intensive industries. Unless the money is transferred overseas, the investment opportunities left would be in the service sector, including the property market. A concentration of investment in the service sector would further strain supplies and raise prices, forcing up overall inflation in the economy.

The deindustrialization of the Hong Kong economy would be incomplete because of the protection given by restrictive foreign import controls, which mitigate against the effects of adverse comparative advantage on the remaining local industries. However, the conversion of the local export-oriented manufacturing economy into a China-dependent service economy is also beset with problems of structural unemployment and inflation. Without strong market competition in the local service sector, its productivity and efficiency would not be raised and the easy access to China's huge pool of cheap labor would also help the economy out by bringing in cheap labor as a substitute for management and technical improvements. The local economy would continue the pattern of extensive growth that was started with the extensive growth of its export-oriented labor-intensive industries in Guangdong, now followed by similarly extensive growth of the service sector in Hong Kong. The scope of operation and integration of the Hong Kong economy has been extended to cover part of Guangdong, to form a so-called "Greater Hong Kong." But this "greater Hong Kong" is increasingly dependent on Guangdong and China, more and more integrated into the regional economic division of labor that centers on the manufacturing base of Guangdong.

In the plans for Guangdong in the 1990s, the secondary import-substitution industrialization program of the province has not incorporated an active role for Hong Kong. Partly this is true because it is the intention of Guangdong to reduce its reliance on outward processing from Hong Kong, which benefits Hong Kong more than the province. It may also reflect the fact that a service sector-dominated Hong Kong would have little contribution to the development of capital and technology-intensive industries that Guangdong aims to build up in the coming decade. If Guangdong is as successful in its secondary import-substitution industrialization as in the primary import-substitution industrialization of the 1980s, the importance of Hong Kong in the region will be reduced further to concentrate on services related to the industrial, trade and investment development of Guangdong and China.

Impact of Guangdong's Economic Development on Taiwan

Taiwan has come to the China scene only recently since 1988, when political and military confrontation between the Chinese government and the KMT government of Taiwan was abandoned. In the mid-1980s, Taiwan was forced by the U.S., because of its huge trade surplus, to appreciate its currency and to liberalize its economy. This has caused a general escalation of production costs in Taiwan, pushing its export-oriented labor-intensive industries to shift to other lower-cost production localities outside Taiwan. Before 1988 Taiwan's outward investment for lower production costs went mostly to the ASEAN countries and to the U.S. and EC to bypass trade protectionism enforced in these markets. When the political change in 1988 allowed Taiwan's investors the choice of China, the flow of outward investment first began to turn to Fujian, the Chinese province next to Taiwan, which has a closer cultural and dialect affinity with Taiwan, and later more to Guangdong, which offers much better investment incentives and convenience than Fujian.

Within three years, by early 1992, over 80 percent of Taiwan's traditional exporting industries manufacturing shoes, bags, toys and umbrellas, etc. had moved their production base to China. The manufacturing work force in Taiwan has also lost about 400,000 persons from 1987 to 1991, including about 300,000 persons in the traditional labor-intensive industries. In turn, the work force employed in services and trade expanded by over 140,000.[35] The same pattern of structural change in the composition of the labor force of Hong Kong mentioned earlier appears to be repeated in Taiwan, though at a later date and on a smaller scale.

In the past few years, Taiwan's trade pattern also shows a similar trend to that of Hong Kong's. Taiwan's overall exports stabilized after 1987, and in 1989 and 1990, annual growth rates were 9.3 percent and 1.4 percent respectively much slower than in the mid-1980s, when Taiwan's exports already suffered from the pressure of currency appreciation and cost escalation. The very modest growth of these years was maintained by a rapid expansion of exports to Hong Kong, most of which were actually sent on to China to circumvent the prohibition of direct trade between China and Taiwan imposed by the Taiwan government. Hong Kong's share of Taiwan's total exports increased steadily from below 8.0 percent in 1987 to 9.2 percent in 1988, 10.6 percent in 1989, and 12.7 percent in 1990.[36]

The growing trade of Taiwan with Hong Kong and indirectly with China has been accompanied by two features. First, the share of traditional labor-intensive industrial products in Taiwan's overall exports has been on the decline. In 1987, the share of textiles and textile articles occupied 16.9 percent, while that of footwear, umbrellas, plastic flowers, etc. constituted 8.1 percent. By 1990, their shares dropped to 15.3 percent, and 6.1 percent. Their volumes experienced an insignificant nominal increase of 0.7 percent (mostly due to the exports of artificial fibers and fabrics to China for export-oriented processing) and 16.0 percent over three years.[37]

Second, Taiwan's trade surplus with the U.S., traditionally its number one market, has stabilized following the smaller growth and declining importance of its exports to the U.S. since 1987. However, its trade surplus with Hong Kong has expanded drastically. In 1987, the trade surplus with Hong Kong was 18.0 percent of the total trade surplus, as compared with the U.S. 85.7 percent share. The Hong Kong share rose to over 39.0 percent in the next two years and further to 56.9 percent in 1990.[38] By 1991, of the total trade surplus of US$13.3 billion, the Hong Kong share was US$10.4 billion, or 78.2

percent.[39] Hong Kong has replaced the U.S. as the main source of Taiwan's trade surplus, even though it is the second largest export market.

The reason for the rapid build up of Taiwan's trade surplus with Hong Kong and indirectly with China lies in two factors. The relocation of Taiwan's labor-intensive export-oriented industries to Fujian and Guangdong has transferred much of Taiwan's original exports to China, reducing its exports and therefore its trade surplus with the U.S. Since the Taiwan government still maintains a very restrictive policy towards imports from China, most of the exports become either direct exports from China to the U.S. and elsewhere, including those transshipped through Hong Kong or re-exports from Hong Kong to overseas markets. Thus, intra-industry trade does not create imports for Taiwan, while the restriction on direct imports from China further exaggerates Taiwan's trade surplus with China.

The relocation of Taiwan's industries to China, particularly Guangdong, where most Taiwanese investment is found, is still in its early stage. Unlike Hong Kong, which does not have upstream industries for its relocated consumer goods industries, Taiwan's export industries have, in the past, been created through the efforts of the government, with a large upstream industrial sector backing it up. The relocation of the industries has eliminated the clients of the upstream industrial sector, as once they are relocated to China, the industries may find more convenient suppliers outside Taiwan. This has created pressure for firms in the upstream industrial sector to follow their clients and to move to China. The latter move has not yet taken place on a large scale, partly because relocation of production in this sector still requires approval from the Taiwan government and the investment would be much bigger and take longer to negotiate and plan. If this should proceed with the tolerance of the Taiwan government, the relocation process would take longer and involve more capital- and technology-intensive industries. The deindustrialization of Taiwan would be of a much larger scale with more far reaching effects than that of Hong Kong. It would also coincide with the secondary import- substitution industrialization plans of Guangdong. The consequence would then be a more fundamental restructuring of the regional pattern of economic integration and division of labor among Guangdong, Hong Kong and Taiwan, which would have a strong impact on the broader regional economic system of East Asia and on East Asia's trade with industrialized nations.

Conclusion

The rapid economic growth of Guangdong in the 1980s has offered new economic opportunities to Guangdong, Hong Kong and Taiwan. Guangdong's import substitution industrialization has built up the economic strength and dynamism of the province, offering a chance to use the relocation of upstream industries from Taiwan to advance secondary import-substitution industrialization in the province. At the same time, the relocation of Hong Kong and Taiwan's labor-intensive export-oriented industries to Guangdong to take advantage of local access to the huge pool of human resources in China has built up a very competitive, export-oriented industrial sector in the province. The two sectors, if merged together through investment from the province and by Hong Kong and Taiwan, would create a dynamic regional economic system that would in turn force a drastic restructuring of the economies of Hong Kong and Taiwan.

Notes

1. *A General Regional Survey of China's Electronics Industry—Guangdong* (Beijing: Electronics Industry Press, 1988: 98-101).

2. Cf. the document approved by the Chinese Party central leadership on 19 April 1978 about the plan for the development of China's foreign trade in the following 8 years, a summary of which may be found in *A Chronicle of Summaries of Major Events about National Economic and Social Development Plans of the People's Republic of China, 1949-85* (hereafter, *Chronicle of Summaries)* (Beijing: Hongqi Press, 1987: 393).

3. See the various documents relating the grand plans for importation of foreign technology in 1977 and 1978. *Chronicle of Summaries:* 383, 393.

4. See Thomas M. H. Chan, *China's Industrial Development, 1978-89,* Working Paper Series No. 91016 (Business Research Centre, School of Business, Hong Kong Baptist College, 1992).

5. *Economic Research Report on Guangdong—A Review of the 1980s and the Prospect for the 1990s* (hereafter, *CERD Report*) (Hong Kong: CERD Consultants Ltd., 1991: 2).

6. *CERD Report:* 3.

7. *CERD Report:* 5.

8. For Special Economic Zone investments by the central government, see Thomas H. Chan, "Financing Shenzhen's Economic Development: A Preliminary Analysis of Sources of Capital Construction Investments, 1979-84," *The Asian Journal of Public Administration* 7, No. 2, December 1985: 170-197.

9. *CERD Report:* 12.

10. *CERD Report:* 12.

11. For the retention system, see Lin Dahui, *Micro-International Finance,* Beijing: Chinese Finance and Economics Press, 1991: 138-171.

12. *CERD Report:* 9.

13. *Statistical Yearbook of Guangdong 1991:* 191, Table 7-1.

14. *Statistical Yearbook of Guangdong 1991:* 29, Table 8-1.

15. *Statistical Yearbook of Guangdong 1991:* 29, Table 8-1.

16. Calculated from *CERD Report:* 14.

17. *CERD Report:* 14.

18. See, for instance, Wan Jieqiu and Li Huizhong, *On Price Mechanism* (Shanghai: Shanghai Joint Publications Press, 1989: 208-248).

19. Thomas M. H. Chan, *China's Industrial Development, 1978-89.*

20. *CERD Report:* 9.

21. *CERD Report:* 10. It was estimated the actual trade volume should be at least 40-50 percent larger than revealed by official statistics.

22. *Statistical Yearbook of Guangdong, 1991.*

23. *Statistical Yearbook of Guangdong, 1991:* 163, Table 5-6.

24. *CERD Report:* 10.

25. *CERD Report:* 14.

26. *CERD Report:* 22.

27. *Statistical Yearbook of Guangdong,* various issues.

28. *Statistical Yearbook of Guangdong,* various issues.

29. *Statistical Yearbook of Guangdong,* various issues.

30. *Statistical Yearbook of Guangdong, 1991:* 154, Table 5-2. The Statistical Communique on Guangdong's economic performance in 1990 issued by the Guangdong Provincial Bureau of Statistics reported that at current prices, the share of exports in gross industrial output in the year was 32 percent, a significant jump from 1989's 26 percent. However, the percentage did not tally with the output figures listed in the Communique. The Communique may be found in *Nanfong Ribao,* 7 March 1991.

31. See Thomas M. H. Chan, "Report on Guangdong," October 1991, mimeo.; for the concept of secondary import substitution, see Chi Schive, "The Next Stage of Industrialization in Taiwan and South Korea," in *Manufacturing Miracles - Paths of Industrialization in Latin America and East Asia,* edited by G. Gereffi and D. L. Wyman (Princeton: Princeton University Press, 1990: 267-291).

32. Census and Statistics Department, Hong Kong Government, *Hong Kong Trade Statistics,* quoted from Research Department, Hong Kong Trade Development Council, *Survey on Hong Kong Domestic Exports, Re- Exports and Triangular Trade,* Hong Kong, November 1991, Appendix 4.

33. Research Department, Hong Kong Trade Development Council, *Hong Kong's Trade by Countries - Statistical Yearbook,* Vol. 1, 1991.

34. Same as note 32.

35. Quoted in *Commonwealth* (Taipei), 1 March 1992: 16, 22.

36. *Statistical Yearbook of the Republic of China, 1991.*

37. *Statistical Yearbook of the Republic of China, 1991.*

38. *Statistical Yearbook of the Republic of China, 1991.*

39. Quoted in *Commonwealth* (Taipei), 1 March 1992: 16.

12

Merchants, Small Employers and a Non-Interventionist State: Hong Kong as a Case of Unorganized Late Industrialization

Tai-lok Lui and Stephen W. K. Chiu

The economic performances of the East Asian newly industrializing economies (EANIEs—Hong Kong, South Korea, Singapore and Taiwan) in the post-war decades have been remarkable. This so-called "East Asian miracle" has sparked off a race among observers—academic and journalist—to search for the winning formula of these EANIEs. By now, research on East Asian capitalism has come to constitute a growing industry of its own. However, while the lessons of economic growth and development in East Asia are still hot topics for debates, the EANIEs have undergone economic restructuring and are facing new problems and challenges. Current research on the topic, with their emphases on the origins of the economic success of East Asian capitalism, rather than the structuring and restructuring of industrial development in the region, simply fail to catch up with recent developments in these EANIEs.

In different ways, newly industrializing economies in East Asia are restructuring their industries in response to changes in their comparative advantages and to the changing environment of the global economy. This process of industrial restructuring poses new questions to current research on East Asian capitalism. First, what were once the competitive edges of these NIEs, particularly low labor costs and attractive terms to foreign investments, have been gradually eroded over time. Second, concomitant to changes in their comparative advantages, the NIEs have to restructure their industries in a changing socio-economic context. Those structural conditions and state policies, which have been conducive to rapid growth and development in the early phase of industrialization, are not necessarily sufficient for tackling new problems arising in the process of industrial restructuring. Indeed, our investigation of the industrial restructuring process requires a new research agenda—one requiring a dynamic analysis of the ups and downs of these EANIEs instead of undertaking further *post hoc* (and often spurious) explanations of well known success stories. In this sense, the industrial restructuring process offers a vantage point both for understanding the factors underlying the economic success of the EANIEs, and for looking ahead to their prospects of maintaining growth and development in a new round of global economic competitions.

This chapter will start with an examination of the restructuring process of Hong Kong's manufacturing activities in the 1980s. Essentially, Hong Kong's industries continue to pursue labor-intensive production and have not been "manufacturing up" to more technologically sophisticated products. Yet, despite the failure to achieve technological upgrading, the manufacturing sector is still able to secure reasonable growth. This enigma of Hong Kong's industrialization is the object of study for this chapter. In the following sections, we shall first examine the conditions of industrial development in the 1980s, and then investigate the structural and institutional factors underlying Hong Kong's failure to upgrade the technology of industrial production, and the continuation of labor-intensive production. In particular, we shall focus on two issues: first, on the character of Hong Kong's industrial economy and the way local small factories respond to changes in the business environment, and second, on the formation of the non-interventionist colonial state in industrial development and its implications for Hong Kong's industrial restructuring process. It is our contention that Hong Kong is a case of unorganized late industrialization. We shall argue that the peculiarities of the case of Hong Kong does not make it simply exceptional and thus irrelevant to our understanding of East Asian capitalism in general. In fact, our case casts doubts on the efficacy of current analyses and throws light on the diversity of development trajectories among the EANIEs.

Given the limited length of this chapter, we shall not go into the details of the historical development of Hong Kong's industries (but see Chen, 1984; Lui and Chiu, 1993, for a brief review). Furthermore, as we are interested in the restructuring process of Hong Kong's manufacturing industries, we shall start our discussion with the landmark of an official attempt to deal with increasing protectionism and to recognize, as put by the Governor in his address to the Legislative Council in 1977, the "urgency to the long term desirability of broadening our industrial base" (The Advisory Committee on Diversification, 1979: 1). Accordingly, an advisory committee was appointed by the Governor to consider: "the principal factors which have contributed to Hong Kong's economic growth over the past 15 years," "the past, present and likely future course of the regulation of international trade," and "the factors which have been influential in attracting or deterring the establishment of new activities in the manufacturing and other sectors of the economy," and "comparative practices in comparable economies which have successfully encouraged the establishment of new industries."

The outcome of this official exercise of reviewing the matter of industrial diversification should not bother us here. Indeed, when *The Report of the Advisory Committee on Diversification* was finally published in late 1979, it "was out of date as soon as it was published because of the new role for Hong Kong as a result of China's opening up in 1977" (Chen and Li, 1991: 41). There are actually two issues we need to note in understanding the restructuring process in the late 1970s. First, China's open-door policy has brought about the revival of entrepot trade and has opened new opportunities for local manufacturing. And as we shall see in subsequent discussion, economic reforms in China constitute one of the most important factors in shaping the course of Hong Kong's industrial restructuring in the 1980s. Second, and equally important, the influx of legal and illegal migrants from mainland China since the mid-1970s has again, like previous waves of migration from the other side of the border, brought Hong Kong a new pool of low-wage labor force for manufacturing production (Greenwood, 1990; Skeldon, 1986). Census statistics suggest that in 1976-81, 58.0 percent of the population growth was composed of net migration. A large proportion of the economically active migrants (73.9 percent) was found in production and related occupations which provide the opportunity for their participation in the local labor market.

What interests us here is not only that the arrival of immigrants has brought about an increase in the supply of labor to Hong Kong's industries. More important, it has the unintended effect of assisting the perpetuation of labor-intensive production in the manufacturing sector. The consequence is, as cogently put by Greenwood (1990: 21), that "the growth of Hong Kong's GDP in the 1960s and 1970s was made up, in significant degree, by the "horizontal" expansion of the labor force, i.e., the arrival of large numbers of relatively unskilled workers, rather than by the "vertical" upgrading of skills of resident employers and employees." However, the fact that successive waves of immigrants from China, particularly relevant here is the immigration in the 1970s, constitute sources of labor supply for coping with the problem of labor shortage, should not lead us to assume that the continuation of a low-wage, labor-intensive production strategy is simply the outcome of "historical accidents." On the contrary, the effects of the "timely" arrival of immigrants on the structuring of local manufacturing has to be explained in the context of an industrial structure dominated by small, local establishments, a government practicing non-interventionist policies, and trade unionism underdeveloped in shop floor bargaining.

Here in this section, we shall concentrate on the characteristics of Hong Kong's industries and see how local industries respond to the challenges of restructuring. Then, in the next section, we shall investigate the formation of the non-interventionist state and its role in industrial development. But before we come to discuss the restructuring of local industries, it would be useful to briefly review the state of industrial development in the 1980s.

As we have pointed out above, the re-opening of the Chinese economy and the "timely" arrival of migrants had the effects of making the industrial diversification program redundant. Local employers are happy to capitalize on the supply of recent migrant labor and continue their labor-intensive production. So, the development of Hong Kong's manufacturing in the 1980s was essentially a continuation of the course of industrialization since the 1970s. First, following the trend started in the 1970s, the contributions of manufacturing to GDP and employment continued to drop in the 1980s (see Tables 10. 1 and 10.2). The general trend is one of de-industrialization, with the tertiary sector assuming greater significance in the economy. Second, with the decline of the textiles industry in the 1970s, garment-making and electronics have come to take the leading positions in terms of employment shares (in 1988, 33.9 percent and 13.0 percent respectively) and share of domestic exports (in 1988, 30.9 percent and 25.5 percent respectively) among local manufacturing industries.

Third, although the number of establishments with direct foreign investments rose from 242 in 1971 to 509 in 1986, these establishments only constitute a very small proportion (509 out of 48,623 in 1986) of the total manufacturing establishments. Of course, in terms of their impacts on Hong Kong's industrial development, the significance of direct foreign investments is greater than this simple number counting of establishments under the ownership of foreign capital (e.g., these establishments accounted for about 10.0 percent of the manufacturing employment). Furthermore, foreign manufacturers are likely to be running bigger establishments and are contributive to technology transfer (Hung, 1984). However, it is still true to say that Hong Kong's manufacturing is mainly operated by local employers. This relates to our fourth point that in the 1980s the manufacturing sector is still dominated by small industrial establishments (Table 12.3). The average size of manufacturing establishments in 1989 was 16 employed persons. Without suggesting size *per se* is a sufficient indicator of organizational character and resources, it is fair to say that these small establishments, which are mainly engaged in labor-intensive production, come close to the descriptions of those secondary or peripheral firms operating in highly competitive environments that we find in the literature on

TABLE 12.1. Hong Kong: GDP by Industry (percentage), 1961-1991

Industry / Year	1961	1971	1981	1986	1991
Agriculture and Fishing	3.4	1.8	0.7	0.5	0.2
Mining and Quarrying	0.3	0.2	0.2	0.1	#
Manufacturing	23.6	28.2	22.8	22.3	15.5
Electricity, Gas and Water	2.4	1.8	1.4	3.0	2.2
Construction	6.2	4.9	7.5	4.8	5.3
Wholesale and Retail Trades, Restaurants and Hotels	19.5	19.5	19.5	21.3	25.4
Transport, Storage and Communication	9.6	6.8	7.5	8.1	9.7
Financing, Insurance, Real Estate and Business Services	10.8	17.5	23.8	17.3	23.0
Community, Social and Personal Services	17.7	18.9	13.3	16.6	15.4
Ownership of premises	6.5	—	9.8	10.7	10.7
Nominal Sector	N.A.	N.A.	-6.5	-4.7	-7.4
Unclassified	—	0.6	—	—	—

Sources: De-liang Zheng, *Xianzai Xiang Gang Jingji* (Modern Hong Kong Economy) (Beijing: China's Financial, Political and Economic Publisher, 1987), p. 123; Census and Statistics Department, *Estimates of Gross Domestic Product: 1966 to 1990* (Hong Kong: Government Printer, 1991), p. 31; *Estimates of Gross Domestic Product: 1966-1992* (Hong Kong: Government Printer, 1993), p. 39.

Key: * Provisional estimates
Less than 0.05%

TABLE 12.2. Hong Kong: Distribution of Working Population (in percentages) by Industry, 1961-1991

	Year			
Industry	1961	1971	1981	1991
Manufacturing	43.0	47.0	41.2	28.2
Construction	4.9	5.4	7.7	6.9
Wholesale and Retail Trades, Restaurants and Hotels	14.4	16.2	19.2	22.5
Transport, Storage and Communication	7.3	7.4	7.5	9.8
Financing, Insurance, Real Estate and Business Services	1.6	2.7	4.8	10.6
Community, Social and Personal Services	18.3	15.0	15.6	19.9
Others	10.5	6.3	4.0	2.1

Sources: Census and Statistics Department, *Hong Kong 1981 Census Main Report, Volume 1: Analysis*, p. 138; *Hong Kong 1991 Population Census Main Report*, p. 95

TABLE 12.3. Hong Kong: Distribution of Manufacturing Establishments and Employment by Size (percentages)

Size of Establishment	Establishment				Employment			
	1961	1971	1981	1989	1961	1971	1981	1989
1 - 9	38.9	51.9	65.4	69.6	6.0	6.9	13.3	16.1
10 - 19	21.6	19.1	15.6	14.6	8.4	7.5	10.9	12.2
20 - 49	18.2	15.5	11.1	9.5	15.1	14.0	17.9	18.1
50 - 99	6.7	6.6	4.7	3.8	12.4	13.2	16.2	16.4
100 - 199	4.0	3.9	2.0	1.5	14.7	15.7	14.4	12.5
200 - 499	2.5	2.1	0.9	0.7	20.3	18.6	13.7	12.8
500 and Over	0.9	0.7	0.3	0.3	22.9	24.2	13.6	11.9

Sources: V. Sit, et al., *Small Scale Industry in a Laissez-faire Economy* (Centre of Asian Studies, University of Hong Kong, 1979),pp. 25-6; Census and Statistics Department, *Hong Kong Annual Digest of Statistics: 1990 Edition,* p. 38.

economic dualism (for instance, Averitt, 1968). They are more likely to be survivors in economic niches than venturers for innovations and structural transformation.

The kinds of problems encountered by Hong Kong manufacturers can be illustrated by a brief review of the two leading industries, namely garment-making and electronics (for a more detailed review, see Lui and Chiu, 1992). In the case of the garment industry, quota restrictions have long been the main concerns of the industry. But what is more critical to the development of the industry has been the problem of rising labor and production costs under inflationary pressures (Industry Department, 1991: 39). The original advantage of the availability of cheap labor has gradually been eroded over time. Despite these pressures on the industry to diversify and upgrade its products, the organization of production for the manufacturing of garments has remained largely unchanged. On the whole, the bulk of the garment-making labor force is composed of semi-skilled (operative) and unskilled workers (see Table 12.4). While computer-aided equipment has been installed (in pattern-grading and marker-making processes), they are mainly found in larger factories (Industry Department, 1989: 33).

As regards the electronics industry, it grew rapidly in the 1970s. The 1970s and the early 1980s witnessed an expansion of radio production and the emergence of the production of fashionable fad products (e.g., electronic watches and clocks, calculators, etc.). Also, in this period, the industry moved into packaging and testing of semi-conductor components (see Henderson, 1989). But then, this was soon overtaken by the assembly of

TABLE 12.4. Hong Kong: Labor Force Composition in the Clothing Industry and the Electronics Industry

	Electronics				Clothing		
Job Categories	1974	1978	1982	1986	1972	1981	1987
Technologist Level	1.5	2.5	3.8	4.0	N.A.	1.4	1.5
Technician Level	6.3	6.7	12.0	14.6	5.4	5.4	7.6
Craftsman Level	11.8	10.2	9.6	9.6	2.2	3.7	4.4
Operative Level	78.3	79.4	71.9	69.1	82.9	76.1	74.2
Unskilled	2.1	1.2	2.7	2.7	9.5	13.4	12.3

Source: Vocational Training Council, *Manpower Survey Report of the Clothing Industry; Manpower Survey on the Electronics Industry,* various years.

computer parts. This cursory review of the development of the industry reveals its strengths as well as weaknesses. No doubt, the strength of the industry lies mainly in its responsiveness and adaptability, to changes in world demands. It moves quickly into the production of many fashion products (e.g., TV games in the late 1970s, and fax machines and memory goods in the late 1980s). However, the other side of this strength of flexibility is that local manufacturers are more capable of playing the role of subcontractor for the international market than of promoting Hong Kong to the status of a regional core of the electronics industry. The constraints of the industry are best summarized by the Industry Department in its *Hong Kong's Manufacturing Industries: 1988* (1989: 48):

> Apart from a few exceptions in the production of transfers, switches, and transistors, Hong Kong does not have a significant process industry for the manufacturing of electronic parts and components from raw or semi-finished materials. . . . The lack of precision metal working capability also restricts Hong Kong's entry into many value-added products such as micro-cassettes, disk drives and printers, which require precision mechanical parts and processing. . . . Hong Kong, while largely successful in competing in the international market as a subcontractor for many electronic consumer products, lacks well-developed supporting industries and a substantial research and development capability. This makes it difficult for the industry to diversify into other areas of knowledge-intensive and potentially high value-added production.

By and large, the electronics industry still relies on a labor-intensive production strategy. Table 12.4 shows the composition of different skill levels of the electronics industry work force. Compared with the garment industry, it is observed that the electronics industry has a larger portion (around 30 percent) in the 1980s) of its labor force engaging in "technologist, technician and craftsman" levels of work. Moreover, there is a trend toward an increase in the proportion of technician level workers and concomitantly a decrease in the operative level workers in the industry. However, these statistics have to be interpreted with caution. First, although there has been a decrease in percentages, the semi-skilled and unskilled workers still constitute the largest component of the work force. Second, the increase in importance, at least quantitatively, of technician level workers does not really suggest a drastic upgrading of the production process. The main occupants of jobs at the technician level are telecommunications technicians whose jobs require the standard of education of either Form 5 (secondary school)/post-secondary diploma or on-the-job training/apprenticeship (Vocational Training Council, 1990). There are few signs suggesting that Hong Kong's electronics industry has significantly improved its technological structure.

Without going further into the details concerning the failure of local manufacturers in re-organizing and upgrading their production, the above discussion of garment-making and electronics production should be sufficient to support our earlier remarks that Hong Kong's manufacturing continues to pursue a labor-intensive strategy in the restructuring process of the 1980s. But then, the intriguing issue is that Hong Kong's industries survive and continue to do well without upgrading their production. On the one hand, as mentioned earlier, the manufacturing sector has difficulties in upgrading its production technology and shifting to higher value-added products. Total value-added as a percentage of gross output of the manufacturing sector in 1985 was 28.5 percent, a figure lower than the percentages of other major economic sectors. In 1989, the percentage dropped to 27.6 percent (Census and Statistics Department, 1992: 40). Moreover, compensation to employees in the manufacturing sector constituted 59.0 percent of value-added of manufacturing industries in 1989. Compared with the figures of other sectors (for instance, the figure for "financing, insurance, real estate and business services" of the same year is 36.4 percent), the percentage of manufacturing was rather high. These statistics clearly show that local manufacturers are producing at small profit margins, and there is a need for them to develop higher value-added products and processes. On the other hand, there are indicators showing that Hong Kong's manufacturing continues to fare reasonably well in the 1980s. In terms of the value of the gross output of local manufacturing, there has been an increase "at an average annual rate of 12.7 percent from HK$136,628 million in 1981 to HK$315,940 million in 1988" (Industry Department, 1991: 7). During the same period, value-added also rose at "an average annual rate of 12.7 percent, from HK$36,049 million in 1981 to HK$83,182 million in 1988." GATT statistics also show that in 1989, Hong Kong moved up to third position among world textiles exporters (from thirteenth position in 1973), making a share of 7.6 percent of total world exports of textiles

(Mytelka, 1991: 116). In short, though Hong Kong's manufacturing has not significantly upgraded its production, it remains competitive in the world market and continues to grow.

The factors underlying this "Hong Kong way" of industrial restructuring are related to the character of the industrial economy of Hong Kong. First of all, it is crucial to note that the spectacular growth of the Hong Kong economy through export-led industrialization is essentially conditioned by the restructuring of the world economy (Dicken, 1986; Landsberg, 1979; So, 1986). Indeed, to a large measure, the development of Hong Kong's manufacturing cannot be abstracted from the emergence of the international subcontracting network which facilitates the incorporation of Hong Kong into the global manufacturing system through the interconnectedness of transnational corporations (Chu, 1988; also see Germidis, 1980).

Here we would like to draw upon a study of the development of garment making in Hong Kong to illustrate the effects of the changing international economy on the industrialization of the colony (Chu, 1988). The gist of the research findings is this. While it is true to say that the influx of Shanghainese industrialists in the late 1940s had brought with them capital and skills which facilitated the growth of manufacturing in general and textiles in particular, their influence on the process of industrialization should not be overstated. There is no evidence to suggest that the textile industrialists have taken an active role in the development of garment production. The influence of these industrialists on production activities besides textiles is more limited than often supposed. Also, though the British merchants and their Commonwealth connections were pertinent to developing markets for local exports in the early 1950s, their role became less significant as the U.S.A. emerged as the major importer of Hong Kong's garment products. Foreign direct investments in manufacturing have been rather insignificant, at least for the initial stage of the colony's industrial development (also see Hung, 1984: 186). Chu's close scrutiny of the validity of the above explanations suggests that the major factor which brings about Hong Kong's industrialization lies elsewhere. Her argument is that "it is the multinational trading groups or the 'commercial form' of the international subcontracting system that has been at work" (Chu, 1988: 74). The international subcontracting system has provided Hong Kong with the opportunities to develop its low-cost, labor-intensive, export-oriented industries.

The incorporation of Hong Kong industries into the world economy through the channel of international commercial subcontracting carries important implications for our understanding of the colonial industrial economy. As mentioned earlier, the role of foreign direct investments in the structuring of Hong Kong's industries is limited. And this becomes even more evident in the process of restructuring in the 1980s. Essentially, the major agents of industrial restructuring remain small local firms. Technological upgrading through attracting foreign capital to selected industries is not and has not been adopted as a strategy for industrial restructuring. Neither is it the practice of the colonial government to give any preference or incentive to foreign direct investments (Wong, 1991: 268-9). Nor is Hong Kong particularly competitive, for instance compared with Singapore, in terms of industrial supports and the structure of industries, in attracting foreign investments to develop technologically sophisticated productions in the industrial colony. The loss of the opportunity to develop into a regional core of the semiconductor industry (see Henderson, 1989 for an analysis of Hong Kong's early achievement and Ho, 1991 for how the opportunity is lost to Singapore) is a revealing case.

Under the pressures for restructuring, local small firms survive by continuing labor-intensive production with higher sensitivities to market changes and greater flexibilities in production. The fact that, compared with other EANIEs, Hong Kong started its export-oriented industrialization early gives local industries some advantages in developing strong commercial ties in their businesses. In the first place, research on Hong Kong industries has long emphasized the role played by trading firms and sourcing agents in the facilitation of industrial development (see, for example, Chan, 1984; Chu, 1988; Sit and Wong, 1989). What is pertinent here is that such a well-developed commercial network provides local manufacturers with the means to reach international markets. More important, such commercial ties shape local manufacturers' sensitivity to the needs of importing markets, especially at the level of retailing. As a result of economic restructuring in advanced industrial societies, production has been increasingly conditioned by the needs of the retailing market (Harvey, 1989; Murray, 1989). In this new world of consumption, the ability to handle such a volatile market is the basic requirement for success. As we have shown in our cursory review of the two major industries of Hong Kong, namely garment-making and electronics (also see Lui and Chiu, 1992), local manufacturers are highly responsive to changes in market needs. Indeed, they possess a good sense of market intelligence and very often are quick to shift their production to new products.

To match the need to respond quickly to changes in the consumption sphere, local manufacturers have been looking for ways to increase their flexibility in production. In the case of garment making, from the time a customer order is placed to when the goods are ready for shipment, small firms in "cut and sew" need 14 days while large firms need 30 days. For knitwear production, the lead-time for small firms is 17.5 days while that for large firms is 35 days (Kurt Salmon Associates, 1987: 143). On the whole, Hong Kong manufacturers are competitive vis-à-vis their international competitors in terms of manufacturing lead time.

Such flexibilities in production are embedded in the "politics of production" (cf. Sabel, 1982) of Hong Kong. The development of garment making in Hong Kong has long been characterized by the predominance of small firms which are interconnected through the subcontracting network. Also, various forms of informal work (such as internal contracting and outwork) have been widely used and are well integrated into the production system of the industry (Lui, 1990 and 1991b). Whereas larger establishments are likely to farm out parts of their production to subcontractors, small establishments rely heavily on such subcontracting activities to maintain their production and, in their turn, shift part of the risk of production to women outworkers. So what lies behind production flexibilities is an urban informal sector wherein women constitute a hidden work force for flexible production (Lui, 1991a and 1991b). However, having noted the informal aspect of production flexibility, it is equally important for us to recognize that local manufacturers have also attempted to re-organize their labor processes for the purpose of increasing flexibility. What is known as the modular production system is gaining in popularity. The idea behind the modular production system is the group work concept (Industry Department, 1990: 39):

> Self-contained work units of 5 to 20 people sew either the whole, or various parts of, a garment. As far as possible, operators are trained to perform a number of tasks within the manufacturing process to achieve maximum flexibility, and appropriate incentives are given for higher performance.

It is suggested that the application of this production system helps improve productivity "of between 10 percent and 40 percent," and reduce "throughput time to one or two days." Although the number of manufacturers who are applying such new production techniques in local production is still small (only 10 out of the 120 manufacturers interviewed by Lau and Chan, 1991, used modular systems in local production), the development of new production processes is a sign showing how local manufacturers take up the issue of flexible production.

In short, the responses of local manufacturers to the changing business environment involve increasing their flexibilities, both in terms of the organization of production and the capability of responding to volatile product markets, than moving towards technological upgrading. As mentioned above, local manufacturers continue to perform the role of subcontractors for international markets and to pursue labor-intensive production. Indeed, it is against this background that we can come to understand two recent developments in Hong Kong's industrial restructuring. The first concerns the importation of foreign labor. Towards the end of the 1980s, it became evident that it was increasingly difficult for Hong Kong's manufacturers to pursue labor-intensive production in the context of rising production costs. The call for importing labor marks the beginning of a new approach to the development of human resources for industrial development. Under pressure from employers in industry and business (see, for example, The Joint Association Working Group, 1989), the government introduced the scheme for importing guest workers in May 1989. Since then, further relaxations concerning restrictions on the number, categories, and wages of guest workers have been made to allow for more flexible importation of labor. In brief, by the end of the 1980s, the government has recognized the strategy of labor importation as a means to tackle the problem of labor shortage and rising labor costs, which was a relief to labor-intensive manufacturers.

A far more important development in recent restructuring processes has been the phenomenon of industrial relocation. Of course, local manufacturer's moves to off-shore assembly are by no means new (see Lau, 1991). Nor are their moves confined to neighboring areas. But what emerges as the most significant development in Hong Kong's manufacturing in the 1980s is the process of industrial relocation to China (especially to the Shenzhen Special Economic Zone and other areas in the Guangdong Province) (Federation of Hong Kong Industries, 1990, 1992 and 1993). One way to look at the significance of off-shore processing in China is to review the statistics concerning re-exports to China for outward processing (Table 12.5). Caveats are in order here. First, the statistics in Table 12.5 do not include figures on materials directly entering China and thus do not reflect the entire picture of Hong Kong's off-shore processing in China. Second, they do not really tell us the actual process of relocation. However, they do show how certain labor-intensive industries can rely on China's labor force for production. Other secondary sources confirm that relocation to China constitutes an important strategy for Hong Kong's manufacturers. According to a survey carried out by Dataquest Incorporated (1991: IV-28), 67 percent of the 116 interviewed electronics companies suggested that they had plants in China for the assembly of semi-finished products, finished products, and parts and components. Production costs and labor shortage were their main concerns in the decision to relocate:

> The main reasons for their establishment of plants and the subcontracting of work in PRC were to solve the labor shortage problem in Hong Kong and to lower the cost of production by making use of the cheap labor and the cheap and abundant supply of land in PRC. . . . They expressed that it was the only means for the electronics manufacturers to survive. In order to stay competitive, they have to move to PRC.

Of course, not all manufacturing productions and production processes can adopt the strategy of relocation. For instance, given the institutional restrictions on qualification for Hong Kong origin status, garment making remains strongly tied to the local base. Such variations in propensity to relocation notwithstanding, the general trend of Hong Kong's manufacturing is one of moving production, especially those relatively labor-intensive processes, to the Pearl River Delta.

TABLE 12.5. Hong Kong: Estimated Values and Proportions of Re-exports to China for Outward Processing Analyzed by Nine Broad Commodity Groups, 1989

Trade Type / Commodity Group	Total Trade Value (HK$ mn.)	Estimated Export Oriented Processing Trade (HK$ mn.)	Percentage of Export-Oriented Processing Trade (%)
Textile materials, yarn, fabrics & textile articles other than textile garments	24,996	17,868	71.5
Articles of apparel and clothing accessories (textile garments)	830	724	87.3
Plastics and articles	7,618	4,417	58.0
Machinery and mechanical appliances, electrical equipment	23,879	5,946	24.9
Sound recorders and reproducers, television image and sound recorders and reproducers	6,773	2,922	43.1
Clocks and watches	1,926	1,801	93.5
Toys, games and sports requisites; parts and accessories	487	293	60.1
Base metals and metal products	6,398	2,420	37.8
Others (excluding commodities & transactions not classified according to kind)	30,064	8,514	28.3
All commodities above	102,971	44,906	43.6

+ These values exclude commodities and transactions not classified according to kind.

Source: Census and Statistics Department, *Hong Kong Monthly Digest of Statistics,* May 1990, p.114.

Both the importation of labor and the process of industrial relocation can be seen as production-cost reduction strategies for assisting local manufacturers in continuing labor-intensive production. What we have been arguing is that the adoption of such restructuring strategies is essentially shaped by the structural and institutional formations of local industries. If it is true to say that the "China factor" (both in terms of the influx of immigrants in the 1970s and the opportunities for industrial relocation in the 1980s) makes the continuation of labor-intensive production viable, it is equally true to note that, given the institutional structuring of Hong Kong's manufacturing, local manufacturers would only appropriate these opportunities without significantly reshaping their production strategies. Undoubtedly, the new resources made available by importing labor and relocating production to China would help to reduce production costs and to maintain the competitiveness of local industries. But this is only a partial answer to our original question: why and how are Hong Kong's labor-intensive industries still alive and doing well? More important, we contend, is the ability of local manufacturers to maintain close contacts with the international commercial subcontracting network and to adjust their productions to meet changing needs. We shall come back to this issue in subsequent discussions.

In our discussion of the industrial restructuring process, we have concentrated on the performances of local small factories. The picture we have been presenting looks as if small local manufacturers have almost been left on their own to cope with problems arising in increasing protectionism, rising production costs and changes in global capitalism. In fact, it is our contention that this actually represents the institutional setting of Hong Kong's industrial economy—Hong Kong is a case of unorganized late industrialization.

More precisely, we contend that local small manufacturers have neither been assisted nor pushed to follow a different course of industrial restructuring. An important component of the institutional environment of industrial restructuring is the financial system. It has been argued that the banking system has been the pillar of the development of manufacturing industries in East Asia (Wade, 1985). Under the state's selective credit policy, banks in Japan, Korea and Taiwan channel large amounts of funds to the industrial sector. Even Singapore has an industrial bank responsible for the provision of long term capital. Yet, Hong Kong seems to be a far cry from this active partnership between finance and industry as in other East Asian economies (also see Ho, 1986: 195-6). Indeed, Hong Kong's situation is closer to that of Britain, where an "institutional separation of finance and industry" is said to exist (Ingham, 1984). There is no industrial bank in Hong Kong. More revealing is the fact that for much of the 1960s, when Hong Kong's industrial growth accelerated, less than 20 percent of the loans and advances issued by the banks were directed towards manufacturing activities (Jao, 1974). The share of loans to manufacturing further declined in the 1970s and 1980s. As one may observe from the statistics from Table 12.6, corresponding figures for the other three EANIEs tend to be much higher. The meager share of Hong Kong's manufacturing in bank loans is obviously not commensurate with their contributions to the national product.

The inadequacy of support from the financial sector is most noticeable when we look at the small and medium manufacturing firms. Only larger firms with substantial collaterals manage to solicit helps from the banks; smaller firms are often denied financial assistance. As a study conducted in the 1960s observed, "the degree of self-financing in Hong Kong industry is indeed abnormally high; a number of substantial firms rely exclusively on their own resources" (Economist Intelligence Unit, 1962: 16). The

TABLE 12.6. Hong Kong: Share of Manufacturing in Bank Loans in East Asia NIEs (percentages)

Singapore		South Korea		Taiwan		Hong Kong	
Year	Share	Year	Share	Year	Share	Year	Share
1967	21.4	1965	42.0	1965	41.5	1965	19.6
1970	34.1	1970	47.5	1970	42.4	1970	19.2
1976	26.7	1975	56.2	1975	68.7	1976	12.8

Source: Singapore: Lee Sheng-Yi, "Financial Institutions and Markets in Singapore," in *Financial Institutions and Markets in Southeast Asia,* edited by M. Skully (London: Macmillan, 1984). South Korea: David Cole and Park Yung-chul, *Financial Development in Korea* (Cambridge: Harvard University Press, 1983). Taiwan: Central Bank of China, *Financial Statistics Monthly* (various years). Hong Kong: Y. C. Jao, "The Financial Environment," in *The Business Environment in Hong Kong,* edited by David Lethbridge (Hong Kong: Oxford University Press, 1980).

same study also pointed out that even for larger firms, long term capital investments are likely to be self-financed and most bank loans are directed to the financing of short term working capital. Later studies also reveal the same pattern of "institutional separation" of small scale manufacturing from the financial sector (e.g., Sit et al., 1979). This institutional feature discourages the adoption of restructuring strategies which require heavy capital investments and encourages capital-saving strategies, especially among smaller firms.

Also pertinent is the fact that local manufacturers are not under any pressure from below to carry out technological upgrading. In other words, they are not constrained by strong unionism in making decisions on restructuring production. A detailed analysis of the development of trade unionism in Hong Kong is beyond the scope of this chapter (but see England, 1989; Turner et al., 1980; Turner, Fosh and Ng, 1991; Levin and Chiu, 1990). Briefly, Hong Kong's union movement is numerically weak, with less than 20 percent of all employees belonging to unions. Union density in the manufacturing sector is particularly weak—less than 10 percent. Unions are also organizationally fragmented into three "federations" of different political persuasions. Shop floor organizations are almost non-existent; unions have very limited power in mobilizing collective actions such as strikes. At the community level, the political clout of unionism is equally limited. Consequently, in devising various strategies of restructuring (for instance, increasing flexibility in production and the use of subcontracting and industrial outwork), local manufacturers are almost completely free of resistance or interventions of unions.

But the most critical institutional factor shaping the "Hong Kong way" of industrial restructuring is the practice of non-interventionism by the colonial state. Essentially, the philosophy behind the management of economic affairs by the colonial government is that of "positive non-interventionism" (Haddon-Cave, 1984: xiv):

> this involves taking the view that, in the great majority of circumstances it is futile and damaging to the growth rate of the economy for attempts to be made to plan the allocation of resources available to the private sector and to frustrate the operation of market forces which, in an open economy, are difficult enough to predict, let alone to control.

However, it is important to point out here that, contrary to the picture portrayed by Friedman and Friedman (1980: 54-5) and other neoclassical economic analysts that the role of the Hong Kong Government in managing economic activities is limited to the minimum, the colonial state is by no means passive in the facilitation of economic growth (Schiffer, 1991; Henderson, 1991). In relation to our present discussion of Hong Kong's industrialization, massive spendings on housing, medical care, education, and social welfare (broadly under the heading of social services) by the colonial government are, no doubt, pertinent to facilitating industrial development. According to a historical review of public expenditure in the postwar decades (Lo-Cheng, 1990: 42ff), "the percentage change in public expenditure on social services remained quite steady, ranging from zero to five percent," and by the financial year 1987/88, it came to constitute 41 percent of total public expenditure. This clearly shows that the government is surely not marginally involved in the provision of social services. More importantly, the massive public housing program established since the 1950s is now widely recognized as one of the crucial factors contributing to the success of local industries (Castells, Goh and Kwok, 1988: Chapter 2). In functional terms, the public housing program (the current population living in public and aided housing, not including those in home ownership estates, is 40.5 percent of the total population) helps tackle the problem of the reproduction of labor power. This question is particularly pertinent as Hong Kong's industries are mainly labor-intensive and their competitiveness depends heavily on the supply of cheap labor. In this context, the public housing program has the effect of subsidizing the wage of the low-wage population—the working class families are able to survive by low wages received from their employers as the latter are indirectly assisted to continue their pursuit of low-wage, labor-intensive manufacturing. In short, the notion of "positive non-interventionism" is not quite the picture of *laissez-faire* conjured up in neoclassical economic texts. As put by Youngson (1982: 132), "Hong Kong and *laissez-faire* have only an occasional acquaintance."

However, while it is one thing to say that the colonial state has an active role to play in facilitating industrial development, it is quite another to assume that it plays the role of a developmental state. Compared with other NIEs in the region (for a brief summary of recent research, see Onis, 1991), the role of the Hong Kong Government falls far short of being a capitalist developmental state. Not only has it not formulated any strategic industrial policy, it also intently refuses to provide any long term rationality for national industrial development or direction for the operation of the market economy. The aforementioned public housing program, as an example of the intervention of the colonial state in the economy, illustrates the strengths and weaknesses of the approach of positive non-interventionism. Whereas the provision of public housing helps to make low wage, labor-intensive manufacturing a viable strategy for industrialization in the 1960s and the early 1970s, this form of indirect intervention does not propel local industries on to the track of industrial restructuring. Under the non-interventionist banner, the emphasis of government policy on industrial development continues to be indirect involvement. These indirect involvements are mainly infrastructural and institutional supports (see Wong, 1991, on the Hong Kong Government's industrial policy). In terms of institutional supports, government expenditure is mainly spent on financing the work of the Industry Department and subventing activities of various industry-related bodies like the Hong Kong Productivity Council and the Hong Kong Design Innovation Company. There are six divisions (namely "development support," "data and services," "infrastructure support," "quality services," "inward investment" and "administration") under the Industry Department. They provide consultancy, information and quality assurance services to local industries. Basically they stay aloof from the operations of industrial production. Their main research outputs are techno-economic case studies of various industries. This clearly illustrates its limited role in supporting local industries.

As regards infrastructural support, the colonial state has long been active in financing education and building communication and transportation networks. But in terms of human resource development, there is no industry-specific manpower training. Generally speaking, coordination between manpower training and industrial development is simply non-existent. Seen in the light of this rather loosely defined infrastructural supports, the development of the Hong Kong Industrial Estates Corporation, with the objective of encouraging technology-and-skill-intensive industries, is a major move in assisting selected industries. However, that said, the impact of the industrial estates program on facilitating industrial restructuring remains to be seen (see Ho, 1986, for some of its problems).

On the whole, the government maintains its detachment from subsidizing any one industry and from directly assisting any particular industrial activity in terms of R&D and other matters related to technological development. Its main objective is to provide the infrastructure for the growth of industrial activities. In the context of industrial development in the 1980s, the government essentially left local manufacturers on their own to tackle the problem of industrial restructuring. The consequence, as mentioned repeatedly, is the perpetuation of labor-intensive manufacturing.

That the colonial state stays aloof from assisting and directing industrial development requires explanation. Here, it is interesting to note that in recent research on East Asian capitalism, particularly those studies emphasizing the pertinence of a state-centered approach, often leave the Hong Kong case of non-interventionism untheorized. Indeed, many state-centered researchers (e.g., Amsden, 1990: 5) simply ignore the case of Hong Kong in their analyses of successful late industrializers. But there is also another kind of treatment which attempts to label Hong Kong as exceptional. Yet, this is an exceptional case which proves rather than falsifies the general rule of the state-centered approach. In his discussion of the "strategic capacity" model of development, Deyo (1987: 243) contends that:

> A deliberate adherence on the part of Hong Kong's colonial elite to laissez-faire principles of political economy seems to preclude application of the strategic model I have suggested. . . . Nevertheless, the recent experience of sluggish industrial transformation alongside rapid growth in finance sectors suggests the usefulness of the model for even this exotic case.

Essentially, two points lead Deyo to suggest that Hong Kong is an "exotic case" which confirms the statist model. First, while Hong Kong successfully industrialized in the early post-war period, its ineffective response to the changing economic environment and the failure to develop high technology are indications of the negative effects of the absence of a developmental state. Second, strategic capacity for economic development does not come from the state (in the narrow sense of the term) alone. "It seems clear that the peak economic associations in Hong Kong have in fact assumed a role of economic tutelage in the development of the colony, which is not surprising if one takes into account the social cohesiveness and unity of commercial, financial, and industrial leaders, on the one hand, and colonial authorities, on the other" (Deyo, 1987: 244). While Hong Kong lacks a strong developmental state, the big banking groups and trading firms provide a perfect surrogate, which, in turn, possesses the strategic capacity requisite for economic growth. In Deyo's view, Hong Kong, far from being an anomaly, in fact gives further credence to a (expanded) statist conception of economic development.

This is not the venue to go into a detailed discussion on the state-centered approach. What we find problematic in the literature is the tendency of either ruling out the relevance of Hong Kong's case of non-interventionism or ignoring its peculiarities. Either way, we believe, will only undermine the explanatory power of the state-center approach to researches on East Asian capitalism. Elsewhere one of us has spelled out the colonial state-industrial capital relationship during the early period of Hong Kong's industrialization (Chiu, 1994). Briefly, the argument is that for a long time, the colonial state has stayed aloof from regulating industrial development. Instances where the government has deliberately stayed away from giving assistance to the development of industries and providing directions for industrial development are many. An important case to comment on, perhaps, is the establishment of an industrial bank in the late 1950s. Since the early 1950s, there had been voices among local manufacturers complaining of inadequate support from the financial sector. Many manufacturers aired their dissatisfactions and worries about the adverse effects of high interest rates on industrial development through the Chinese Manufacturers' Association (CMA) and news media.

Then, in 1958, a resolution on industrial development was passed in an executive meeting of the CMA, which requested the government to set up a special agency responsible for industrial lending. Under pressure, the government announced, in late 1958, that the proposal to establish an industrial bank was under consideration. Later in 1959, a committee was appointed to review the whole issue. However, after one and a half years' deliberation, it was suggested in the report of the committee, submitted in July 1960, that

> The Committee has . . . been presented with no evidence of any concrete case where an industrial development had failed to secure finance in Hong Kong but could properly have secured it from a specialized industrial bank. This, taken in conjunction with the evidence of the very considerable role played by banks in the expansion of industry in recent years, has led us to the conclusion that the need for an industrial bank for the finance of industry in Hong Kong is not proven. (Quoted from Chiu, 1994: 80)

The decision to shelve the idea of an industrial bank serves well as an illustration of the effects of the specific configuration of state capacity and the state-capital alliance on economic policies. The financial capacity of the colonial state was limited internally, on the one hand, by the low tax and tariff policy, and on the other hand, by the private control of crucial resources in the economy. Externally, the British Government also had an interest in the financial health of the colonial state to guard against the possibility of a massive increase in state expenditure by deficit budgeting.

But state capacity alone does not explain the abandonment of the plan to establish an industrial bank. Equally critical here was the lack of political support for the proposal. The point to note was the conspicuous absence of manufacturers in the top rung of the bourgeoisie and the limited access that industrial capital had on the state elite. An indicator of the distance between the industrial bourgeoisie and the center of state power can be found in the composition of unofficial members in the Executive and Legislative Councils. The appointment of unofficial members by the colonial state to the two councils had always been done by selecting the most important and powerful capitalists in the economy. None of the unofficials in the Legislature and the Executive Council in 1951 was an industrialist, nor was anyone in the 1961 cohort (Chiu, 1994: 53). Most of the unofficial councilors were hong merchants, bankers, proprietors of major utilities companies, and property magnates. The first unofficial member of the Legislature coming from the manufacturing sector was not appointed until 1964, and the Executive Council had to wait until 1972 for its first industrialist unofficial. Throughout most of the 1950s and the early 1960s, when Hong Kong's export-oriented industrialization was taking off, the industrial bourgeoisie was not represented in the top decision making bodies. And this under-representation of the interests of industrial capital persisted in the 1970s and 1980s (Davies, 1977; Leung, 1990). Differently put, the established finance-trading power bloc occupied a privileged position in the center of decision making within the state machinery, as a result of the gradual emergence of a close alliance between large-scale financial and commercial interests and the colonial administrative elite. Due to these political alignments, the interests of the manufacturers are not as significant as those of finance and commercial capital in the political calculus of the state elite. Such a constitution of the state-capital relationship, i.e., a coalition between the colonial state and finance as well as commercial capitals, explains why the colonial state is more prone to intervene in some areas of economic activity and less so in the area of industrial development.

Not only has the colonial state systematically kept its distance from assisting industrial development, the big banking groups and trading companies in Hong Kong also, contrary to Deyo's argument, do not constitute a "functional alternative" to the state for providing the centralized strategic capacity for industrialization. As we have shown in the earlier discussion of industrial restructuring, it is actually fair to say that "rugged individualism"—and not the "visible hand" of the state—prevails in the Hong Kong economy. The manufacturing sector is filled with a multitude of small firms which follow no administrative orders of the state but only the market signals of profit making. Furthermore, neither is it true that Hong Kong's industrialization is directed by the strategic minded banking groups and trading companies. Throughout the process of industrialization, as noted earlier, manufacturers have been complaining about insufficient supports from the financial sector. The major banks, originating from the entrepot trade of the past century, have been more accustomed to finance trading rather than manufacturing activities (Chiu, 1994; Industrial Banking Committee, 1966). There is actually an "institutional separation" of industry and finance; hardly can we see any function of economic tutelage by finance and commercial capitals in directing industrial development. Also, the role of the British origin trading companies in leading industrial development has been overstated. Instead of having these large "hongs" providing some kind of centralized guidance to the manufacturers, Hong Kong is a genuine case of decentralized industrialization. The major marketing channel of manufacturing products has not been these large "hongs" but the large number of small and medium-sized import-exporters (the average size of import-exporters in 1984-89 was about 6 persons per establishment). The Indian trading firms had played an important part in marketing clothing exports in the earlier period, while the mostly small Chinese import-export houses have been the major driving force behind the tremendous expansion of manufacturing exports.

In the case of Hong Kong, there is no developmental state to assist local manufacturers in coping with industrial restructuring. Nor has the process of late industrialization necessarily converted the colonial state to the adoption of a more developmentalist approach toward economic development. Under non-interventionism, local small manufacturers have developed their own special ways to tackle industrial restructuring—continuing their labor-intensive production with increasing their market intelligence, enhancing production flexibility and drawing upon the resources of China by relocating their plants across the border.

To sum up, the key elements of the Hong Kong model are:

1. The way Hong Kong's industries are incorporated into the world economy through the network of international commercial subcontracting;
2. Merchant capital actually plays an important role in facilitating linkages between Hong Kong's industries and overseas buyers, and the strong commercial ties strengthen local manufacturers' ability to respond to changes in product markets;
3. Hong Kong's manufacturers are predominantly small, local employers; their competitive edge lies in their flexibility in production, which helps adjust to volatile markets;
4. Industrial capital remains detached from the state elite, the government is selective in intervention in economic affairs, unionism is underdeveloped in terms of shop floor bargaining, and most local employers running small production plants have all been contributive to the continuation of labor-intensive manufacturing, especially when manufacturers can capitalize on the abundant supplies of cheap labor and land in the Pearl River Delta.

So our answer to the enigma of Hong Kong's industrialization is this. Hong Kong industries survive in the world economy by responding to the changing global market for manufacturing products. This stretches back to the origins of the success of Hong Kong's industrialization. The comparative advantage of Hong Kong's industries lies not in their ability to supply advanced technology for new production, but in their ability to ride on the crest of the waves of changes in consumption. The continuation of labor-intensive production hinges mainly on Hong Kong's position in the commercial network of international subcontracting.

We believe there are, at least, two important lessons that can be learned from the case of Hong Kong. First, that Hong Kong's labor-intensive industries continue to survive and fare reasonably well can be taken as a case to cast doubt on the assumption that in order to maintain growth and development, the NIEs must upgrade their technology and/or move up to the upper end of the commodity chain (cf. Gereffi, 1989; Gereffi and Korzeniewicz, 1990). Indeed, it is our contention that the question of economic development is more open-ended than what the existing literature suggests. Placing our study of Hong Kong in the context of the analysis of East Asian capitalism, our case shows the diversity of development trajectories—diversity in the sense that the EANIEs respond differently to global restructuring, as each of them is shaped differently by domestic institutional and organizational arrangements—and that development is not a "success or failure" issue but rather that there are different ways for individual economies to find their niches in global capitalism. In a world of changing patterns of consumption, Hong Kong's industries can survive and do well by strengthening their market intelligence and increasing production flexibility without really shaking off labor-intensive production.

Second, following our point on the diversity of development trajectories, the case of Hong Kong suggests that there are different paths of late industrialization. In the recent research on late industrialization in East Asia (e.g., Amsden, 1990), there is the central assumption that for late-comers, a centralized approach to industrialization is more appropriate than that of decentralization. Indeed, the more backward a country when it embarks on industrial development, the more central direction the economy requires (cf. Gerschenkron, 1966). For the late-industrializers, there is the need for a more centralized mechanism for capital mobilization, and the existing stock of technology favors capital-intensive and large-scale production. Individual firms are difficult to grow autonomously because there is simply too much to "catch-up" on before they can become competitive. The state is then called forth to play a more active role in providing capital and guidance to individual firms. We find such a view of late industrialization evolutionist and functionalist. To industrialize on the basis of "borrowed technology" (Amsden, 1990) does not necessarily bring the state into the center of industrial development. In the first place, there are different ways to borrow technology (cf. Wade, 1992: 300-301). In the case of Hong Kong, small local manufacturers are more capable of acquiring and using existing innovations and technology, and putting various components into new products than doing their own R&D. And they survive by quickly moving from one trendy product to another to meet market needs. Moreover, whether the state will assume a developmental role in industrial development depends on the political configuration of power coalitions for industrialization and is not an automatic outcome of late development. Late industrialization can be unorganized and de-centered. Unless we continue to conceive the case of Hong Kong simply as exotic and thus irrelevant to the theorization of East Asian development, more attention to the constitution of development trajectories is a prerequisite for learning the lessons of East Asian capitalism.

References

Amsden, A. "Third World Industrialization." *New Left Review* No. 182. 1990.

Averitt, R. *The Dual Economy.* New York: Norton. 1968.

Castells, M, L. Goh, and Y. W. Kwok. *Economic Development and Housing Policy in the Asian Pacific Rim.* Berkeley: Institute of Urban and Regional Development, University of California. 1988

Chan, T. S. *Distribution Channel Strategy for Export Marketing: The Case of Hong Kong Firms.* Ann Arbor: UMI Research Press. 1984.

Chen, E. "The Economic Setting." In *The Business Environment in Hong Kong,* edited by D. Lethbridge, 2nd Edition. Hong Kong: Oxford University Press. 1984.

Chen, E., and K. W. Li. "Industry Development and Industrial Policy in Hong Kong." In *Industrial and Trade Development in Hong Kong,* edited by E. Chen, M. K. Nyaw, and T. Wong. Hong Kong: Centre of Asian Studies, University of Hong Kong. 1991.

Chiu, S. "The Politics of Laissez-faire." Occasional Paper No. 40. Hong Kong Institute of Asia-Pacific Studies, The Chinese University of Hong Kong. 1994.

Chu, Y. W. "Dependent Industrialization: The Case of Hong Kong Garment Industry." M. Phil. thesis, Sociology Department, University of Hong Kong. 1988.

Dataquest Incorporated. Techno-economic and Market Research Study on Hong Kong's Electronics Industry, 1988-1989. Hong Kong: Industry Department. 1991.

Davies, S. "One Brand of Politics Rekindled." *Hong Kong Law Journal* 7, No. 1. 1977.

Deyo, F. "Coalitions, Institutions, and Linkage Sequencing - Toward a Strategic Capacity Model of East Asian Development." In *The Political Economy of the New Asian Industrialism,* edited by F. Deyo. Ithaca: Cornell University Press. 1987.

Dicken, P. *Global Shift.* London: Harper & Row. 1986.

Economist Intelligence Unit. *Industry in Hong Kong.* Hong Kong: South China Morning Post. 1962.

England, J. *Industrial Relations and Law in Hong Kong,* 2nd edition. Hong Kong: Oxford University Press. 1989.

Federation of Hong Kong Industries, Industry & Research Division. *Investment in China.* Hong Kong: Federation of Hong Kong Industries. 1993.

____. *Hong Kong's Industrial Investment in the Pearl River Delta.* Hong Kong: Federation of Hong Kong Industries. 1992.

____. *Hong Kong's Offshore Investment.* Hong Kong: Federation of Hong Kong Industries. 1990.

Friedman, M., and R. Friedman. *Free to Choose.* Harmondsworth: Penguin Books. 1980.

Gereffi, G. "Development Strategies and the Global Factory." *The Annals of the American Academy of Political and Social Science* No. 505. 1989.

Gereffi, G., and M. Korzeniewicz. "Commodity Chains and Footwear Exports in the Semiperiphery." In *Semiperipheral States in the World Economy,* edited by W. G. Martin. Westport: Greenwood Press. 1990.

Germidis, D., ed. *International Subcontracting.* Paris: OECD Development Centre.

Greenwood, J. "Hong Kong: The Changing Structure and Competitiveness of the Hong Kong Economy." *Asian Monetary Monitor* 14, No. 6. 1990.

Haddon-Cave, P. "Introduction." In *The Business Environment of Hong Kong,* edited by D. Lethbridge, 2nd edition. Hong Kong: Oxford University Press. 1984.

Harvey, D. *The Condition of Postmodernity.* Oxford: Blackwell. 1989.

Henderson, J. "The Political Economy of Technological Transformation in the Hong Kong Electronics Industry." In *Industrial and Trade Development in Hong Kong,* edited by E. Chen, M. K. Nyaw, and T. Wong. Hong Kong: Centre of Asian Studies, University of Hong Kong. 1991.

____. *The Globalization of High Technology Production.* London: Routledge. 1989.

Ho, K. C. "Studying the City in the New International Division of Labor." Department of Sociology Working Paper No. 107, National University of Singapore. 1991.

Ho, Y. P. "Hong Kong's Trade and Industry: Changing Patterns and Prospects." In *Hong Kong in Transition,* edited by J. Cheng. New York: Oxford University Press. 1986.

Hung, C. L. "Foreign Investment." In *The Business Environment of Hong Kong,* edited by D. Lethbridge, 2nd edition. Hong Kong: Oxford University Press. 1984.

Industrial Bank Committee. "Report of the Industrial Bank Committee." Mimeo. 1960.

Industry Department. *Hong Kong's Manufacturing Industries.* Hong Kong: Industry Department. Various years.

Ingham, G. *Capitalism Divided?* London: Macmillan. 1984.

Jao, Y. C. *Banking and Currency in Hong Kong.* London: Macmillan. 1974.

Kurt Salmon Associates, Inc. "Final Report on Techno-economic and Market Research Study on the Textiles and Clothing Industry for Hong Kong Government Industry Department." Mimeo. 1987.

Landberg, M. "Export-led Industrialization in the Third World." *Review of Radical Political Economy* 11. 1979.

Lau, H. F. "Development Process of the Hong Kong Manufacturing Companies: With Special Reference to the Garment Firms." In *Industrial and Trade Development in Hong Kong,* edited by E. Chen, M. K. Nyaw, and T. Wong. Hong Kong: Centre of Asian Studies, University of Hong Kong. 1991.

Lau, H. F., and C. F. Chan. "Structural Adaptation: The Response of Hong Kong Garment Manufacturers." Paper presented at the symposium on "Industrial Policy in Hong Kong." Hong Kong Institute of Asia-Pacific Studies, The Chinese University of Hong Kong. 1991.

Leung, B. "Power and Politics." In *Social Issues in Hong Kong,* edited by B. Leung. Hong Kong: Oxford University Press. 1990.

Levin, D., and S. Chiu. "Dependent Capitalism, Colonial State and Marginal Unions: The Case of Hong Kong." Mimeo. 1990.

Lo Cheng, S. S. *Public Budgeting in Hong Kong.* Hong Kong: Writers' & Publishers' Cooperative. 1990.

Lui, T. L. "Waged Work at Home." In *Selected Papers of Conference on Gender Studies in Chinese Societies,* edited by F. Cheung, et al. Hong Kong: Hong Kong Institute of Asia Pacific Studies, The Chinese University of Hong Kong. 1991a.

____. "Now You See It: Industrial Outwork as a Form of Urban Informal Activity." *The Annals of Japan Association for Urban Sociology.* 1991b.

____. "The Social Organization of Outwork." In *Between East and West,* edited by E. Sinn. Hong Kong: Centre of Asian Studies, University of Hong Kong. 1990.

Lui, T. L., and S. Chiu. "Industrial Restructuring and Labor Market Adjustment under Positive Non-Interventionism." *Environment and Planning* A 25, No. 1. 1993.

____. "A Tale of Two Industries: The Restructuring of Hong Kong's Garment-Making and Electronics Industries." Paper presented at the workshop on "Industrial Restructuring and Regional Adjustments in the Asian NIEs." National University of Singapore. 25-27 March 1992.

Murray, R. "Fordism and Post-Fordism." In *New Times,* edited by S. Hall and M. Jacques. London: Lawrence and Wishart. 1989.

Mytelka, Lynn K. "Technological Change and the Global Relocation of Production in Textiles and Clothing." *Studies in Radical Political Economy* 26. Fall 1991.

Onis, Z. "The Logic of the Developmental State." *Comparative Politics* 24. 1991.

Sabel, C. *Work and Politics.* Cambridge: Cambridge University Press. 1982.

Schiffer, J. "State Policy and Economic Growth: A Note on the Hong Kong Model." *International Journal of Urban and Regional Research* 15, No. 2. 1991.

Sit, V., and S. L. Wong. *Small and Medium Industries in an Export-oriented Economy: The Case of Hong Kong.* Hong Kong: Centre of Asian Studies, University of Hong Kong. 1989.

Skeldon, R. "Hong Kong and Its Hinterland." *Asian Geographer* 5, No. 1. 1986.

So, A. "The Economic Success of Hong Kong: Insights from a World-System Perspective." *Sociological Perspective* 29. 1986.

The Advisory Committee on Diversification. *Report of the Advisory Committee on Diversification.* Hong Kong: Government Printer. 1979.

The Joint Associations Working Group. "Report on Hong Kong's Labor Shortage." Mimeo. 1989.

Turner, H., et al. *The Last Colony: But Whose?* Cambridge: Cambridge University Press. 1980.

Turner, H., P. Fosh, and S. H. Ng. *Between Two Societies: Hong Kong Labor in Transition.* Hong Kong: Centre of Asian Studies, University of Hong Kong. 1991.

Wade, R. "East Asia's Economic Success: Conflicting Perspectives, Partial Insights, Shaky Evidence." *World Politics* 44, No. 2. 1992.

____. "East Asian Financial Systems as a Challenge to economics." *California Management Review* 27. 1985.

Wong, T. "A Comparative Study of the Industrial Policy of Hong Kong and Singapore in the 1980s." In *Industrial and Trade Development in Hong Kong*, edited by E. Chen, M. K. Nyaw, and T. Wong. Hong Kong: Centre of Asian Studies, University of Hong Kong. 1991.

Youngson, A. J. *Hong Kong: Economic Growth and Policy.* Hong Kong: Oxford University Press. 1982.

Index

About the Book

This book explores the foundation and nature of the relationship between capitalist accumulation and the state in East Asia and Latin America that has profoundly influenced industrialization and macroeconomic performance. Scholars from both sides of the Pacific offer critical perspectives on the differing fates of the two regions, especially over the last decade. Considering the role of markets, developmental states, location, ethnic networks, dynamic comparative advantage, and competitiveness, this pioneering volume draws comparative lessons from the East Asian experience for the developing world.

About the Contributors

Diana Alarcón-González received her Ph.D. in Economics from the University of California, Riverside. She has been a Research Associate at El Colegio de la Frontera Norte in Tijuana, Mexico, since 1988 and is currently on sabbatical working as a research economist at the International Labor Organization in Geneva. She has published articles on different aspects of trade liberalization, the distribution of income, and poverty in Mexico and is author of *Changes in the Distribution of Income in Mexico and Trade Liberalization.*

Anuwar Ali is Director, Universities Division, Ministry of Education, Malaysia, and former Deputy Vice-Chancellor and Professor of Economics in the National University of Malaysia. Among other publications, he is author of *Malaysia's Industrialization: The Quest for Technology.*

Alejandro Alvarez Béjar is a Professor of Economics at the National University of Mexico (UNAM) in Mexico City. He has authored and edited many books, including *La crisis global del capitalismo en México, La Inserción de México en la Cuenca del Pacífico* (co-edited), and *México 1988-1991: ¿Un Ajuste Económico Existoso?* (co-authored).

John Borrego is an Associate Professor of Community Studies at the University of California, Santa Cruz, where he teaches global political economy, regional integration, and community development. His current research is focused on how North American integration and transnational production are restructuring daily life at the community level. His publications include a co-edited book, *La Insercion de México en la Cuenca del Pacífico.*

Thomas M. H. Chan is currently Head of China Business Centre of the Hong Kong Polytechnic University. He has followed economic development and reform in China closely. His present research projects include foreign direct investment and foreign trade in China; China's auto industry and pharmaceutical industry; and economic integration of China, Hong Kong, and Taiwan.

Stephen W. K. Chiu is a Lecturer in Sociology at the Chinese University of Hong Kong. His research interests include industrial relations, social movements, and the comparative study of the East Asian newly industrialized countries. His latest publication is a co-authored book, *East Asia and the World Economy.*

Lynne E. Guyton graduated from Cambridge University with a Ph.D. in Economics ("Japanese FDI in Southeast Asia: The Transfer of Consumer Electronics Production to Malaysia") in March 1995. She is currently working in Global Foreign Exchange for Deutsche Morgen Grenfell in London.

Hsin-Huang Michael Hsiao is a Research Fellow of the Institute of Sociology and Associate Director of the Program for Southeast Asian Area Studies, Academia Sinica and Professor of Sociology, National Taiwan University. His current research focuses on the middle classes in East and Southeast Asia. His major publications in English include *Agricultural Policy in Post-War Taiwan* (co-author), *In Search of an East Asian Development Model* (co-editor), *Taiwan: A Newly Industrialized State* (co-editor), *Taiwan 2000: Balancing Economic Growth and Environmental Protection* (co-author), *Discovery of the Middle Classes in East Asia* (editor), and *The East Asian Middle Classes in Comparative Perspective* (forthcoming).

Dae-Hwan Kim has a Ph.D. in Economics from the University of Oxford and is a Professor in the Department of Economics at Inhua University, Inchon, Korea. His research focus is on sustainable development, privatization, ownership and workers' participation. His published books include *Economic Development, Regulations on Privatized Enterprises in Britain,* and he is co-editing a new book, *Korean Peninsula in Transition.*

Victor D. Lippit is Professor of Economics at the University of California, Riverside, where he teaches economic development, comparative economic systems, and political economy. His books include *The Economic Development of China* and *Radical Political Economy: Explorations in Alternative Economic Analysis.*

Tai-lok Lui is a Lecturer in Sociology at the Chinese University of Hong Kong. His research interests are the formation of the middle class in Hong Kong, industrial restructuring, and economic sociology. He is the author of *Waged Work at Home: The Social Organization of Industrial Outwork in Hong Kong,* and articles on economic restructuring and urban politics.

Antonio Gutiérrez Pérez was Professor and former Head of the Graduate Division of the Faculty of Economics at the National University of Mexico (UNAM) in Mexico City. His publications include "The Financial Power of the United States in the 1980s: Hegemonic Reaccommodations and their Impacts on Latin America," "Reorganization financiere aux années quatre-vingts," and "The American Financial System: Globalization and the Free Trade Agreement."

Rajah Rasiah has a Ph.D. in Economics from the University of Cambridge, teaches in the Faculty of Economics, National University of Malaysia, and is author of many articles and two books, including *Foreign Investment and Industrialization in Malaysia.*

Jomo K. S. is Professor in the Faculty of Economics and Administration, University of Malaya in Kuala Lumpur. He is the author and editor of many books, including *A Question of Class, Growth and Structural Change in the Malaysian Economy, Islamic Economic Alternatives, Industrializing Malaysia, Trade Unions and the State in Peninsula Malaysia, Malay Peasant Women and the Land, Japan and Malaysian Development, Privatizing Malaysia,* and *Malaysia's Political Economy.*

Tan Kock Wah is a Lecturer in Economics in the Faculty of Social Sciences, Universiti Malaya Sarawak in Kota Samarahan, Sarawak, and has completed a manuscript on industrial policy in Japan, South Korea, and Taiwan.